The Inside Story

The Inside Story

A Narrative Approach to Religious Understanding and Truth

Paul Brockelman

State University of New York Press

Published by
State University of New York Press, Albany

© 1992 State University of New York

For information, address State University of New York Press,
State University Plaza, Albany, N.Y., 12246

Production by M. R. Mulholland
Marketing by Bernadette LaManna

Library of Congress Cataloging-in-Publication Data

Brockelman, Paul T.
    The inside story: a narrative approach to religious understanding
and truth / Paul Brockelman.
        p.   cm.
    Includes bibliographical references and index.
    ISBN 0-7914-1019-6 (CH : acid-free). — ISBN
0-7914-1020-X (BH : acid-free)
    1. Knowledge, Theory of (Religion) 2. United States-
-Religion—1960- 3. Postmodernism—Religious aspects. 4. Story
-telling—Religious aspects. 5. Self-perception. 6. Faith and
reason. I. Title.
BL51.B755   1992
200'.1—dc20
                                                                91-4092
                                                                CIP

10 9 8 7 6 5 4 3 2 1

———————— To the memory of my mother, ————
Estelle Brockelman,
whose spirit shapes and informs much of this essay.

2779211

Contents

Preface

Several years ago, I was invited by the University of New Hampshire to deliver a public address on the topic, "The Renewal of Our Religious Traditions." The groundswell of public fascination with Joseph Campbell's reflections on mythology had just begun to become evident and seemed to indicate a widespread interest in such matters. Furthermore, Robert Bellah's de Tocqueville-like survey of America's current spiritual condition had been recently released, and it confirmed that many Americans from various classes and sections of the country felt rather strongly that our culture and religious traditions were in disarray. They voiced a sense of rootlessness and overall disorientation which made the subject of religious renewal seem appropriate for such a public address.

In preparing the address (and subsequently this manuscript), it became obvious to me that the question of religious renewal raised all sorts of ancillary issues. What, for example, are these traditions to renew? And what does such renewal mean? Does it mean simply reviving and going back to some earlier interpretive version—to the medieval scholastic interpretation of St. Thomas Aquinas in Christianity, for example, or Moses Maimonides in Judaism? Or, on the contrary, does it mean doing away with past versions in favor of an interpretation which presumably better fits and meets the needs of today or even tomorrow? What is an interpretation anyway, and how does one decide which is more suitable or correct within a particular tradition? How do we know when an interpretation (or renewal) is 'true'? What kind of 'truth' is this? How are we to evaluate (never mind choose between) different and even contradictory truth claims within a tradition or between various traditions? In a well-armed and yet shrinking world, these issues are neither gratuitous nor merely academic.

I delivered the lecture and it was well received. Several friends and colleagues thought the topic, with all of its cultural and spiritual ramifications, important enough to urge me to expand it into book form in order to address the issues raised in a more leisurely fashion. I decided to take their advice and set out to expand and deepen my thinking about religious renewal. The more I reflected on the subject, the more it seemed to explode into a veritable nebula of interlocking perplexities. Yet one fundamental issue which seemed to pervade or underlie all the others—the ether, if you will, in which they all moved—began to emerge. It was the question of religious knowledge and truth. Any solution to the issues of renewal and interpretation, for example, seemed to depend on an appropriate or correct conception of such religious understanding.

What, in fact, do we mean when we talk about religious understanding and truth? There seems to have been, at least until recently, an assumption among scholars and (it seems to me) most other people that such religious knowledge is not unlike scientific knowledge. Just as scientific knowledge embodies true or false assertions about the processes of nature, so religious knowledge, the assumption goes, embodies true or false beliefs about the existence and nature of God, although of course He is so 'wholly other' that He is not present in the same sense as nature. Is knowledge of God like that? Is it really like a hypothesis in biology, for example, or the big bang theory in astrophysics? Is God simply a *being* who is so withdrawn in His transcendence that our assertions about Him—although in other respects just like empirical statements about nature—cannot be verified or falsified like their empirical cousins? Is religious knowledge really hypothetical and propositional at all—i.e., true or false judgments within assertions concerning an absent entity, God? Is faith so heady, so cognitive? And is God an entity, or even *like* an entity for that matter? Does religious truth entail a correspondence, so to speak, between the beliefs we hold and God? The more I reflected on this, the more such a conception of religious understanding seemed naive, stupifyingly ill-matched to actual religious experience, and spiritually inefficacious. It seemed naive because it is too simple-minded to meet our religious needs, ill-matched because it is out-of-sync with our real religious practices and lives, and inefficacious because it seems to lead to the attenuation or even demise of genuine religious life in either skepticism or dogmatism.

With respect to the last point, the traditional assumptions about religious understanding seemed to lead us, on the one hand, to a kind of fanatical absolutism and exclusivism with very dangerous implications for our shrinking world. On the other hand (and at the same time), it seemed to leave the more aware and well-educated of us in religious limbo—that is, in a spiritual state in which we are relegated to painful lives of relativism and even skepticism. In such a state, one certainly cannot 'renew' a religious tradition because one cannot even begin to accept it as a viable option. That, in fact, seems to be just the spiritual condition in which we find ourselves—a modern world in which we have been witnessing the parallel growth of skeptical meaninglessness and fanatical dogmatism.

The cluster of interlocking issues, then, seemed to come down to epistemological ones in two senses. First, an inadequate (and yet very common) conception of religious understanding has been set loose in our culture which seems not only false to religious life but also politically dangerous and spiritually damaging. That, secondly, seemed to demand the development of an alternative view of such religious understanding, one which is more faithful to religious experience and supportive of the practice of genuine religious understanding as well as mutual respect and toleration between the various interpretations and traditions. This dual endeavor, then, underlies the following essay: (1) a critique of what I think is a wrong-headed but by now very common conception of religious knowledge, and (2) the development of an alternative model which, I hope, is pregnant with new possibilities to help us meet the needs of our time.

I should note at this point that my reflections on these issues have been shaped to a large degree by what seems to be a sea change in our understanding of understanding itself; a change brought about by the remarkable cultural and intellectual shift from modernity to postmodernity. Along with a number of other philosophers, I believe we are presently living through one of the most fundamental shifts in our history—a change in the modern belief structure of Western, industrial society which has characterized our tradition at least since the seventeenth century. Just as the Copernican revolution and the Cartesian program triggered the advances of modern industrial and technological society, so too our present awareness of some of the implicit interpretive assumptions on which it rested and which it systematically avoided making conscious has led to a cultural and intellectual paradigm shift which some have termed 'postmodern.' In particular, the broadened and deepened understanding of human, interpretive understanding (hermeneutic) which lies at the heart of this postmodern attitude has, I believe, direct and important significance for our present-day conception of religious understanding and renewal. Putting it another way, I think we can say that the paradigm trans-formation from modernity to postmodernity opens up vast new possibilities of and for spiritual understanding today. Certainly, it makes possible a new understanding of the nature of religious knowledge—and philosophical knowledge, for that matter. But at the same time, and perhaps more importantly, it makes available a universe and Being filled with wonder and awe. That, in turn, permits an alliance between science and religion in which, for the first time in three hundred years, they can not only focus on the same reality (the universe), but to a large degree tell the same story about it. As we will note later, this has important implications for both our spiritual lives as well as for the fate of the environment of which we are presently such a critical (and seemingly disastrous) part.

One more point. In thinking through the nature of this alternative conception of religious understanding, I was greatly influenced by the contemporary work going on in what has been called "story" or "narrative" theology, particularly that which has been developed by Stanley Hauerwas, Paul Ricoeur, Hans Frei, Sallie McFague, Terrence Tilley, and (to a lesser degree) David Tracy. I, myself, had recently published a monograph (*Time and Self: Phenomenological Explorations*[1]) in which I argued not only that the self is a kind of unfolding story, but that it is the existential condition for human stories as such—e.g., novels, dramas, case studies, myths, and so on. In retrospect, it seems natural enough that that interest in narrative would influence these subsequent reflections on religious understanding, as indeed they have. In fact, one could characterize what follows as an attempt to develop a postmodern, narrative model of religious knowledge and inter- pretation which might enable us to better address the spiritual issues and needs we face today, thereby (hopefully) 'renewing' our religious traditions. The attempt is not to do away with the cognitive significance of religious life, but rather to get at the peculiar kinds of cognitive claims religious understanding entails. Stanley Hauerwas puts this very well.

> I am interested in "story"...not because the narrative form may be a way of avoiding how religious convictions may or may not be true. Instead I hold the more positive view that the story quality of the gospels provides the appropriate context to raise the issue of truth at all.[2]

But before setting out to tell the story of religious stories, I want to thank Dean Stuart Palmer and Associate Dean Ted Kirkpatrick of the College of Liberal Arts at the University of New Hampshire for their sustained support of the writing and ultimate preparation of this manuscript. Although all-too-often unacknowledged, such support is indispensable to the real life of the mind.

Introduction

I look upon religion as potentially a powerful force for global consciousness. But I am aware that if it is interpreted in fundamentalist or fanatic terms, it can be the antithesis of that global consciousness. That is why it is too important to be neglected.

> Karan Singh, Indian Ambassador to the U.S.
> and founder of *Virat Hindu Samaj*,
> an Indian movement to modernize Hinduism

1. First the Good News

There is something in the intellectual atmosphere today which, like a sweet desert breeze wafting from the groves of Mamre, has an air of fertile promise about it. Stale issues and perspectives which have characterized the human arts and sciences for a century or more seem to be dissolving like morning mist, and they are being replaced by remarkably new and exciting approaches to understanding in the arts, humanities, and social sciences. I am referring, of course, to the new ways of understanding what 'understanding' and 'interpretation' are all about in those human arts and sciences—what some have called a postmodern paradigm. It is an approach to human life and understanding which, in my opinion, is revolutionizing our interpretation of literature, art, philosophy, history, sociology, and psychology, not to mention the various natural (or hard) sciences. Because the field of religious studies in its various aspects is clearly one of those human sciences, it will come as no surprise to the reader to discover that this postmodern approach and perspective has already contributed significantly to our interpretation of religious attitudes, language, and practices.

From this postmodern perspective, one of the most pernicious errors promulgated during the Enlightenment (and characterizing 'modernity' ever since) was to divide and reduce human experiential reality (what we shall later call "the world of ordinary experience") to either subjectivity (*res cogitans*) or objectivity (*res extensa*), thereby rendering actual, lived experience quite invisible and opaque. The subsequent history of modernity, as we all know, would attempt to reduce the subjective or mind side of things to a secondary or epiphenomenal aspect of objective reality, thereby reducing Being to objects present to us—referred to as "the forgetfulness of Being" in Heidegger's haunting phrase. Along with this, of course, went an epistemology which limited knowledge to the relevant discovery of the 'external' world through the empirical sciences or mathematics and the use of language to those forms of discourse appropriate to dealing with external 'things.' This immediately pitched any conception of religious knowledge and truth into deep trouble by forcing it to claim to be either empirical (or deductive) in nature or simply nonepistemic— i.e., a subjective illusion. More important, though, is the fact that it made the understanding of religious life quite impossible. It dissolved and blinded us to the only context in which that religious life makes any sense at all—the world of ordinary experience.

We can put the same point another way. To try to fit God or faith into a world of objects is like expecting fish to exist without water or birds without air. It can't be done. And just as we can't imagine fish living without water or birds living without air, so from a postmodern perspective our religious lives and practices are inconceivable outside the context of the overarching meaning and interpretive understanding we find in the world of ordinary experience. I believe that we are presently living in an exciting intellectual period. It is a period which has rediscovered what had for so long been hidden—the world of ordinary experience along with its fundamental structure of interpretive understanding or meaning. As water is for fish and air for birds, such a world is for our understanding of religious knowledge and practice. This is a time of great possibility and fresh hope for deeper (and sometimes new) understanding of religious phenomena. The great mist of modernity, a mist which permitted unparalleled technological advancement but obscured and nearly destroyed the spiritual side of our lives, has begun to lift. And behold! What was before either entirely hidden or at best obscured is gradually becoming recognizable and clear. It is indeed an exciting time for religious studies!

2. Now the Bad News

The bad news is that our contemporary religious situation still seems structured and defined by the kinds of spiritual issues and ways of seeing things inherited from the Enlightenment. There seems to be a growing sense in our modern, industrial societies—whether capitalist or communist—that we have lost our spiritual and moral bearing. There is a widespread sense that there is nothing left to believe in, that all spiritual claims are merely relative, and that the only sensible position to take is outright skepticism or even nihilism. And along with this spiritual emptiness has been an evident disregard for nature which in turn has permitted a technological and industrial proliferation which has put the planet as a whole in grave jeopardy.

At the very same time, there is a growing prevalence around the world of fundamentalist and fanatical sects and movements which not only claim absolute truth but harshly condemn and even threaten alternative religious views and traditions. The modern world is haunted by the twin specters of meaninglessness and fanaticism. It is a heady, potent, and extremely dangerous mix.

Let us first briefly explore the contemporary sense of skepticism and meaninglessness. Contemporary observers such as Wolfhart Pannenberg point to anomie and a spiritual malaise following a loss of our traditional faith:

> The feelings, so widespread today, of an all-pervading sense-lessness, together with the related questing after meaning, indicate that, for many persons and for broad segments of the public consciousness in our secular culture, the traditional answers of Christianity are no longer adequately functioning as a comprehensive interpretation of the experience of the world's reality and of the life problems that contemporary people face.[1]

Others such as Peter Berger trace the causes of our spiritual disorientation to the encroachments of modern thought patterns and perspectives developed in the Enlightenment, perspectives which make such traditional faith seem naive and unfounded:

> It is my position that modernity has plunged religion into a very specific crisis, characterized by secularity, to be sure, but characterized more importantly by pluralism. In the pluralistic situation, for reasons that are readily visible to historical and social-scientific observation, the authority of all religious traditions tends to be undermined. . . . The individual comes to experience himself as being alone in a way that is unthinkable in traditional society—deprived of the firm solidarity of his collectivity, uncertain of the norms by which his life is to be governed, finally uncertain of who or what he is.[2]

Along with the mindless explosion of technology and the secular way of life it promotes, such social commentators as Berger believe that our lives have become trivial and vacuous, a wilderness of spiritual superficiality and disorientation. They have the sense that we are adrift in a hollow (albeit air-conditioned) land where material acquisition and technological power seem to be the only goals worthy of struggle and sacrifice. A young woman recently voiced to me just this sense of meaninglessness and disorientation when she defended the need for a constitutional amendment to protect the nation's flag from desecration. "Nobody gives a damn about anything anymore", she said. "Something has to count. Something has to matter beyond one's own narrow needs if we are going to survive as a nation."

The well-known evangelical theologian Carl Henry made the same point recently in a more explicitly theological manner.

> The West has lost its moral compass and sinks in neo-pagan naturalism that says nature alone is real, that man is essentially only a complex animal, that distinctions of truth and good are temporary and changing. . . . Repudiation of divine purpose in reality leads people to play gods themselves, bringing the blight of meaninglessness that plagues Western culture.[3]

Interestingly, it is not just Western commentators who bemoan this loss of faith and consequent skepticism and spiritual emptiness. In a parallel way, the Gorbachev era has witnessed in Soviet literary journals the emergence of a host of writings pointing to a spiritual crisis in the USSR and condemning the moral and spiritual degradation of the Soviet people. Writers such as Vasily Bykov, Viktor Astafyev, and Chinghiz Aytmatov—like Solzhenitsyn before them—see the roots of moral decline in the demise of the Russian religious tradition and think the revival of that tradition is the only way out of their presently stifling spiritual situation. "What happened to us?" asked Astafyev in a recent article.

> Who hurled us into the depths of evil and misfortune, and why? Who extinguished the light of goodness in our soul? Who blew out the lamp of conscience, toppled it into a dark, deep pit in which we are groping, trying to find the bottom, a support and some kind of guiding light to the future?. . . They [the Communists] stole it from us and did not give anything in return, giving rise to unbelief, an all-encompassing unbelief. . . . [4]

This contemporary sense of moral and spiritual rootlessness— whenever and wherever it finds voice—is undoubtedly fostered and supported by the explosive growth (if we are to believe the media) of random violence and human abuse, even at the heart of our families. Carl Henry points out that there seems to be an atomization and relativity of human value and attitude that leaves us breathless and in fear for the future and the commonweal. It has even shown up in the recent yuppie sense of exorbitant individualism and lack of civic concern—a view which seems to hold that if each of us takes care of him or herself, everything else will take care of itself, no matter the social cost. As Philip Rieff puts it:

> Quantity has become quality. The answer to all questions of "what for?" is "more". The faith of the rich has always been in themselves. Rendered democratic, this religion proposes that every man become his own eleemosynary institution. Here is a redefinition of charity from which the inherited faith of Christianity may never recover. Out of this redefinition, Western culture is changing already into a symbol system unprecedented in its plasticity and absorptive capacity. Nothing much can oppose it really, and it welcomes all criticism, for, in a sense, it stands for nothing. . . . Individuals learn to feel that they owe nothing to any man, they expect nothing from any man; they acquire the habit of always considering themselves as standing alone, and they are apt to imagine that their whole destiny is in their own hands.[5]

Of course, as we are increasingly aware, it is not just a lack of concern for the social commonweal in favor of a myopic individualism that has infected the culture. An equally distressing and perhaps more threatening lack of concern for the interrelated commonwealth of nature has brought us—some think—to the edge of extinction.

In his brilliant analysis of the moral and spiritual condition of contemporary America, Robert Bellah recently documented this widespread sense of disorientation and disaffection among ordinary Americans from various traditions and classes across the country. Listen to his summary of the situation:

> Our problems today are not just political. They are moral and have to do with the meaning of life. We have assumed that as long as economic growth continued, we could leave all else to the private sphere. Now that economic growth is faltering and the moral ecology on which we have tacitly depended is in disarray, we are beginning to understand that our common life requires more than an exclusive concern for material accumulation.

Perhaps life is not a race whose only goal is being foremost. Perhaps true felicity does not lie in continually outgoing the next before. Perhaps the truth lies in what most of the world outside the modern West has always believed, namely that there are practices of life, good in themselves, that are inherently fulfilling. Perhaps work that is intrinsically rewarding is better for human beings than work that is only extrinsically rewarded. Perhaps enduring commitment to those we love and civic friendship toward our fellow citizens are preferable to restless competition and anxious self-defense. Perhaps common worship, in which we express our gratitude and wonder in the face of the mystery of being itself, is the most important thing of all. If so, we will have to change our lives and begin to remember what we have been happier to forget.[6]

The mirror image (and twin specter) of such spiritual skepticism and disorientation today is a propensity around the world toward dogmatism, absolutism, and exclusivistic religious groups, denominations and ideologies. Indeed, as we shall see later when we trace these contemporary phenomena back to their Enlightenment roots, these twin phenomena—disenchanted meaninglessness and dogmatic certainty and fanaticism—are but two different and schizoid sides of a single modern spiritual malady. The spiritual dilemma we face seems to limit our religious choices (and that means how we live) to either meaninglessness or fanaticism. As with the menu in a Chinese restaurant, no third choice is permitted. And, of course, these dangerous spiritual choices are made in the context of a growing industrial drift toward ecological disaster.

Given the amount of media coverage devoted in the past few years to an unprecedented explosion of religious dogmatism (and even fanaticism) around the world and within all of the major religious traditions, few of us can remain unaware of it. It would seem, as Peter Berger has pointed out, that one reaction to the skepticism and resultant insecurity (and even anxiety) fostered by the modern situation is for religious groups to dogmatically (or "deductively," as Berger puts it) assert the truth of their views, regardless of contradictory claims by others and a glaring lack of evidence beyond the assertions themselves.[7] As we just said, the more we become aware of alternative religious views, the more a sense of relativism and even meaninglessness seems to emerge. And the more such skepticism and disorientation is manifest, the more we find various forms of fundamentalism and dogmatism emerging against it as an *a priori* denial of it.

In Israel, for example, Jewish fundamentalists are changing the face of Israeli politics. "Jewish fundamentalism remains ideologically the single most coherent and vigorous political force in Israel," according to Dartmouth professor Dan Lustick.[8] In Islam, fundamentalism has become the most potent theological, cultural, and political force today. This is true not only of the Sh'ia in Iran and Lebanon, but also within the mainstream Sunni sect in, for example, Pakistan and Egypt. And, of course, fundamentalism has become a remarkable presence on the American scene in both the Moral Majority movement and creationism.

Sometimes (although not always, of course), such fundamentalism becomes violent and fosters terrorism. The very air we breathe today, it seems, is a mixture of incense and gunsmoke, from Sri Lanka to Ireland and Lebanon to Tibet. Of course, violence in religion is not unique to our time. Words such as *assassin, zealot,* and *thug* entered our vocabulary from fanatical groups in Islam, Judaism, and Hinduism centuries ago. Even Luther advocated violence in the face of the peasants' revolt. Yet, not since the Dark Ages has there been more killing in the name of God than in this allegedly secular century. Religious violence today, as is plain from a cursory reading of our daily press, is a global phenomenon with extensive theological, cultural, and political significance.

All of this is actually a symptom of the underlying growth of dogmatism and fanaticism in our day. In the Roman Catholic context, for example, we find the Vatican claiming doctrinal purity in the name of the Magisterium (the teaching function of the church) by silencing (or attempting to silence) such different interpretations of the tradition within its own ranks as those of Hans Kung, Leonardo Boff, and Richard Curran (of Catholic University). This is necessary, according to Auxiliary Bishop Patrick V. Ahern of New York, because "we're really in a crisis of diversity right now and what we're looking for is a presence of uniform teaching on major issues of dogma and morals."[9]

This sort of attitude has led various bishops to threaten excommunication to parishoners who actively condone or advocate abortion. That Bishop Ahern and others think diverse interpretations add up to a "crisis" and that there ought to be "uniform teaching" indicates that they equate faith with a single and exclusively true set of doctrines. Such an assumption, as David Tracy has put it, may sound sensible, but it has dangerous implications for it leads to book banning, theological coercion and intimidation, and—at the extreme—crusades.[10]

Obviously, not all Roman Catholics are dogmatists, and dogmatism is certainly not limited to Roman Catholicism. It can be found as well within various (especially evangelical) strands of Protestantism. Listen to the evangelical theologian Francis Schaeffer, for example, who (if we are to believe his words) thinks that his version of Christianity is absolutely and exclusively true. In life, he says,

> You have to have absolutes, or nothing has meaning. . . . What we are talking about is the philosophic necessity, in the area of being and existence, of the fact that God is there. That is what it is all about: He is there. . . . The truth of Christianity is that it is true to what is there. . . this is not the *best* answer; it is the *only* answer[11]

Even Karl Barth, whom one might expect to be a bit more open-minded and tolerant, claimed such absolute and exclusive truth for Christianity—or his version of it, at any rate. He said, "The Christian religion is true, because it has pleased God, who alone can be the judge in this matter, to affirm it to be the true religion."[12]

Theologian Hendrik Kraemer, a Dutch missionary and student of Barth's, took a more nuanced and yet equally dogmatic and exclusivistic position. For him, "God has revealed *the* Way and *the* Life and *the* Truth in Jesus Christ, and wills this to be known through all the world."[13] And for both Schaeffer and Kraemer, precisely because Christ's message is true, alternative, non-Christian claims must be false. Non-Christian life, Kraemer tells us, "the lofty and the degraded, appears to lie under the divine judgment, because it is *misdirected.*"[14] Such dogmatic exclusivism reminds one of the story of Karl Barth who took a similarly intolerant position. When asked by a friend how he knew Hinduism was false, he replied, "*A priori!*"[15]

My claim, here, however, is not just that many religious people today are dogmatists. My claim is rather that the ordinary view of religion by the average man or woman on the street—whether believer or non-believer—is precisely that it consists of true or false doctrines about the existence and nature of God. Revelation, from this point of view, is propositional: the Bible (or the Koran or whatever) is the inspired word of God. That means that God communicates his truths to us through his inspired prophets and priests. The Bible is not primarily testimony in various social contexts to the saving power of Jesus as the Christ, but a set of true doctrines (propositions) concerning the demands of God. In Billy Graham's famous phrase, "God had thirty secretaries."

During twenty-five years of university teaching, I have been continually and inevitably struck by the assumption and remarkable pervasiveness among my students of this view of religion and revelation. It is a view, I believe, which finds its roots in an inadequate notion of knowledge and truth which we have inherited from the Enlightenment. That view of truth, I am claiming, has brought us to the intolerable spiritual situation we have been trying to explore here, a situation in which our religious options have become disastrously constricted by being limited to either a rootless skepticism and meaninglessness or dogmatism and even fanaticism.

3. More Bad News: The Ecological Crisis

As if this constricted and idiotic cultural menu which limits spiritual life either to meaninglessness or dogmatic and sometimes fanatical exclusivism weren't enough, the modern industrial world in which it is taking place has brought us to the brink of ecological disaster. The very drive for economic and material progress has led to a paradoxical situation in which it seems that the only way a run-away human population can be clothed and fed adequately is to further devastate the natural resources on which we are terrifyingly dependent, thereby making the sustenance of such industrial progress (never mind the natural world) quite impossible. Our earth is poisoning itself with acid rain and chemical and nuclear waste. It is an earth whose atmosphere is heating up, an earth reeling in the wake of the extinction of over seventeen percent of recently existing plant and animal species, an earth becoming denuded of its topsoil and increasingly emptied of its nonrenewable metals and minerals. We have drained and dug away the oil and coal stored beneath our land in order to feed the engines of modern industry which propel the so-called progress demanded by our consumer societies.

The bill is coming due, of course, for (to use Solzhenitzyn's devastating image) a host of worms can gnaw on a rotten (finite) apple for only so long. In spite of the fact that many people would prefer not to believe it, the earth is not infinite in its resources. There are limits to the industrial and economic growth to which we have grown accustomed and which the earth can sustain. We have already done irreparable harm to our natural environment; in fact, some would maintain that it is already beyond saving.

So the modern world is doubly ill: it has come down with the very painful and dangerous spiritual disease of meaninglessness (and its attendant fanaticism) at the very moment that its technological and industrial power has devastated the natural world on which it is so dependent.

4. The Roots of the Problem

What has caused this dual malady? I believe it can be traced back to the attitude toward life which emerged during the Enlightenment and which, in the form of modernity, has spread around the globe. I will argue later that only a radical change in that attitude, a shift in the way we view and interpretively understand nature and our place and destiny within it, can hope to overcome this spiritual and ecological malaise. It is possible that without such a radical shift in our thinking, there will be no future at all.

The modern world emerged in the seventeenth and eighteenth centuries around the vision that human history was the story of how humanity gradually came to know how to control nature by coming *to know how to know*. Knowledge, as Francis Bacon put it, is power; it is through such knowing that nature will be forced to divulge her secrets and mankind will be able to control and transform reality for his own ends.

Thinkers such as Descartes, Newton, Locke, and David Hume gave substance to Bacon's insight by limiting genuine scientific or objective knowledge to empirical induction or mathematical deduction—matters of fact or matters of reason. As we shall see in more detail later, this not only did away in a stroke with the traditional notion of religious or spiritual understanding but also limited such understanding—as it did all human understanding—to just these two possibilities. Because of this, religious understanding was either reduced to a propositional and empirical kind of 'fact' or it was viewed as not epistemic at all—i.e., a subjective illusion or perhaps a mere emotion. That meant, of course, that religious knowledge either took on the character of an empirical hypothesis (including its form of verification), or its assertions were taken to be meaningless. Furthermore, because two contradictory empirical hypotheses can't both be true, the same held for religious beliefs. By this means, we have been led to the twin specters of exclusivistic dogmatism or meaninglessness.

As if that were not enough, the difficulties thrown in the way of living a spiritual life were compounded by the evident explosion of modern technological and industrial power and the consumer society that attends it. Progress was envisioned (and measured) in terms of the increasing control of nature through the application of empirical and mathematical knowledge in the form of science and technology (the application of science for practical ends—i.e., the manufacture of useful human products such as medicine, food, and consumer products of various kinds). Supporting this conception of progress was the Enlightenment (Cartesian) separation of mind and matter. *Mind* was reserved for religion and morality (and, in any case, dropped from view as modernity unfolded), and *matter* became the realm of science and mathematics. That meant that nature was desacralized and was pictured as a meaningless and merely mechanical reality which was free to be exploited for the endless progress fueled by the engine of the consumer-industrial world.

All of this led to the ecological disaster we are presently facing. It also brought the various traditional religious cultures (however attenuated and conceived as fact-like dogmatic assertions about an absent entity—God) into collision with one another while at the same time arming them to the teeth. It is hard to imagine a more dangerous situation. At the same time, of course, the industrial-consumer society which has emerged in the modern world rests upon and supports the very modern vision of life and epistemology which has led to the impossible spiritual and environmental dilemmas we have been discussing. This is a gruesome, painful and intolerable religious situation. We find ourselves in what appears to be a spiritual wasteland, a wasteland which we have in turn imposed on a devastated nature, a wasteland wherein "ignorant armies" enthused by ignorant models of religious understanding "clash by night."[16]

5. The Question of Religious Truth

Interestingly, most of the world's great religions (and some of their more creative periods of development) seem to have originated in times of religious pluralism and contention. Think, for example, of the situation at the time of Abraham or the conquest of Canaan. Or those of Gotama, Jesus, and Mohammed, not to mention the complex religious situation in the Hellenistic world of early Christianity, the thirteenth century encounter of Latin Christianity with Islam, or the religious melting pot of the Renaissance and the Reformation. It may even be that such pluralism is challenging and thereby conducive to genuine religious creativity and development. It's certainly not farfetched to think so. Yet, the religious pluralism and conflict which we are presently witnessing around the world seems of a different kind and extent. Perhaps because our fragmented religious cultures are in much closer contact and at the same time very heavily armed, they seem more violent, deeply entrenched, and exclusivistic than earlier species. Whatever the reasons, we certainly don't seem to have grown accustomed or adjusted our thinking and behavior to it.

This very comingling and proximity in a shrinking world confronts us with the question of religious truth. After all, what we call a religious "belief" seems to be a belief only in so far as it tacitly holds that something is in fact true. It doesn't take very long for us to get to the question of religious knowledge and truth, then. The very religious pluralism which has brought us the kind of religious freedom and choice unthinkable to our parents and grandparents at the same time raises the reflective issue of religious knowledge and truth. On the surface, it would seem that we could choose from this rich menu of religious options the way we choose careers or fashions. One result of this increased freedom, however, is the emergence in very direct form of the question of religious understanding and truth: all those different religious traditions are either explicitly or implicitly claiming such truth. Thus it occurs to all of us (sometimes in a painfully existential way) to ask what precisely is meant by such understandings and truths and if they are mutually exclusive. If one is true, does that mean the others are false?

Putting the same point more dramatically, the question of religious truth obtrudes itself when we consider such common phenomena today as the fact that, for many Shiite Moslems, America is 'the great Satan.' Of course, for the Reverend Moon and certain American fundamentalists, the great Satan is Communism and secular humanism, and America is seen as the special vehicle of God's providence. In fact, however, when we step back from these immediate passions to see the broader picture, the idea that one or another of these alternative traditions might be considered true and all the others false seems naive, quaintly old-fashioned, and absurdly dangerous.

Such a view seems naive because it posits an eternal and unchanging set of dogmatic truths with absolutely no recognition of the historical, cultural, economic and gender relativities which unavoidably enter into any particular interpretation of canon and tradition, including this one. For anyone who has actually studied the historical development of the various world religions, such contingent historical interpretations seem to be not only unavoidable but essential aspects of a tradition. Indeed, we are all aware that what appears to be today's dogma was yesterday's contingent interpretation.

The view that just one set of religious doctrines is true and all others false appears old-fashioned because it seems to be a view of religious truth designed for another time and place. As Peter Berger puts it:

It seems highly improbable, to say the least, that the millennia of Hindu and Buddhist experience can be subsumed under the heading of idolatry or illusion. Conversely, it seems most implausible to look upon the prophet Isaiah as an infantile intimation of what every ordinary Tibetan monk takes for granted. *How could it be possible that both types of religious experience are true?*[17]

Finally, the view appears dangerous because, in a shrinking and violent world, it hands dogmatic epistemological weapons to traditions which are already in head-on cultural, economic, and political collision. It is also dangerous because it contributes nothing toward ameliorating the present level of environmental devastation. Indeed, it is part of a mind-set which fosters such devastation.

And yet, to fall back into a sort of universal skepticism in which none of the various traditions are true at all and in which truth claims are simply relative seems spiritually impossible, for it makes the pursuit of religious understanding and life a kind of contradiction and absurdity. How can anyone commit him or herself to the difficult discipline of spiritual development over time without thinking that, in some sense or other, what one is doing is true? If it's all simply a shot in the dark, why do it?

Such skepticism seems self-defeating in more than just a conceptual sense, for it entails a way of living which seems to be a painful contradiction of the human need for meaning. Aldous Huxley claimed somewhere that "the central question for humanity is the quest for grace." If that is the case, as I think it is, then to deny its possibility is to live a kind of contradiction in terms. Since it appears to fly in the face of our own nature, such an existential contradiction is probably quite impossible to sustain in the long run.

Furthermore, all of the various religious traditions involve a recognition in some form or other of an ultimately meaningful dimension of life—the sacred. That sacred, by whatever name, is considered to be above all real, indeed *reality* itself. By definition, knowledge has to do with a consciousness, representation, or perception of reality. For if it were not about the real, then it would be about what is *not* (i.e., nonreality), and thus would be not knowledge, but illusion or error. It would seem, then, that human beings (of whatever culture or tradition) have a deep need to believe that the religious views and standards they hold are in fact true, that they are rooted in the fundamental and unchanging nature of reality itself. Were it not so, how important could they really be? Yet how can we hold that our particular truths are true when others hold such different and seemingly antithetical ones? In the modern context, we seem damned if we do and damned if we don't. That certainly sounds like a no-win spiritual situation.

Faced with such a spiritual dilemma, what are we to do? The choice of either relativism or a myopic and self-enclosed absolutism seem inadequate and, as we have said, existentially self-contradictory. As human beings, we have the questions. It's the answers that are inadequate or simply lacking. In the words of Peter Slater:

> My own experience in public universities has been that for many students, religious questions are alive but traditional answers are dead. For many others the traditions still live, but in corners cut off from the rest of their experience.[18]

This is the underlying spiritual dilemma into which the modern world has been thrown. The roots of the dilemma, as we have just seen, can be traced back to an inadequate and certainly dysfunctional conception of religious knowledge developed (or at least hardened) during the Enlightenment. That schizoid limitation of our spiritual choices to either meaninglessness and existential incoherence or dogmatic exclusivism—all within the context of the ecological crisis which it has helped to foster—is, of course, not something anyone desires. My claim in this book is that a new, postmodern model of religious understanding might be able to help heal the spiritual and ecological malaise presently overwhelming us.

The world's religious traditions all point to a dimension that is in danger of being closed off in our technological, industrial societies. That dimension—the sacred, by whatever name—is in nature, personal relationships, our cities, factories, schools, everywhere, if we can but perceive it. But we seem increasingly blind to it, perhaps because (as we have been claiming) our picture of religious understanding and truth makes it seem naive and untenable. Religious people see the same world as nonreligious people, but they see it in the light of that sacred dimension. Testimony from all religious traditions makes clear that to live in the light of that sacred dimension is to find all things new and to discover love and compassion for all beings—including nature, of course.

If it is fair to say that the purpose of our various religions is to commend that sacred dimension in such a way that it is made available once again to our people, then we must come to grips with whatever stands in the way of that task. It seems quite clear that the inadequate view of religious truth imposed on us by the Enlightenment, a view which constitutes part of the very substance of modernity, does in fact stand in the way. It either erodes all traditional visions of meaningful life or it transforms them into isolated and insulated pockets of dogmatism—all the while fostering a notion of industrial and economic progress and development which threatens the earth itself.

We need to develop an alternative conception of religious knowledge then, one which will permit us to overcome modernity's propensity to obliterate traditional culture in favor of renewing it. It is important here to emphasize *renewal*. Such a postmodern model of religious understanding will neither do away with the traditional conception of meaningful life nor simply reduce our understanding of it to a set of static and unchanging doctrines. To do that would be to fall into the painful, modern dilemma we have been attempting to outline. Rather, this alternative conception should permit us to come in between the horns of that dilemma, to reassess and appropriate our traditions in such a way that we can address the situation of our own time and place—including, of course, the painful spiritual and environmental dilemmas we are presently facing. Putting it another way, we need to construct a theory of religious understanding which neither locks us into the past nor critically discards that past. We seek neither dogmatism nor critical emptiness, but rather a critically informed view of religious understanding and truth which will enable us to appropriate and revitalize our traditional cultures at a higher, postmodern stage.

The time seems ripe for such a postmodern model of religious understanding because (some claim) modernity itself has been transcended into a postmodern situation in which alternative conceptions of human understanding and destiny have come to the fore. We need no longer reduce reality to objects in nature and knowledge to their apprehension. A wider, postmodern perspective has come into view, a view which strives to see and explore religious practice and understanding from within the world of ordinary experience. Such a perspective, I believe, is pregnant with a conception of religious understanding which can help us to renew our religious lives—but at a critical, postmodern level. In the words of Robert Bellah:

> If our high culture could begin to talk about nature and history, space and time, in ways that did not disaggregate them into fragments, it might be possible for us to find connections and analogies with the older ways in which human life was made meaningful. This would not result in a neotraditionalism that would return us to the past. Rather, it might lead to a recovery of a genuine tradition, one that is always self-revising and in a state of development. It might help us find again the coherence we have almost lost.[19]

6. Here's the Story

Max Weber thought that traditional religious culture was "an enchanted garden" compared to the "flat and disenchanted" modern, technological culture that replaced it. The nub of this essay is to tell the story of how we got into such a disenchanted cultural situation with the kinds of pervasive, persistent, and nagging spiritual issues indicated above and to sketch out an alternative, postmodern conception of religious understanding which may help us come to grips with it.

Put as succinctly as possible, I argue that underlying the modern period of the European tradition was a form of narrative (mythological) interpretive understanding on which it was founded and of which it remained unaware. That attitude toward life pervaded the modern world and cultures and led to disastrous consequences for our spiritual lives as well as for the natural environment which was utilized to sustain it. The recognition of that mythological, interpretive understanding underlying the modern world constitutes the initial step into what some have called the "postmodern" era. The emerging awareness that this alternative form of narrative, interpretive understanding is an essential aspect of human life comes to characterize postmodern philosophy and understanding in general. Furthermore, it provides a model of religious understanding which is not only more consistent with what we know about religious life, but at the same time may permit us to deal more effectively with the spiritual and ecological maladies which have poured down upon us in the modern world.

This overall argument can be broken down into the following specific steps:

1) An analysis in which I trace these modern maladies back to their origin in the Enlightenment vision of nature and reality (and the human place within it) as well as the model of human understanding which accompanied this vision.
2) An indication of the place such a modern view occupies within the larger story of our European tradition's conception of religious understanding.
3) An attempt to show how a postmodern conception of interpretive (hermeneutical) understanding in the humanities and social sciences grew out of that modern conception as a critique of it.
4) An argument that this postmodern conception of interpretive understanding has great significance for the development of a narrative model of understanding based on the kind of interpretive knowledge involved in stories of various kinds.

5) An attempt to draw out and specify in some detail the nature of such a postmodern model of narrative, religious understanding, and truth.

6) A summary of our contemporary religious situation in which I show how this view of religious knowledge provides us with new and more adequate ways to deal with the spiritual issues which we have inherited from the Enlightenment and which are so stubbornly pervasive and pernicious today.

The overall argument of the book can be put in another way. We are all aware of the recent explosion of scholarly interest in what has been termed 'story theology.' Such prominent and yet diverse thinkers as Alysdair MacIntyre, Stanley Hauerwas, Paul Ricoeur, Sallie McFague, Johann Baptist Metz, Hans Frei, and Terrence Tilley have explored the narrative foundations and grammar of theology and religious life in general. This has constituted an important new direction in theology, one which has led to a deepening of our understanding of various aspects of our spiritual condition. In particular, it has helped us to recognize what hitherto went unnoticed—that religious understanding or truth is an alternative kind of knowing beyond and outside of science and mathematics, a broad kind of narrative understanding which founds and structures the various human 'worlds' which populate human history. I myself recently published a phenomenological study in which I tried to show how narrative is the form of personal identity and that such a story-shaped self constitutes the ontological or existential condition for the possibility of human stories of any kind—novels, narrative history, psychological case-studies, dramas, and (of course) religious mythology and historical revelation.

This book is an attempt to think through the specific nature of religious understanding and truth in light of that basic, narratively structured self and then to consider the significance of that understanding of religious knowledge for our contemporary religious situation.

Specifically, my thesis is that religious knowledge involves two kinds (or aspects) of narrative understanding: (1) the narrative disclosure in myth, historical revelation, and metaphysical system of possible modes of meaningful existence, and (2) faith or the actual living out of a particular story or personal identity in light of that disclosure. I argue that these two aspects of religious understanding together constitute a unique form of interpretive human understanding, a form with its own particular criteria of evaluation and truth. This conception of religious understanding has only recently become philosophically available in our postmodern world. It has, I believe, immediate and important consequences for religious life today. It can support the active pursuit of spiritual understanding and life as well as foster tolerance and dialogue between different religious symbol traditions. In a shrinking world where major religious traditions and ideologies are coming into increasing contact and conflict, such spiritual understanding and tolerance have become critically important.

The book is divided into three sections. In Part One, ''The Historical Story,'' I trace the history of Western religious understanding from its beginnings in mythology and historical revelation through the flowering of modernity in the seventeenth and eighteenth centuries to the postmodern critique of that modernity and emergence of an alternative kind of interpretive understanding which is neither inductive nor deductive. It is this model of interpretive understanding which, I believe, has great potential for the development of a postmodern conception of religious knowledge and truth. Modernity, with all its difficulties for religious understanding, was in fact based upon a nonempirical story about the 'progress' of human history. This, in turn, led to a postmodern situation in which a new understanding of a broader kind of narrative and interpretive knowing in the humanities and arts has emerged as both a powerful critique of modernity and a means of acquiring a deeper understanding of what and how we can be said to truly 'know' in these human (or humane) disciplines.

Part Two, ''The Heart of the Matter,'' constitutes the core of the book in which I develop this postmodern view of religious knowledge in light of the basic narrative structure of personal experience and identity. That knowledge, I argue, is a unique form of interpretive understanding in narrative, mythological form—a disclosure of different ways human beings see life as a meaningful whole and through which they come to actually live in oriented cultural 'worlds.' Such interpretive understanding involves unique evaluative criteria and renews (in different form) the ancient tradition of an encompassing kind of human wisdom or knowledge.

Finally, in Part Three, ''Denouement,'' I outline how such a view of religious knowledge and truth can help us move beyond the constricting and debilitating spiritual issues generated by the modern world view.

To begin the argument, then, we must first come to terms with the history of our own tradition's varying attitudes toward religious knowledge and truth. We can't do that by means of a kind of scientific process in which we move from observations to causal hypotheses and explanations to experimental testing of those hypotheses. Such a procedure would entail the tacit acceptance and reduction of that history to the framework of modernity—the very framework we are trying to get beyond. What we need, then, is to 'see' that modernity along with its constricted understanding of human knowledge and destiny within the larger framework of history. Historical, interpretive understanding is called for here, and that entails telling the whole story of our Western conceptions of religious knowledge in such a way that we can 'see' the sequence of views as a whole over the evident temporal changes which characterize it. We will see why that is the case later. In the meantime, however, it ought to come as no surprise that an essay dedicated to attempting to understand religious knowledge as a form of narrative insight into life begins its argument with the *story* of the historical development of that religious knowledge.

Part I

The Historical Story

1

From Myth to Modernity

It is not easy...to see realities that one's cultural world-view is not calibrated to perceive. It is one of the presuppositions of thought that a revision is requisite, if we are to think more truly about the world and our life together.

Wilfred Cantwell Smith

1:1 Mythology

We begin our story with the traditional cultures of ancient Greece and the Near East. Surprisingly, what was until very recently the common, modern view that mythology is nonscientific fable, invention, and fantasy directly contradicts the attitude of the traditional cultures that myth is not only significant but true. As Mircea Eliade has put it, mythology "is considered to be absolutely true" in its original cultural context "because it is concerned with realities."[1] Mythology, then, constitutes the first and most fundamental form of religious knowledge, a form which emerged at the traditional or archaic beginnings of our religious and cultural tradition.

Mythology comes from the Greek word *muthos,* which means a story or something said. As opposed to legends and other forms of folktale, myths are stories about the sacred and the relationship of the world and human beings to it.[2] Mythology, then, bifurcates reality into two levels—a transcendent or deep level of meaning (heaven, the abode of the gods, etc.), and the fallen, dependent, and ordinary world of nature and the tribe—what Eliade calls the "sacred" and the "profane."

In short, myths reveal that the World, man, and life have a supernatural origin and history, and that this history is significant, precious, and exemplary.[3]

The deep level is considered real, whereas the ordinary level is thought of as a less real and dependent reflection of it:

> The man of archaic societies tends to live as much as possible in the sacred...because for primitives...the sacred is equivalent to a power, and, in the last analysis, to reality. The sacred is saturated with being.[4]

Furthermore, the sacred is construed to be perfect, ideal, eternal, unchanging, and holy, whereas the ordinary world of nature and human experience is, as it were, fallen—a lesser, changing, and temporal reality, which is dependent upon the sacred for its existence as well as for any meaning, unity (or order), and success achieved within it. Mythology (especially creation mythology), then, discloses a human awareness of a transcendental reality beyond this world but reflected within it:

> Primitive man might be said to view the encounter with "otherness" as a mode of access to what Emerson called "a world elsewhere" which, though revealing itself within the sphere of the profane, is nevertheless assumed to originate from beyond it. Just because of its stability and perdurance, this "other world" is assumed to be the "real" one and thus serves as model and norm for all that transpires in the unreal haphazard realm of historical time.[5]

Avery Dulles associates this transcendental reality known by myth with metaphysics into which (as we shall soon see) it will be translated through the allegorical method.

> In every civilization there have been thinkers concerned with the ultimate basis of reality, meaning, and value. In some traditions this basis has been viewed as an invisible and transcendent order in which our empirical world is somehow rooted. This view, which may be called metaphysical or religious, is held in common by many of the Greek philosophical systems, the Eastern religions, and the Western religions.[6]

Jean Seznec expresses this sense of two worlds very well when discussing the particular and astonishing development of astral and gnostic cults in the late Roman period.

The idea of "two worlds" was part of the religious topography of man in late antiquity. For pagans and Christians alike, the "other world" was the seat of a supreme God, infinitely remote from the human world.[7]

This discovery and display of the sacred level of being in mythology is (as we shall argue in more detail later) the first step in the long process whereby human beings came to orient their lives in the light of an interpretation (Hermeneutic) of the meaning of being. Human beings don't just exist; they exist and act in the light of some ultimate sense of what it means to be. In a very real sense, religious mythology moves and shapes people's lives by helping them to notice the difference between what is in themselves and the world and what might or ought to be, thereby helping them to discover an ultimate vision of what they are living for. *Heaven* expresses the important fact that our human reach exceeds our grasp, that we construe (or see) our ordinary lives in terms of an ideal perfection we discover through our founding myths. We know of no human beings or cultures which do not involve some human sense of what life means—what it is for—and it is these overarching interpretations of life which configure and found the variety of human cultures or worlds. As Robert Oden put it recently:

Many scholars have proposed that any society's myths are an integral part of the ways in which that society presents to its members and to the wider world a full articulation of its deepest values and beliefs.[8]

1:2 Myth and Historical Revelation

But what about the Biblical tradition of historical revelation? Is it too mythological, or does it (as many adherents have claimed) lie entirely outside myth as a historical and 'factual' disclosure of God's nature and will?

If by historical revelation we mean the disclosure of God in and through real historical events, then I believe we can say that it is an extension of myth to covenantal history. As we have already indicated, by 'mythology' we don't mean lies or falsehoods, but rather the narrative disclosure of ultimate meaning for our lives—in this case, through historical events.

'Sacred history' is not a mere chronicle of events, but an *interpreted* account of what those events mean within a narrative historical construal or 'reading' of them. In other words, we 'see' the events of history in the light of a narrative plot which links those events into a meaningful whole. As Arthur Danto argues, because narrative organization and meaning involve a telos which could not have existed at the time of those events, it is not something lying within historical events themselves, but of necessity is something which a later historian brings to the events in terms of 'temporal wholes.' [9] We can say then that, although revelation may involve real historical events, the *meaning* of those events is not itself objective as much as a narrative, interpretive framework in which the events become mythologically disclosive of an overarching and transcendent dimension of life. Donald Polkinghorne has argued that literary, mythological, and historical narratives are all the result of cultural attempts

> to impose a satisfactory, graspable, humanizing shape on experience. The historical narrative takes the types of plots developed by literature and subjects them to the test of endowing real events with meaning. The knowledge provided by narrative history is what results from the application of the systems of meaning originally elaborated by cultures in their myths and (in some cultures) later refined by their literatures. Historical narratives are a test of the capacity of a culture's fictions to endow real events with the kinds of meaning patterns that its stories have fashioned from imagined events. Thus, historical narratives transform a culture's collection of past happenings (its first-order referents) by shaping them into a second-order pattern of meaning.[10]

There is no question that the great covenantal, historical tradition has discovered something new and important; and yet, for all that, it still remains a mode of mythology. It has discovered a mythological dimension to history, an interpretive story in which individual events become windows through which we can encounter the ultimate meaning of our lives. The Bible is not so much a set of doctrines as it is a collection of stories about historical events which make the meaning of those events narratively available to the reader. Sacred history is the shaping of (past) historical events into a narrative pattern of meaning. In other words, we come to 'see' the events of history in the light of a narrative plot which links them into a meaningful whole.

> One simply has to realize sooner or later how much of the truth about historical people and events requires the imagination of the story-teller, the creativity of the literary artist, for its telling.[11]

The Biblical scholar Robert Alter makes this point explicit in his recent book, *The Art of Biblical Narrative.*

> As odd as it may sound at first, I would contend that prose fiction is the best general rubric for describing biblical narrative. Or, to be more precise...we can speak of the Bible as *historicized* prose fiction....Let me hasten to say that in giving such weight to fictionality, I do not mean to discount the historical impulse that informs the Hebrew Bible. The God of Israel, as so often has been observed, is above all the God of history: the working out of His purposes in history is a process that compels the attention of the Hebrew imagination, which is thus led to the most vital interest in the concrete and differential character of historical events. The point is that fiction was the principal means which the biblical authors had at their disposal for realizing history.[12]

1:3 Allegory and Metaphysical Knowledge

The next step in the story of Western understanding of religious knowledge was tied up with the religious reform which attended the development of classical Greek philosophy, from Anaximenes, Heraclitus, Pythagoras, and other pre-Socratic cosmologists to the great systems of Stoicism and Neoplatonism. The reform involved the allegorical method of interpreting the (by that time) classical myths and mythological history, especially with the Stoics, but also with Philo Judaeus and (later) Origen. We should keep in mind from the outset that that allegorical method—whether in the hands of the Stoic Chrysippus or the later Christian, Origen—is a hermeneutical or interpretive method, indeed *the* method of scriptural interpretation in Christianity at least until the seventeenth century and in Judaism until the present day.[13]

As H.A. Wolfson has put it, ''The allegorical method means the interpretation of a text in terms of something else....''[14] Myths (and later scripture) are polysemic. That is, they embody another (or several other) level(s) of allegorical meaning beyond the literal meaning of the text. The naive religious myths and biblical history were interpreted or 'seen as' implicit allegories which could be translated into explicit scientific or metaphysical insights and systems. As we noted earlier, mythology expresses a two-level reality—a transcendent or sacred level of reality (what Emerson called ''a world elsewhere'') and the lesser, dependent reality of nature and ordinary life. The simple mechanism for this allegorical interpretation was to replace that transcendent, deep-level sacred with principles (*Archai*), natural law (*Logos*), mind (*Nous*), or eternal ideas. The great Greek philosophers picked up this notion of a bifurcated reality and 'saw' this life (the many particulars in motion) as a dependent reflection of an ultimate metaphysical reality (the One which is eternal) known by the mind. Plato, for example, defined the ''ideas'' as

> an unchanging and harmonious order where nothing can do or suffer wrong, where all is in order according to reason.[15]

> These ideas are as it were patterns fixed in the nature of things; the other things are made in their image and are likenesses; and this participation they come to have in the ideas is nothing but their being made in their image.[16]

Mircea Eliade's comments on the religious reform which Plato's idealism constituted could be said of the allegorization of myth in Greek philosophy in general.

> The distance between Plato and the primitive world is too obvious for words; but that distance does not imply a break in continuity. In this Platonic doctrine of Ideas, Greek philosophy renewed and re-valorised the archaic and universal myth of a fabulous, pleromatic *illud tempus*, which man has to remember if he is to know the *truth* and participate in *Being*. The primitive, just like Plato in his theory of *anamnesis*, does not attach importance to *personal* memories: only the myth, the exemplary History is of importance to him. One might even say that Plato comes nearer than Pythagoras to traditional thinking: the latter, with his personal recollections of ten or twenty previous lives, is more nearly in line with the 'elect'—with Buddha, the yogis and shamans. In Plato it is only the pre-existence of the soul in the timeless universe of Ideas that matters; and the truth (aletheia) is the remembrance of that impersonal situation.[17]

The 'something else' in terms of which reality is interpreted, to use Wolfson's terminology, is a philosophical or cosmological system. The myth is thus given a metaphysical reading or gloss, and traditional Greek religion is thereby reformed and made acceptable to its more sophisticated members.

Indeed, the allegorical interpretation began with the sixth-century B.C.E. Greek cosmologists who found the literal meaning of Homer's and Hesiod's stories of the gods literally incredible. Rather than simply reject these by now traditional and authoritative myths, thinkers such as Heraclitus, Anaximenes, Pythagoras, and Anaxagoras translated the stories allegorically into one or another version of natural law or mind (*Logos* and *Nous*). Even Plato and the Neoplatonists who followed much later, while belittling the exuberance and exaggeration of allegorical interpretation (both Plato and Porphyry do that), clearly indulged themselves in such allegorical interpretation of traditional religious myths, practices, and terminology. But it was the Stoics who finally perfected the method and passed it on to the Hellenistic Jews through Philo Judaeus and the Christians through Origen. For the latter, scriptural interpretation involves three levels of meaning—the 'flesh,' the 'soul,' and what he called 'pneumatic nomos.'[18] In spite of a tendency toward interpretive exaggeration and the emergence of inconsistency between the interpretive levels (the problem of 'double truth' in the Medieval period), the method of an allegorical discovery (some say a "reading into") of philosophical understanding and perspective within the scriptures led to the synthesis of Athens and Jerusalem which was the heart of Medieval culture and theology and fundamental to the development of European culture and religion. As I have already indicated, the allegorical method remained *the* method of critically interpreting religious texts and stories at least until the seventeenth century.

I believe the significance of this development for the Western tradition's conception of the nature and status of religious understanding cannot be overemphasized. There is a traditional and perennial knowledge or wisdom[19], this allegorical method seems to imply, that can be expressed in at least two forms—that of religious stories for the common people and that of a parallel philosophical or metaphysical understanding for more intellectual devotees. In whichever form, we have here a conception of an encompassing sort of spiritual wisdom, clearly and closely associated with religious truth. It was a wisdom which had to do with understanding how life might be lived fully in the light of a vision of ultimate reality disclosed narratively or allegorically. Such wisdom both encompassed and exceeded mathematical and empirical forms of knowledge, which were envisaged as subsets within it. Rather than a kind of technical understanding which seeks to subordinate nature to human drives and ambition, then, this was an insight which insisted on integrating human life into an overarching cosmic order. It was this model of an encompassing religious understanding which (disastrously, I believe) was destined to be set aside during the Enlightenment.

1:4 Modernity

It was when the so-called "modern" period emerged that the story of religious knowledge took a rather bizarre turn. "Modernity" is the name commonly given to that worldview which emerged in seventeenth-century Europe with the development and eventual domination of modern science and technology; and which, outfitted in secondhand European clothing, has in the meantime spread around the world. It should be noted here that by "modernity" I do not mean the movement in artistic, architectural, and literary circles in the late nineteenth and twentieth centuries called "modernism." Rather, the term *modernity* (or the modern world) indicates the worldview and concrete technological and industrial culture which developed from the Cartesian, Galilean, Baconian, and Newtonian views of science, nature, and human destiny, as well as Adam Smith's conception of economics. *Postmodern,* then, indicates a contemporary worldview and possible cultural evolution which—although certainly not setting aside science and technology—critically goes beyond the modern premises and presumptions concerning knowledge, nature, and human life in general.

We might define a worldview as a culture's overarching and encompassing sense of the meaning, purpose and essential point of human living. Perhaps we can borrow Clifford Geertz's now-classic definition of religion to spell out what we mean in more detail. A worldview is a cultural "blueprint or template," he tells us,

(1) a system of symbols which acts to (2) establish powerful, pervasive, and long-lasting moods and motivations in men by (3) formulating conceptions of a general order of existence and (4) clothing these conceptions with such an aura of factuality that (5) the moods and motivations seem uniquely realistic.[20]

The dominant worldview of a people or age—their fundamental outlook on life—colors their thoughts, behavior and beliefs.

In the last analysis, it is the ultimate picture which an age forms of the nature of its world that is its most fundamental possession. It is the final controlling factor in all thinking whatever.[21]

From a phenomenological and Heideggerian perspective, a worldview is the symbolic hermeneutic or interpretation of the meaning of Being which constitutes the ultimate horizon of the various human 'worlds' in which people happen to live.[22] Using a structuralist manner of speaking, we could call it the code or deep grammar which conditions and delimits the variety of thought and activity which takes place within it in much the same way that the rules of the game condition and delimit all the baseball games actually played out.

Like any other worldview, modernity was not just a matter of thinking. Rather, it entered concretely into how people shaped their environment, built their homes, and ordered their political lives; what ultimate sense of right and wrong they held; how they saw themselves as men or women, family members, or citizens of this or that nation-state. As we shall argue later when discussing the hermeneutical, religious foundations of culture, it was not so much thought about as lived and behaved. It was an attitude toward life which cast a mood and structured a whole epoch and world with meaning, at least until recently. It established cultural and intellectual limits as well as opportunities which characterized the modern period as such. As Langdon Gilkey puts it, it was a worldview which

> at the deepest level...has been founded on a new philosophy of history, a philosophy built on faith in knowledge and its power to control, on the triumph through knowledge of human purposes over blind fate, and on the confidence that change, if guided by intelligence informed by inquiry, can realize human fulfillment in this life. Such a view of history as guided by science and shaped by technology was the implicit 'religion' of the West until a few decades ago.[23]

What emerged in the Enlightenment, then, was an overarching hermeneutical (and mythological, I shall claim) interpretation and picture of reality, self, history, and the human role and destiny within nature.

In his brilliant analysis of the origins and roots of modernity, *Cosmopolis: The Hidden Agenda of Modernity*, Stephen Toulmin points out that a more tolerant and nondogmatic (skeptical) period in European culture before 1610 fractured on the nightmare of the Thirty Years War (1618–1648). The result was a failure of nerve on the part of the new philosophy, for it in effect proposed to address that bloody and painful crisis by establishing a philosophical methodology and view based on certainty and unambiguous language. What they proposed, in short, was to overcome ambiguity and conflict by establishing an apodictic, foundational theory beyond the contradictory and inflamatory claims and passions of the various faiths and cultures involved in the nightmare. By this means, the new philosophy swept away the previous, more humble skepticism of sixteenth-century thinkers such as Montaigne in favor of foundations which were taken to be certain to the degree that they were (initially) mathematically 'proven' or (ultimately) empirically traceable back to 'facts.' From this point of view, philosophy itself was to be foundational by being rationally grounded on abstract, universal, and timeless concepts. By doing this, Toulmin points out, the new philosophy decontextualized its own thought and science, and devalued the real and the particular (in short the concrete world of ordinary experience) in favor of an abstract and ideal theory.

> The three dreams of the Rationalists thus turn out to be aspects of a larger dream. The dreams of a rational method, a unified science, and an exact language unite into a single project. All of them are designed to 'purify' the operations of human reason by decontextualizing them: i.e., by divorcing them from the details of particular historical and cultural situations.[24]

The word *modern* is etymologically derived from a Latin word meaning "contemporary" or "of this time." The English word seems to have two principle meanings: (1) that which is contemporary, and (2) the present era which is thought to be new (novel) and different from the traditional culture which preceded it. Thus, the general sense of the term is to name the cultural period in which we are presently living, a period which has developed beyond the pre-modern and pre-industrial culture by critically standing outside of and over/against it. Thus, modernity is sometimes referred to as "the critical era" insofar as it consciously holds up the earlier traditional (and religious) culture for critical analysis.

Within this overall characterization, the modern worldview is generally thought to incorporate the following attitudes and ways of seeing life and human destiny.

1. *Human destiny lies in its increasing domination and control of reality.* God only knows (if you'll excuse the pun), but it seems like ever since being expelled from the Garden of Eden for picking the fruit of the Tree of the Knowledge of Good and Evil (in other words, a long time ago), human beings have sought to recapture their lost security by discovering a way of knowing—an aggressive and controlling form of knowing—which would permit them to dominate and order all of reality. "If we can master our earthly environment," they seem to be saying, "we can at last feel secure: the more control, the more security."

This search for a controlling form of knowledge led at first to the creation of special tools and techniques to force a niggardly nature to yield more than she seemed willing to give on her own. The next step along the road to the modern, industrial world was taken at the beginning of the seventeenth century.

In 1620, Francis Bacon published his *Novum Organum*, which defined genuine knowledge as the fundamental tool in the human arsenal for mastering nature. He called for a new, objective scientific method which would permit human beings not only to avoid egregious error fostered by subjective passions ("idols of the mind"), but to achieve a genuine and practical kind of understanding of nature "from which must necessarily follow an improvement of their estate, and an increase of their power over nature."[25] And Descartes, in his *Discourse on Method*, echoed this sentiment when he indicated that by knowing how to know we can become "masters and possessors of the earth." True knowledge permits a kind of control which assures human security.

This attempt to control and dominate nature in ways which other (traditional) cultures could never and did never achieve has become a characteristic element of modern life. We moderns seek control and order through our technologies (the practical application of scientific understanding) not only over the cruel accidents and perfidy of nature, but over the disruptive ambiguities and pains of society as well. Witness the host of such social technologies as criminology, education, journalism, public relations, marketing, advertising, and so on. In fact, astonishingly enough, we seem bent at present on trying to order and master our own bodies and selves through genetic engineering.

2. *History is progressive*. The notion that history is progressive and that things are getting better and better for human beings is an important and rather unique aspect of modernity. In all probability, the notion was inherited in germinal form from the earlier, traditional Judaeo-Christian worldview, but it was quickly shaped and adapted to fit into the modern situation.

Human history is not simply the endless, natural, cyclical repetition (as with the seasons) of what has been before; rather, it is linear. It starts somewhere and is progressing toward a human goal and destiny of perfect—or at least expanded—security. Such progress, then, entails the emergence of genuine novelty, and that novelty is envisioned as progressively better and better.

Although environmentally disastrous in its anthropocentric point of view, this notion (humanly speaking) is profoundly optimistic, perhaps naively and dangerously so for those of us here at the end of the twentieth century. When this concept of progress is combined with the drive for control discussed above, we are left with the typically modern view that human history displays as its inherent nature and telos the unending development of human control and security by knowing how to know. The rewards of that kind of mastering and dominating knowledge, we are told, will continue to pour down upon us as we extend it throughout nature and human society.

3. *The reduction of knowledge to technical understanding.* For purposes of this essay, the most fateful step in the development of the modern worldview was to limit knowledge or even rationality itself to a kind of calculating reason—i.e., careful observation based on matters of fact along with an equally careful and clear use of deductive reason. In other words, 'knowledge' was limited to matters of fact or matters of reason. This is, of course, what some have referred to as the fetishizing of fact and deductive logic. The social sciences, arts, and humanities, in this context, must either utilize just those methods of knowing or be banished from the arena of 'knowledge' and 'rationality' entirely. According to Rorty:

> Since the Enlightenment, and in particular since Kant, the physical sciences had been viewed as a paradigm of knowledge, *to which the rest of culture had to measure up.*[26]

All that was left for the nonscientific, human arts and sciences, then, was value—either moral or esthetic. However it is expressed, a radical distinction emerged between genuine science and the leftover 'human arts'—including, of course, religion and theology.

> Science is radically different from art. The former is cognitive, the latter imaginative. The former discovers, the latter creates. Science is *hard,* art *soft.* Many find this disjunction tremendously important, for without it there seems no way to distinguish between matters of fact and matters of taste, between "objective" and "subjective," between "what is true" and "what I like."[27]

However interesting and even inspiring they may be, these human arts and sciences (once again, including religious understanding) are construed as emotive decoration, matters of taste or subjective feeling and attitude projected upon a meaningless nature, but certainly not ways of 'knowing' anything. Put more bluntly, we learn nothing from our great paintings or music, nothing from religious myths or practices, perhaps nothing even from our great philosophical essays—because knowledge or learning is *a priori* limited to matters of fact and matters of reason.

4. *Modernity is critically anti-traditional.* This is true in two senses. First of all, the modern reduction of human understanding to scientific and mathematical knowledge assures a critical scrutiny of those earlier, traditional claims to religious wisdom or understanding. Embodied in this critical approach, then, is what has been called a "hermeneutics of suspicion," in which the modern observer not only puts the tradition at a distance, as it were, but also simply obliterates its claims to truth of any kind. In other words, the entire religious endeavor is suspected of sheer fantasy. Indeed, 'mythology' in this context is interpreted as 'lie' or 'scientific error:' It is often said that something is "just a myth." This of course leads to the typically modern interpretive antithesis of either a return to some version or other of tradition or a reduction of the tradition to modern terms and understanding. Ultimately, of course, I shall argue that this interpretive dilemma is characteristically modern and must be transcended in any postmodern conception of our relation to our various traditions.

Second, by critically questioning and distancing itself from the earlier tradition, modernity frees itself from its social and moral constraints. To be modern, then, means to be free from traditional social, class, institutional, and even national definitions of who we are. A characteristic element of modern culture is the sometimes painful and sometimes exhilarating sense of sheer freedom and possibility which is ours—a dizzying sense that our morality, vocations, and perhaps our very selves (for Sartre, for example) are matters of freedom and choice.

Modernity, then, introduced a cultural climate which separated it from the traditional point of view preceding it. It is a climate which seems to dissolve any possibility of spiritual life in the harsh glare of its critical suspicion, and which leaves us fascinated with and yet distraught by freedom.

> To be modern is to find ourselves in an environment that promises us adventure, power, joy, growth, transformation of ourselves and the world—and, at the same time, that threatens to destroy everything we have, everything we know, everything we are. . . . it pours us all into a maelstrom of perpetual disintegration and renewal, of struggle and contradiction, of ambiguity and anguish. To be modern is to be part of a universe in which, as Marx said, "all that is solid melts into air."[28]

5. *Modernity desacralizes nature.* As everyone knows, Descartes split reality into two essentially distinct kinds or forms; *res extensa* and *res cogitans*—matter and mind. In the overall economy of his ontology, Descartes envisaged 'mind' as the appropriate domain for religion and morality, whereas 'matter' (nature) was reserved for genuine scientific understanding. This, of course, has led not only to the desacralization of nature but also to the typically modern sense that science and theology have nothing to say to one another. Furthermore, because 'mind' gradually disappeared as modern culture unfolded, reality was increasingly pictured as made up of independent things or objects 'out there' which are knowable as they are 'in themselves' only by genuine science. Epistemologically, the problem was to show how the ideas we have in our minds about those things hook up with and "mirror" (to use Richard Rorty's phrase) what is actually there. In this cultural context, of course, God and theology have neither a role to play in understanding nature nor a 'real' home they can call their own. The earlier Christian tradition had conceived of nature as sacrosanct. Think of the Augustinian and Neoplatonic tradition—in St. Bonaventure, for example, or mystics such as Meister Eckhart, or, more concretely, the ordinary Trinitarian notion of the Holy Spirit. Now, however, nature was stripped bare of any possible epiphany.

Descartes considered matter (nature) to be simple extension and thus geometrically rule bound. In fact, he says somewhere that "God is a geometer," thereby implying that He generated nature at creation by simply embodying the geometric design of it that He had already within his mind. This not only empties nature of anything spiritual, but (at best) pushes God off into a nebulous and ultimately self-contradictory realm 'before' creation and 'time.'

Newton added mechanics to this stark vision of nature. Although nature in itself is made up of meaningless bits, it constitutes an ordered whole structured by the principles of mechanics. Nature, then, is thought of as a machine the parts of which are ordered by mechanical law. As with Descartes, it seems that the only place and role for God in this picture is as the deist creator of the machine. As a machine, of course, nature (like any other machine) can be utilized for our own use. We can best control and utilize her for our ends by scientifically grasping the principles which inform her motion.

This means not only that nature was given over to mathematical (calculus) physics, but that theology was all the more rigorously excluded from trafficking with her. Science was separated from the earlier natural theology of which it had been a part and the modern slogan became: "What science has put asunder let no mere thelogian attempt to rejoin.'' So nature was increasingly desanctified and, to the degree that it was pictured as a machine ready for use, prepared for the industrial and technological revolution which was soon to follow.

6. *The economic base for modern industry.* Just as Newton saw nature as made up of bits which were organized into a machine-like whole by the natural law of mechanics, John Locke viewed human society analogously. Society, according to Locke, was made up of individual persons (bits) whose singular purpose is to perpetuate themselves by fulfilling their own needs. But just as with nature, there is a natural social law which harmonizes and orders the bits into a machine-like whole. Adam Smith, of course, drew the appropriate economic lesson: the common good of society is fostered by each individual seeking his or her own material advantage because a natural law of supply and demand (the famous 'invisible hand') regulates the organic whole of these bits of economic activity.

The scene was thus set for the development of modern industrial society. Nature was desacralized and pictured as a meaningless machine ready for human use. Human society itself was thought of as being made up of individuals whose chief good was to maximize their own economic control and success. Everything else would take care of itself.

1:5 The Spiritual Blues of Modernity

The modern worldview, then, was set in place and began its long evolution up to the present day. In fact, as I shall emphasize in more detail in the next chapter, it was founded upon a story. We humans, the story goes, have always wanted to achieve genuine knowledge, for such knowledge would bring us control over nature and a consequent security in life. Heretofore, we have had only pallid and useless mythological and metaphysical counterfeits of the authentic understanding of nature. But recently we have learned how to know. We have discovered that true understanding is limited to matters of fact and matters of reason. That in turn has revealed that nature is fundamentally mechanical and 'objective' in nature. It is not in any case the location or occasion for religious understanding or experience of any sort. This *knowing how to know,* the story concludes, makes possible the human dream of achieving a heaven on earth by dominating and ordering both nature and society. Put simply, language, ontology, and epistemology were placed in service and limited to those ways of speaking, that conception of reality, and those kinds of understanding which were effective in gaining mastery over the universe.

We should note at this point that this modern worldview led to many important and positive benefits for human life—its critical questioning of unsubstantiated claims, its demand for 'rational' analysis and evidence, its evident technical advances in medicine, agriculture, manufacturing, and so on. In fact, I shall argue later that the critical and interpretively 'suspicious' side of modernity should not only *not* be set aside but should be expanded and applied to modernity itself! However, if modernity entailed positive benefits (as I think it did), it also introduced a host of disastrous, dysfunctional consequences for spiritual life—what I call "the spiritual blues of modernity." It is precisely these difficult spiritual aspects of the modern world, of course, which the postmodern concept of religious understanding I will outline in Part Two must address and (hopefully) help to ameliorate. What were these spiritually dysfunctional aspects of the modern worldview?

1. *First of all, modernity broke the tradition of perennial wisdom.* In a stroke, the earlier tradition which saw religious understanding and metaphysical knowledge as forms of a single, encompassing 'wisdom'—a wisdom in which empirical knowledge and mathematics were but aspects—was overturned and irrevocably broken. This was important for at least two immediate reasons. First, as we have seen, that wisdom had to do with understanding how to live a meaningful and qualitatively rich life as opposed to a merely technical understanding which in effect reduced human destiny to power, control, and security. What was lost, then, was a form of hermeneutical understanding which involved an overarching sense of what human life was all about and how it ought to be lived. What replaced that kind of wisdom was an implicit (and assumed) sense that all that matters in life is order and security and an insistence that in the light of that, the only form of human understanding worthy of the name was that which was useful in achieving it. This was a remarkably blinkered and constricted view of human understanding.

But secondly, this overturning of the traditional sense of wisdom entailed a critical attitude which in effect not only undercut and obliterated the various traditions but also insisted that the only possible alternative to them was the modern view itself. This either/or situation—either a return to the traditional views and life or an insistence that the only alternative worldview and life is the modern one—is not only characteristic of modernity but (I shall argue) an inadequate and overly constricted conception of historical possibility.

2. *Modernity lost sight of the world of ordinary experience.* Modernity was a view which suppressed the world of ordinary experience in favor

of a picture of reality as a collection of object-things (matter) present to observers (mind). Thus, our immediate and ordinary experience of being-in-the-world was suppressed and in effect replaced by these two substances or realities. This not only blinded us to the relational field which *is* experience, but actually constituted an abstraction out of it in favor of one or the other pole within it—subjective perceiver and objective perceived. This left what many consider to be the main problem of modern philosophy, the bifurcation between subject and object and the consequent construction of philosophical perspectives on either the subjective and idealistic pole or the objective and realistic pole. With the rock-bottom presupposition of these two 'realities,' modern philosophy seemed to swing back and forth between constructing the world 'out there' either from the structures and contents of the knowing mind or reducing that knowing mind to a passive reception of the world as it was imagined to be 'in itself.' And while modern philosophy was limited in this way, at the same time it was simply unaware of the actual bipolar horizon of immediate experience. This constituted what Heidegger calls "the forgetfulness of Being"—the willy-nilly interpretation of being—not as concrete experience 'in the world'— but as either a worldless 'mind' or an equally worldless 'matter' construed as things 'in themselves.'

Stephen Toulmin refers to this remarkable blindness to ordinary experience as the "decontextualization" of understanding. From his point of view, modernity set aside the uncertainties and ambiguities of life (what I am calling "the world of ordinary experience") acknowledged by such sixteenth-century skeptics as Montaigne in favor of an abstract, timeless (eternal) and 'rational' understanding and certainty.

> That change of attitude—the devaluation of the oral, the particular, the local, the timely, and the concrete appeared a small price to pay for a formally "rational" theory grounded on abstract, universal, timeless concepts. In a world governed by these intellectual goals, rhetoric was of course subordinate to logic: the validity and truth of "rational" arguments is independent of *who* presents them, *to whom,* or *in what context*—such rhetorical questions can contribute nothing to the impartial establishment of human knowledge. For the first time since Aristotle, logical analysis was separated from, and elevated far above, the study of rhetoric, discourse and argumentation.[29]

This is not a merely parochial dispute between philosophers about 'ordinary' versus 'ideal' language, for it has immediate and important consequences for our understanding of religious knowledge and behavior. From the postmodern point of view I am trying to articulate in this essay, to lose sight of and suppress that experiential world of ordinary experience is to take away the only context and framework in which religious life and understanding make any sense whatsoever. It is a kind of 'category mistake' then, an intellectually illicit attempt to grasp religious realities in categories which are appropriate only to things. This not only distorts the religious realities we are trying to get at; it also blinds us to those categories embedded within ordinary experience which seem more useful in coming to understand them.

3. *It introduced the twin specter of meaninglessness and fanaticism.* As we have seen, modernity insisted on the reduction of valid knowledge to inductive hypotheses (matters of fact) and deductive conclusions (matters of reason). Physics and mathematics were increasingly viewed as the very paradigm of human understanding; all other cultural claims to understanding had to measure up to this model.

One consequence of this shift in paradigm was that religious understanding was increasingly construed as either a relative and noncognitive illusion or a kind of matter-of-fact knowledge (true beliefs) about the existence and nature of an absent, entity-like God.

On the one hand, attempts by rationalists and empiricists to force religious understanding or belief into either the deductive or inductive molds failed for rather obvious reasons. Because of this, as modernity evolved, such understanding increasingly was assigned to the trash heap of emotion and decoration, matters of taste and subjective feeling rather than any sort of genuine understanding of life and its demands. Religious belief (along with any understanding claimed by literature, history, the arts, and even philosophy) was banished from the realm of knowledge altogether. We learn nothing from gospel and myth.

We can put this another way. Because the inductive and deductive forms of understanding in terms of which religious belief was being judged were based on an implicit commitment to control and order, any form of understanding not in the service of the mastery of nature was simply considered irrelevant. We might call this a methodological atheism, for all talk of God was excluded in principle in a world dedicated to calculating, ordering and controlling 'things.'

Given that exile from the epistemic kingdom, then, any claims to truth by various religious traditions or scriptures were seen to be merely relative, perhaps sheer 'subjective' illusion, but in any case a matter only for the weak, mentally enfeebled, or childishly naive. There was no true religious belief. And because no particular tradition could actually validate its truth claims, life itself became meaningless. In fact, this sense of skepticism about any and all religious claims and a consequent sense of meaninglessness has come to haunt the modern world.

On the other hand, against the relativizing and subjectivizing of religious understanding, some defenders claimed willy-nilly that religious knowledge (like science) is 'objective,' in spite of the fact that there was neither empirical nor validly deductive evidence for it. It was thought to be 'objective' because this seemed to be the only kind of knowledge available and the alternative (mere subjectivity) seemed so unthinkable. It was thought to be absolute and increasingly exclusive both because the Aristotelian laws of logic meant that it couldn't be both true and false, or that contradictory truths couldn't both be true, and because revelation in any case gives a particular religious interpretation a supernatural seal of approval. In that case, religious understanding was pushed toward dogmatism if not outright fanaticism. As Pope Leo XIII put it in his 1879 Encyclical, *Aeterni Patris*:

> Reason declares that the evangelical doctrine has shone as the light from its very beginning, by signs and miracles which are infallible proofs of infallible truth.[30]

Not to be outdone in this sordid matter, various contemporary evangelical Protestants have taken the same, inflexible position. Francis Schaeffer, for example, claimed recently that Christianity is not only true, but is exclusively so.[31]

The *Lusanne Covenant* of 1974 carried the same thought even further toward a kind of exclusivistic intolerance between various interpretive, religious traditions.

> We also reject as derogatory to Christ and the Gospel every kind of syncretism and dialogue which implies that Christ speaks equally through all religions and theologies. Jesus Christ, being himself the only God-man, who gave himself as the only ransom for sinners, is the only mediator between God and man. . . . To proclaim Jesus as 'the savior of the world' is not to affirm that all religions offer salvation in Christ. Rather it is to proclaim God's love for a world of sinners and to invite all men to respond to him as Savior and Lord in the wholehearted personal commitment of repentance and faith. Jesus Christ has been exalted above every other name; we long for the day when every knee shall bow to him and every tongue shall confess him Lord.[32]

Modernity, then, forced religious understanding to be conceived of as either an inductive matter of fact (or deductive conclusion) or nothing—i.e., a mere illusion and whim of human fancy (not a kind of understanding at all). No alternative was permitted to this stark dilemma, because understanding was willy-nilly limited to matters of fact and matters of reason—and only those. Because of this, a difficult and painful spiritual dilemma was imposed upon us: spiritual life seemed to be limited to either a meaningless and disoriented relativism and skepticism or a kind of matter-of-fact knowledge about the existence and nature of an absent (because 'transcendent'and, in any case, removed from nature) God. The twin specter of relativistic meaninglessness and dogmatic fanaticism came to haunt the modern world.

4. *Modernity made the pursuit of religious understanding and development almost impossible, especially for the educated.* As we have already indicated, the interpretive framework of modernity forced observers to see religion as either objectively true (like science or math) or merely a subjective illusion. Thus, the entire phenomenon of religious understanding was pushed into an alien interpretive framework which made either horn of the dilemma spiritually difficult. If you chose the emotive horn, as did such 'liberal' theologians as Freiderich Schleiermacher, then you seemed to take religious interpretation and practice right out of the game of understanding and truth altogether. This is apparently why Hegel, in a critical review of the first half of Schleiermacher's *Glaubenslehre*, heaped invective upon Schleiermacher's apparent retreat from traditional religious truth claims with his notion that religion is a mere feeling of dependence. As Hegel sarcastically (and humorously) put it,

> If religion in man is based only on a feeling, then the nature of that feeling can be none other than the feeling of dependence, and so a dog would be the best Christian, for it possesses this [feeling] in the highest degree.... [33]

This subjective horn of the dilemma, then, seems intolerable, because if there is not some form of understanding and truth involved, why bother to pursue it?

On the other hand, if you chose the objective horn of the dilemma—as did the post-Tridentine Roman Church or various forms of evangelical or fundamentalist Protestantism, you increasingly found yourself sounding rather fanatical by asserting that your own views just happen to be absolutely and exclusively 'true' in spite of a lack of any reasonable evidence for them and in spite of the evident contradictory claims of such 'truth' by various religious traditions.

The result, then, was that religious understanding increasingly came to be seen as either an absurd illusion or a literal, absolute, and exclusive truth. Spiritual possibility found itself limited to either a leap in the dark or a doctrinaire and intolerant fanaticism. That meant, especially for the more educated, that pursuing any spiritual path toward deeper and fuller understanding was no longer a live option.

As if that were not trouble enough, it was at just that moment that modernity helped us become aware of religious traditions other than our own, thereby multiplying our religious options. As Peter Berger puts it,

> One of the elements of modern consciousness...is...the multiplication of options. Put differently, *modern* consciousness entails a movement from fate to choice.[34]

This merely exacerbated the spiritually painful dilemma facing modern man: as spiritual freedom increased it became increasingly difficult to exercise it due to a parallel increase in scepticism.

> Modern man is faced with the necessity of choosing between gods, a plurality of which are socially available to him. If the typical condition of premodern man is one of religious certainty, it follows that that of modern man is one of religious doubt.[35]

5. *Modernity reduced the notion of interpretation to factual truth.* This was due to the modern reduction of all understanding to matters of fact and matters of reason. It eventuated in modernity's seeming blindness to interpretive understanding in general. Put another way, this was the attempt to reduce all discourse—including metaphorical speech—to just those forms which were relevant to the calculative mastery of nature. The loss of a sense of interpretive, metaphorical discourse led to limiting interpretive understanding to fact. And if an interpretive understanding of an event or text was not factual—or demonstrable as such—then the only alternative was that it must be factually false (i.e., merely human concoction).

I shall argue in more detail later that this is a plain misunderstanding and distortion of what such interpretive understanding is all about. Furthermore, this collapse of interpretation into fact or illusion led to modernity's remarkable myopia concerning the interpretive understanding founding its own story—i.e., the whole foundational enterprise. It certainly led to the poverty-stricken limitation of interpretive understanding of events such as the Resurrection as well as entire sacred texts such as the Bible to a choice between fact and human projection. In fact, until recently modern Christian scholarship resisted the view that the Bible involved mythological (interpreted to mean 'factual error') elements and rather arbitrarily insisted that it was historical 'fact' not only that Jesus lived but that he was the Christ. But that simply misses the metaphorical character of both mythology and scripture and leaves us a sorry choice between those who say (in the words of the bumper sticker), ''God said it, I believe it, and that settles that,'' and those who simply throw up their hands in despair at the relativity of it all. In effect, then, the collapse of interpretive understanding into matters of fact led to a truncated conception of what scriptural understanding is all about.

Just as importantly, it covered up what in hindsight seems not only obvious but very significant for actually interpreting Biblical scripture—its narrative form and character. Since that narrative form is not only evident with respect to the Bible, and since there has been a tradition for at least a century of literary criticism which has pointed out the obvious differences in form and interpretive procedures between literature and science, such an omission seems all the more remarkable and (to say the least) inefficacious.[36]

Perhaps even more importantly, this paucity of interpretive sophistication led to what might be called a religious hardening of the arteries. Religion was increasingly seen as literally (read 'factually') true or false beliefs concerning a God-entity 'up there' who issues commands and whose commands it is our duty to obey. Thus, a literalistic interpretation of religion as 'fact' gradually replaced the earlier tradition's notion of 'wisdom' understood as an allegorical, metaphorical interpretation and vision of how best to live life. The reduction of all interpretation to empirical understanding, then, resulted in rather flat and certainly narrow interpretations of life, history, and scripture.

6. *Modernity attenuated the conception of religious renewal.* The notion of interpretive understanding was radically constricted by modernity. If a historical event or scripture was not factually (demonstrably) true, then remarkably enough the only interpretive alternative was that it must be false—a human invention or imaginative projection upon reality. Furthermore, we have just seen that the modern focus on the kind of (empirical) understanding useful in controlling and transforming nature

led to a literalist and nonmetaphorical picture of religion in general. All of this had direct bearing upon the modern view of religious renewal and reform.

Insofar as a renewal of religious tradition depended upon an interpretive understanding of the nature of that tradition, and insofar as such understanding was limited to the empirical form, then any religious reform or renewal entailed getting back to true (factual) origins. By this means, the nineteenth century became the occasion for scholarly attempts to find and found faith upon the real or 'historical Jesus' back before the gospels were redacted or before the emergence of the New Testament Church. That one could never get back to such a solid, factual understanding precisely because all human understanding involves an interpretive, mythological construal of whatever facts there might be seems rather evident from our postmodern perspective. One could never get free from such interpretive frameworks because they are an essential aspect of human being-in-the-world. All of that, however, remains to be articulated.

Of course, from the modern point of view, even if we could get back to an original, founding faith, we might find it an alien and bygone attitude toward life, or at least couched in alien and bygone terms. For example, we might find that as a result of his cultural *Sitz-im-Leben*, Jesus undoubtedly believed in spirit possession as well as the three-tiered universe. Must we accept such nonempirical and alien 'mythology' (interpreted in the modern context as 'factual errors') in taking up the original faith? For many in the modern world, that seemed ludicrous. Instead, they suggested that we should "demythologize" (Bultmann) that ancient faith, cleanse it of these alien (to us) elements, and rephrase it in modern terms so that it would be understandable and acceptable in today's world. But if we do that, what remains of the original faith? Have we lost it in favor of making it interpretively acceptable to the modern world?

'Renewal,' then, was so shaped by the modern conception of interpretation that it seemed to swing endlessly between conservative and liberal understandings of the term. On the one hand, the conservative view was that one could in fact get back to an original and true faith, a faith which remains eternally unchanged and the same. This view, of course, ignores the evident fact that any tradition is necessarily a history of interpretations and that there is no original point of view, for any such point of view would of course be merely another interpretive understanding. It would simply be one more mythological and hermeneutical interpretation of life and human destiny—another human story—and would itself have to be interpretively understood by us.

On the other hand, the liberal approach to renewal in, for example, the tradition of Schleiermacher and the German theologians who followed him insisted that whatever the faith had been earlier, it must be framed in a way that modern men and women could understand and accept. Thus, the liberal churches seemed to swallow modernity whole and to reduce the tradition to present-day terms and attitudes. If that is the case, where in such a denial of the historical past is the 'faith'? Has it not been done away with in favor of a here-and-now modern point of view?

The notion of religious renewal and reform in the modern context, then, seemed to swing back and forth between choosing either a past unconnected to today or reducing that past (or pasts with their various interpretive understandings) to today's point of view. In this dialectic, we are stranded with either a past interpretation insulated from the present or a present interpretation isolated from the past. This of course does terrible violence to our actual situationality within history, a situationality which is always embedded in a tradition and at the same time necessarily involved in new interpretive possibilities for understanding it. Clearly, a postmodern conception of religious myth and revelation as interpretive understanding must break out of this overly simplistic dilemma imposed upon us by modernity. It must articulate a third conception of religious renewal, a conception which is neither simply conservative nor liberal, an alternative which includes both but is still more.

7. *Modernity has brought us to the brink of ecological disaster.* The word *ecology* comes from the Greek stem, *Oikos*, which means 'house' or 'place in which to live.' Thus, ecology is the study of organisms within their home—the interconnected life systems which constitute the earth. It is becoming increasingly clear that the industrial, consumer societies which have emerged within the modern period have created an ecological crisis which may in fact destroy that home.

We have seen that the modern drive for security was enhanced by learning how to know—that is by introducing a kind of empirical knowledge which could ensure control and domination over nature. From this point of view, history was nothing but the arena in which the progressive mastery of nature by mankind through the practical application of such knowledge (technology) would take place. The purpose was to transform nature into an unending cornucopia of useful products for human consumption.

From its very beginnings, modernity subordinated nature to human ends. This anthropocentric attitude was heightened when nature was desacralized. The split between mind and matter turned the former over to theology and the latter to science and technology, and that insured that neither one would have anything to say to the other. It also destined religion to be cut off from nature and science from spiritual and moral values. God (the Holy Spirit) withdrew from nature to become (merely) the distant designer and creator of it. Having desacralized nature, and having insured that she was not the locus of spiritual value (reverence), nature increasingly came to be viewed as merely bits of matter ordered by the principles of mechanics. David Klemm puts this very well.

> Critical consciousness. . . makes the sacred power in the symbol vanish. Religious objects, texts, institutions, and pictures of the world lose their unquestioned authority and innocence when the historical and psychological processes infusing sacrality to the symbol are 'exposed' and brought into the light. The result of critical reflection is the desacralization of the world.[37]

So nature was made ready for the industrial revolution. Adam Smith completed that preparation when he envisioned the market economy as the social arena for maximizing the industrial production and consumption of the manufactured products aggressively and sometimes violently extracted from the body of nature.

All of this of course has led us to possible ecological disaster. In fact, the modern story (mythology) concerning the nature of ultimate reality and human destiny is a story which has led to the sorry spiritual condition in which we presently find ourselves. In direct proportion to the degree that we have emptied the universe of the sacred, we have narrowed our already spiritually attenuated lives. Having accomplished that remarkable feat, we then set out to further degrade nature by treating her as the field for our endless economic exploitation. We have poisoned our air and water, polluted our earth, dug up and drained away earth's nonrenewable resources, and crippled our own spiritual relationship to nature. An immense body of scientific literature has documented this process and ought to lead us to very sobering conclusions. If we continue these processes at the same or greater rate as in the past, we are in grave danger of killing all life on earth— including ourselves, of course. The story of modernity may end in disaster. That is surely a significant spiritual issue of our time.

8. *Modernity blinded us to the real spiritual idolatry and danger of our time—the pursuit of technological power and progress.* As Francis Bacon

realized, science is the means for humans to exercise power and control over both nature and themselves through the technological remaking of the world. 'Knowing how to know' permits us to take our rightful place as masters of the universe. This myth of human destiny and inevitable progress (as many have noted) is the orthodox worldview which characterizes and dominates our present technological and industrial cultures, both capitalist and communist. In fact, as Langdon Gilkey observed, it has been "the implicit 'religion' of the West." That modernity, with its industrial (and now biogenetic) technological developments, is not spiritually neutral vis-a-vis other religious visions. Rather, it is itself a hermeneutical or mythological interpretation of what human life and destiny are all about. To the degree that it remains unaware of that fact, it becomes a particularly vicious form of orthodoxy. The modern, industrial, consumer world has been a sort of technological bewitchment or altered state of consciousness which has led not only to the enfeeblement of spiritual life but to the severe damage of our basic life systems. Unless and until we wake up from that dangerous entrancement, it is difficult to have much hope. Just when there is a proliferation of religious traditions available in modern life, and just when the choice of any of those options seems most difficult, the world appears to be swept up in an orientation toward technological and industrial control which, because it is not seen as a spiritual choice at all, has become a dangerous orthodoxy with astonishing and dangerous implications for all our lives.

The addition to the modern worldview of the dangerous myth of an inevitable historical 'progress' brings to this volatile mix an ingredient of uncontrolled and perhaps irresponsible growth. In an atmosphere in which progress is assumed to be both necessary and inevitable, there seem to be no moral, ecological, or spiritual limits or constraints to the explosive growth of technology and industrialism. We seem headed toward some sort of ecological, military, or biogenetic catastrophe because we are at once blind to alternative spiritual possibilities, swept up in the vision of technological power, and fascinated by the endless promise of inevitable progress.

9. *Modernity fostered a multiplicity of religious traditions and practices in conflict with one another.* Spread across the spiritual landscape of the modern world are a plethora of apparently irreconcilable, squabbling traditions and practices, all claiming 'truth'. In the meantime, modern technology and industry have changed the very conditions in which they exist by economically and politically shrinking the world, thereby bringing these different religious cultures into head-on collision with

one another. At the same time, of course, modern technology supplied each of them with weapons and armaments of appalling violence with which to 'defend' themselves. When you add to that volatile mixture the tendency toward dogmatism and exclusivism, the result is the present world we know all too well. It is not only a world fragmented into different and often antagonistic religious traditions, but also a world in which those religious cultures are often deeply and bitterly at war with one another. The shouting and killing—all in the name of one deity or another—seem disproportionate to the universal religious appeal for mutual understanding and love. Indeed, as James Mackey has put it:

> Religion, with its claims and counter-claims, is all too frequently divisive; it frequently sucks the life out of human love, the truest and noblest of our emotions, by insisting that we love only God and love our fellows only for God's sake and for God's purposes, and it can engender long-sighted selfishness in the service of an ultimately selfish God.[39]

The gods, then, seem locked in battle in our time: It is Christ versus Allah, or Christ version #1 versus Christ version #2, Allah version #1 versus Allah version #2, Allah versus Brahman, or technological control and power versus all the rest. And this strife, religious turmoil, and fanaticism are happening around the world—Israel, Syria, Lebanon, Turkey, Egypt, the Sudan, Northern Ireland, Nigeria, India, Pakistan, Indonesia, Sri Lanka, The Soviet Union, and (yes) the United States. Whereas at one time many of the world's religions were for the most part safely distant and protected from one another, in today's smaller world we not only face dizzying religious options, but the different traditions are squeezed together in hostile and sometimes dangerous proximity. All of this is of critical importance today. In place of this explosive situation, we need to develop across the differences some common human sense of worship, a shared gratitude and wonder (in a variety of forms) at the miraculous gift of existence and life. According to Mackey, "The world we know demands immediate attention to the problem of the unity of humankind across all religions and ideologies."[40]

2

A Postmodern Story about Human Understanding

Art...is the becoming and happening of truth.

Martin Heidegger

2:1 A Shift in Worldview

As we have seen, in the seventeenth and eighteenth centuries a new story and vision about a better order of human progress through scientific and technological knowledge was promulgated by Francis Bacon, Descartes, and other Enlightenment philosophers and scientists. This story of progress and control became embedded in the industrial and technological revolution and ultimately led to a world of impoverished spiritual lives and significant environmental degradation. The more 'progress' there is, it seems, the more life systems become threatened and the less genuine religious understanding seems possible at all.

It is perhaps fair to say that the deepest crises societies experience are those moments of change when an old story becomes practically inadequate to meet the spiritual and cultural needs of the present and its possible future. I believe it is just that perceived inadequacy of the modern paradigm which is pushing us toward a postmodern story.

It was Nietzsche who observed that, unlike political upheavals, revolutions in thinking come silently on dove's feet. A wide variety of contemporary observers—from Stephen Toulmin to Daniel Bell, Richard Rorty, Jacques Derrida, and Jean-Francois Lyotard—believe that at the end of the twentieth century we are in fact undergoing just such a sea change in how we think about ourselves and our place in nature. Huston Smith expresses this momentous revolution in our worldview quite succinctly.

Quietly, irrevocably, something enormous has happened to Western man. His outlook on life and the world has changed so radically that in the perspective of history the twentieth century is likely to rank—with the fourth century, which witnessed the triumph of Christianity, and the seventeenth, which signaled the dawn of modern science—as one of the very few that have instigated genuinely new epochs in human thought. In this change, which is still in process, we of the current generation are playing a crucial but as yet not widely recognized part.[1]

To begin with, we need to distinguish postmodernity from romanticism which in some ways it resembles. Romanticism was a nineteenth-century cultural movement which dialectically defined itself over against the Enlightenment or the modern, industrial world in general. As such, it was essentially a protest of the individual against the abstract and mechanical laws of modern science, of feeling against the paradigm of reason put forth by the Enlightenment, of life forces against the dead hand of industrial technology, and of a romanticized, idealized past as opposed to the tawdry and oppressive present. Like romanticism, postmodernity is a contemporary cultural movement and worldview which in many respects rejects modernity and in fact has developed over and against it. On the other hand, unlike romanticism which pretty much remained a countercultural movement that defined itself by rejecting modernity as a whole, we need to emphasize here that the postmodern worldview does not do away with many positive and still useful elements of modernity which it incorporates into its own perspective. It does not reject science and technological understanding, for example, in favor of intuition or pure feeling. Nor does it recommend a luddite-like return to a romanticized past. It does (albeit in somewhat different form) continue the characteristic modern search for truth in terms of thought and criticism. In this sense, we might say that, while it is a development beyond the assumptions and limitations of modern culture, it is at the same time heavily influenced and indeed conditioned by it.

At the same time, the postmodern worldview radically separates itself (as we shall see) from the constricted modern conception of understanding and truth as well as from the typical modern bifurcation of reality into 'subject' and 'object'. It is a worldview of great import to all of the human arts and sciences and indeed to our understanding of who we are and where we are headed at this moment in history. More to our point, it is a perspective that holds great intellectual promise for a more adequate interpretation of religious understanding in general and a more effective way to deal with the spiritual and environmental issues presently threatening us.

As opposed to the modern limitation of knowledge to matters of fact and matters of reason, such postmodern thinkers as Martin Heidegger, Richard Rorty, Hans-Georg Gadamer, and Paul Ricoeur have pointed out that that modern limitation of knowledge (astonishingly enough) is not itself either a matter of fact or a matter of reason. In other words, the modern notion of knowledge (as well as its consequent view of the human arts and sciences) is not 'true' within the epistemological framework of the modern perspective itself, but a simple bias and untested assumption—itself a mere matter of taste, subjective projection, or even a form of self-deception. In the words of Stephen Toulmin: "Far from being categorical and unconditioned, its [the modern viewpoint] validity proves on a closer look to be hypothetical and circumstancial."[2] And Gadamer has made the same point:

> The overcoming of all prejudice, that global demand of the Enlightenment, will prove to be itself a prejudice the removal of which opens the way to an understanding of our finitude.[3]

We can put this another way. According to Timm Triplett, "foundationalism" maintains

> (1) that there are propositions that are epistemologically basic in the sense that they are justified directly or immediately, without dependence on other propositions for their justification, and (2) that every justified empirical proposition is either basic or it derives at least part of its justification from the fact that it stands in an appropriate epistemic relation to propositions which are basic.[4]

Foundationalism, then, is the view that knowledge claims are either 'basic' or 'nonbasic,' that all nonbasic assertions must only be accepted on evidence that can be traced back to basic assertions, and that by basic assertions we mean those which are either self-evident, or incorrigible or perceptually evidently the case.

The assertion here—that all knowledge claims must be limited to matters of fact and matters of reason—seems to be precisely such a classically foundationalist claim. And yet, the claim itself is not 'basic.' It is neither self-evident, nor incorrigible, nor perceptually evidently the case. The assertion itself, then, that knowledge is limited to inductive or deductive kinds of statements must be nonbasic and, as such, must be traced back to some other set of basic assertions on which it rests. But what possible kinds of more basic assertions could there be? It is hard to imagine. That the foundationalist 'feels' or 'assumes' that such an assertion is 'self-evident,' of course, does not make it so. In all probability, all we have here is an unjustified (and one suspects unjustifiable) belief that it is indeed the case.[5]

Modernity tried to replace mythology with objective reason and truth, to claim that modern culture had gone beyond mythology and in fact outgrown the need for it. What modernity actually did, however, was to cover up and forget the mythological basis for its own views. The view that knowledge can be limited to matters of fact and matters of reason and that the mythological dimension of human life was now transcended, a story to end all stories, was itself just another unscientific and mythological story.

> The plot was given in capsule by August Comte: first came religion in the form of stories, then philosophy in the form of metaphysical analysis, and then science with its exact methods. The story he tells in outline is set within another elaborated by Hegel, to show us how each of these ages supplanted the other as a refinement in the progressive development of reason. So stories are prescientific, according to the story legitimating the age which calls itself scientific. Yet if one overlooks that budding contradiction, or fails to spell it out because everyone knows that stories are out of favor anyway, then the subterfuge has been worked....[6]

As James Wiggins has said: "The plot to end stories can now begin to be seen as the plot of the story about trying to end all stories."[7] Modernity rested on a myth, a dream, a human vision of the possibility of control and security through scientific, technological, and industrial progress. It was certainly not 'rational' as that term was understood within the story itself. It was probably the most powerful dream that has ever taken possession of the human imagination, although at the end of modernity we can now see that insofar as it led to spiritual and ecological crisis, it may have been a disturbed dream.

Having developed and articulated such a remarkable story, the modern world promptly proceeded to forget it, thereby becoming oblivious to the kind of narrative and mythological understanding which (this writer believes) it entailed.

A central claim of postmodern hermeneutics is that understanding has been forgotten. Like a misplaced house key or pen, something we rely on and notice only when it is missing, understanding is "here somewhere," although momentarily hidden. The simile is helpful only to a point, however, for understanding is not a tool for our use in life, like a house key or a pen, but rather the fundamental mode of our being in the world. As humans, we are always already understanding ourselves, our world, and God as the ground of self and world. If understanding has been lost or misplaced, the resulting condition is more like amnesia or forgotten identity than frustration over a broken or lost tool. Understanding is more basic to our humanness than our use of tools. Indeed, understanding makes possible our use of tools and, beyond that, our social life and its cultural expressions.[8]

In part because of this widespread recognition of the mythological foundations of the modern worldview concerning science and human knowledge, we have recently witnessed the near demise of its twentieth-century version (positivism) and its replacement with various postmodern philosophies of science. In 1962, Thomas Kuhn published *The Structure of Scientific Revolutions,* in which he argued that, far from being founded upon firm and unchanging foundations, science depends on changing historical frameworks of understanding that shape different periods of scientific history, what he called "paradigms." Within postmodern philosophy of science, then, science is thought to be based upon changing historical paradigms rather than apodictic axioms and postulates. Rather than there being a single method of science, we find that there are a number of different methods to fit different circumstances. And rather than a formal logic of scientific discovery, we find historical explorations of different concepts and approaches at different times.[9] In other words, the sciences themselves are now seen to be interpretive human projects or social constructs within the human context or world of ordinary experience. Facts and hypotheses based upon them are theory- and value-laden. There can be no complete, objective truth in this human life precisely because we—our minds, our bodies, and our sense of what is meaningful—are involved in whatever we come to know. Furthermore, this awareness of the limits of our scientific understanding—the awareness that in principle we can never grasp nature as it is in itself precisely because we can only know it perspectively and through senses and instruments which condition it and as agents with particular interests—is itself the result of that science.[10] Indeed, the very concept of modernity, its vision and program, no longer carries anything like the conviction it once did. It is not just positivist philosophy of science that is ending; it is the modern era itself.

Second, this widening postmodern perspective has led to a fresh exploration and understanding of the kind of alternative form of discourse and cognition which not only was involved in the mythological foundation and development of modernity, but which is basic to historical, literary, philosophical, and religious understanding:

> Scientific inquiry does not represent the sole cognitive relation that men and women possess with what is actual. As Whitehead argues, like the sensory experience on which it is based, scientific method abstracts for certain purposes from the totally encountered world, from our constitutive relations with things, from awareness of the subject of knowing, awareness of natural beings around us, and awareness of persons as persons. To confine knowing to this one significant but objectifying method is to strip natural objects of their inherent reality and value, and persons of their selfhood, their creative freedom, and their humanity. Science must, therefore, see itself as only one aspect— to be sure, a most important and valuable aspect—of human cognitive creativity, and thus one supplemented by and dependent upon other aspects, if it is to take its rightful and not dominating role in our cultural life. Such a reassessment implies an acquaintance with other modes of cognition: in literature, in social science, in the arts, in philosophy, and in religion....A corresponding reassessment of scientific knowledge in relation to the other cultural modes of encountering, knowing, and shaping reality would set science among the humane arts and thus help to humanize rather than to dehumanize our common world.[11]

Postmodern thinkers have gone on to actually look at what and how we 'learn' and 'know' in the human arts and sciences (including religious life) by phenomenologically evoking and articulating our real experience within them. That has led to a broad postmodern conception of human interpretation and understanding, including narrative understanding, a conception which has revolutionary implications and possibilities for our analysis of religious understanding and truth in later chapters.

2:2 A Postmodern Conception of Knowledge

When we do reflectively focus upon that experience, it seems patently clear that we learn about and understand it through such human arts and sciences as historical monographs, paintings, psychoanalysis, poetry, novels, philosophy, and (of course) religious myth and theology. Although they are not empirical or mathematical modes of knowing, these works are realms of discourse which display or make manifest the meaningful texture of various aspects of that experience—what it's like to live right here and now or (sometimes) anywhere and anytime. They *e-voke* (speak out) the actual sense or meaning of this or that experience or event as we (or some agent) live it through. Barbara Mossberg has put this poetically and yet powerfully in a discussion of the humanities proper.

> This terrain of worry, dreams, and hopes is the humanities—that is . . . our ability to use language and logic, to express and to know ourselves, to be self-conscious, to worry, to dream, to imagine, to create, to despair, to laugh, to wonder. The tree outside this building doesn't wonder what it all means. It doesn't worry over its self-image (does the squirrel like me?), it doesn't worry about its honor, or its role in the family. . . . The dog doesn't face retirement or say "to be or not to be." The sand doesn't worry about being loved; grass doesn't tell mother-in-law jokes, or laugh when someone slips on a banana peel. But we do. And out of this come words, thoughts, ideas which enable us to explore ourselves and, in the process, gain a new awareness and appreciation of what it means to be human.[12]

In fact, beyond those works which evoke particular aspects of our experience, some of those arts and sciences give voice to a human sense of an overarching and ultimate destiny—i.e., they make manifest a way of seeing life and history as a meaningful whole. As we shall soon see, this is particularly true of literature, philosophy, and religious myth.

Although each of the arts and humanities manifests the manifold of experiential meaning in its unique way, they all involve 'texts' or (for lack of a better word) 'works' such as poems, paintings, stories, concertos, dramas, sociological monographs, philosophical essays, or religious scripture and ritual. Such works are formed and shaped materials (paint, sound, behavior, words) which embody and display what Paul Ricoeur calls a "surplus of meaning" to those who can actually enter into dialogue with them. That is, they make manifest to our understanding more of that experience than we understood before.

For example, Goya's *May 3, 1808* is an arrangement of pigment and form on canvas. It is about a historical event, namely the massacre of some Spanish guerrillas in northern Spain by Napoleonic troops, but of course it means 'more' than simply that historical event. If we can enter into the world of the painting and 'hear' its particular 'voice,' we can recognize that it is a sort of visual language which displays something meaningful about our lives—human cruelty, the unexpectedness of death, our childlike fear in the face of death, our ultimate aloneness, and so on. It's not so much a representation of our lives as a re-presentation of them which makes manifest aspects to which we normally pay scant attention. We don't look at the painting so much as we look at our lives through it. Through it we come to see and understand more about our lives than we understood before.

Of course, different artistic traditions constitute different languages (replete with their particular grammars and vocabularies) through which we come to 'see' reality in unique ways. For example, Gombrich's *Art and Illusion* juxtaposes an English lithograph of the Romantic period with a Chinese rendering by Chiang Yee of the same countryside in Derwentwater in England. The Chinese painting is structured around a vocabulary which acts as a screen to focus our attention on features of the pastoral which can be expressed only in that particular idiom. The scene looks quite different from the corresponding English lithograph. In fact, it looks remarkably like a gnarled and rocky Chinese landscape along a river.[13]

Let's take a look at a second example of a significant work in the human sciences, this time from philosophy. Spinoza's *Ethics* is a classic philosophical text which takes the peculiar form of geometrical demonstration—i.e., "definitions," "axioms," "propositions" and "demonstrations" which follow deductively, and "corollaries" which those demonstrations logically entail. As with any such geometric demonstration, the intention is not only that every proposition be demonstrated necessarily true if the axioms are true, but that the whole chain of reasonings hang together as a total and comprehensive truth. With this geometric form of argumentation, Spinoza sets out to demonstrate and display in the text itself an overarching sense of what our human lives are all about. True human happiness, he ultimately tells us, comes from the intellectual love of God whereby we understand that everything (including ourselves) is necessarily "in God and conceived through Him" (*Deus sive Natura*). To attain this intellectual love of God, to "conceive things...under the form of eternity," is to attain true human freedom and happiness.

The *Ethics*, of course, is a unique work in philosophy. I have purposely chosen it because it is a good example of an Enlightenment attempt to reduce understanding to inductive or (in this case) deductive logic. Even in this instance, it is not so much that it logically demonstrates what life is about as much as through that peculiar form it displays it. And what is true in the case of Spinoza, I claim, is true *mutatis mutandis* for other great works of philosophical reflection, even though their argumentative styles and notions of philosophical understanding vary considerably from that of Spinoza.

Our third example is a brief story from Nikos Kazantzakis' *Report to Greco*. By framing all of nature and human history in a plot which is awkwardly and painfully evolving into a future state of meaningful being beyond plant life, animality, and our present form of humanity, the story narratively displays an overarching interpretation of the meaning of being. Through its re-presentation of life in story form, we can see our lives (and all of reality) as a meaningful whole. It is a story which lies at the boundary of literature and religious myth.

Blowing through heaven and earth, and in our hearts and the heart of every living thing, is a gigantic breath—a great Cry—which we call God. Plant life wished to continue its motionless sleep next to stagnant water, but the Cry leaped up within it and violently shook its roots: "Away, let go of the earth, walk!" Had the tree been able to think and judge, it would have cried, "I don't want to. What are you urging me to do! You are demanding the impossible!" But the Cry, without pity, kept shaking its roots and shouting, "Away, let go of the earth, walk!"

It shouted in this way for thousands of eons; and lo! as a result of desire and struggle, life escaped the motionless tree and was liberated.

Animals appeared—worms—making themselves at home in water and mud. "We're just fine here," they said. "We have peace and security; we're not budging!"

But the terrible Cry hammered itself pitilessly into their loins. "Leave the mud, stand up, give birth to your betters!"

"We don't want to! We can't!"

And lo! after thousands of eons man emerged, trembling on his still unsolid legs.

The human being is a centaur; his equine hoofs are planted in the ground, but his body from breast to head is worked on and tormented by the merciless Cry. He has been fighting again for thousands of eons, to draw himself, like a sword, out of his animalistic scabbard. He is also fighting—this is his new struggle—to draw himself out of his human scabbard. Man calls in despair, "Where can I go? I have reached the pinnacle. Beyond is the abyss." And the Cry answers, "I am beyond. Stand up!" All things are centaurs. If this were not the case, the world would rot into inertness and sterility.[14]

To say that such a story tells us nothing about life and reality, and invokes no human understanding of our situation in nature and our destiny, seems *prima facie* false. Of course, its particular form of understanding is not like a scientific hypothesis or a mathematical demonstration. Still, if one can enter into the narrative universe it makes available, one can 'see' the whole of reality 'as' a remarkable spiritual evolution from inert matter through plant, animal, and now human life to something spiritually beyond. Our particular interest in this essay, of course, will lie in the peculiar kind of interpretive religious understanding tied up with just such stories—i.e., founding myths which narratively make available such a vision of the whole.

2:3 Metaphor

How do such texts in the human arts and sciences work? How is it that they are able to increase our understanding of various aspects of our concrete experience, including (as we have just seen) our ability to view it as a meaningful whole? How do they accomplish this miraculous "surplus of meaning" in such a way that through them we can understand our own lives more than we did before them? One important postmodern perspective on this issue claims that we accomplish this through symbol, image, and metaphor,—that is, through the remarkable human ability in different realms of discourse to extend meaning (and thus insight into what is going on in our experience and lives) by seeing one thing through another or as like another. If, as is the case with Paul Ricoeur, we mean by 'symbol'

any structure of signification, in which a direct, primary, literal meaning designates, in addition, another meaning which is

indirect, secondary, and figurative, and which can be apprehended only through the first...,[15]

then we can include symbol and image in this metaphorical process.

Metaphor is nothing but applying to one thing or experience
characteristics or descriptions conventionally applied to another on the
grounds of an implicit similarity between the two. For example,
'passion' becomes 'flame.' In this broad sense, of course, it
encompasses analogy and simile as well as metaphor more narrowly
construed. Ordinary life and language are full of such metaphorical
extensions of meaning. A person describing her night's sleep might
say, "I slept like a log," thereby transferring and extending the
characteristics of an inert piece of nature to her night's sleep.
Metaphorical extension of meaning, as Max Black has pointed out, is
carried out when a conventional wisdom associated with some ordinary
context or experience is made to serve as a screen or grid through which
to see another.[16]

A number of scholars have recently pointed out that the Western
concept of soul or mind was developed in just this metaphorical way
"from such terms as *psyche, thymos,* and *pneuma,* terms that originally
referred to concrete bodily functions having to do with breathing, the
flow of blood, the rumblings of the stomach, movement of the limbs,
and so on."[17] As we have seen, the allegorical method was just such
a reading of one reality (myth) in the light of another (a cosmological
or philosophical system), while 'modernity' was constructed mythologically by 'seeing' human history and destiny 'as' a struggle to
achieve human control of our lives through scientific and mathematical
understanding. The very act of 'seeing' life 'as' or 'in the light of' an
overarching meaning presented by Kazantzakis in the story of the Cry
is just such a metaphorical activity. Indeed, such a metaphorical
enterprise lies at the heart of religious and mythological interpretive
understanding in general.

Effective texts or works in the human arts and sciences, then,
display new meaning and thus new understanding of what life is about
by metaphorically 'seeing' (note the metaphor!) one aspect of
experience in the light of other more conventional experiences. Sallie
McFague presents us with a marvelous example of this sort of
metaphorical extension of meaning in an analysis of the Paolo and
Francesca scene from Dante's *Divine Comedy* (Canto 5, 11, 46–50): "And
as the cranes go chanting their lays, making of themselves a long line
in the air, so I saw approach with long drawn wailings shades borne
on those battling winds."

This is technically a simile, not a metaphor, for it has the 'as...so' construction; but that is really incidental, because metaphorical power is present. The cranes and the shades of Paolo and Francesca become one, so that the feeling and insight conveyed in the passage is an amalgam of the eerie, lonely cries of the serene long lines of cranes and the wailings of the lost lovers riding 'the battling winds.' There is no embellishment or adornment there; the knowing that takes place is inseparable from the images used and is conveyed only through them. Cranes and dead lovers are mutually illuminated and there is no way to extricate out a meaning; the meaning is held in solution in the metaphor.[18]

To cite another example, we often see the sacred and spiritual dimension of our lives through such metaphorical images as sky, clouds, oceans, mountains, or even parts of the body. In his magnificent poem, "God's Grandeur," Gerard Manley Hopkins powerfully expresses the presence of God in just this way.

> There lives the dearest freshness deep down
> things;
> And though the last lights off the black West went
> Oh, morning, at the brown brink eastward,
> springs—
> Because the Holy Ghost over the bent
> world broods with warm breast and with ah!
> bright wings."[19]

We even find this use of metaphor to manifest mood and meaning in the concrete [sic] form of architecture. Vitruvius, who in the first century A.D. wrote a major treatise on the different forms (or 'orders') of column in classical architecture (a major step in establishing the language and grammar of the European classical tradition of architecture), described the Doric order as exemplifying "the proportion, strength and grace of a man's body," the Ionic as displaying "feminine slenderness," and the Corinthian as imitative of "the slight figure of a girl." As John Summerson puts it, these

> ...orders provided a sort of gamut of architectural character all the way from the rough and tough to the slim and fine. In true classical designing the selection of the order is a very vital point—it is a choice of mood. What you do with the order, what exact ratios you give its different parts, what enrichments you put in or leave out, this again shifts and defines mood.[20]

Sallie McFague has pointed out that

> When we turn to the sciences, whether mathematics or the natural
> or social sciences, we also find metaphor to be central. Perhaps
> it is most surprising to those who suppose that metaphor belongs
> only in the arts and religion to discover it at the most basic level
> in mathematics: the numerical analogue. Seeing the similar
> number among otherwise disparate entities is a metaphorical act,
> as in six apples, six moons, six ideas, six general acts. In the social
> sciences the ubiquity of metaphor is obvious: the human being
> has been seen as a child of God, as half-angel and half-beast, as
> a machine; the state has been viewed as an organism, and a
> mechanism; the brain has been understood through the metaphor
> of the computer and vice versa. When one turns to physics, the
> evidence for the importance of metaphor in the form of models
> is extensive. . . . Jacob Bronowski speaks for many philosophers
> of science when he insists that ideas in science, as in any other
> field, are derived from images. . . . [21]

A work or text within the human arts and sciences, then, is an
ordered arrangement of material such as sounds, granite, pigment,
words, or human behavior which metaphorically displays or makes
manifest a surplus meaning about life or some aspect of life to a person
capable of entering into its form of discourse and participating in its
universe of meaning. Put another way, we have come to realize in the
postmodern period that there is a form of human understanding made
available through such texts which, although it seems to underlie the
sciences and mathematics, is not itself reducible to scientific or
mathematical modes of understanding.

At this point, we should be very clear about one thing: the subject
of the text and its meaning is seen *through* the metaphorical expression
and is not merely represented or pointed to by the metaphor. For
example, and I mean this phenomenologically, we directly encounter
the meaning of a play or painting through the figurative or metaphorical
'language' involved. We 'see' it directly as through a window rather
than 'inferring' it from the discourse and behavior of the play or the
formed pigment of the painting. Maurice Merleau-Ponty expressed this
point very well when discussing the cave paintings at Lascau:

> I do not look at it as I do at a thing; I do not fix it in its place.
> My gaze wanders in it as in the halos of Being. It is more accurate
> to say that I see according to it, or with it, than that I see it.[22]

The human arts and sciences, then, encompass those significant works of thought and expression which articulate and display the human condition to those who are open to them. It is not entirely an exaggeration to say that human experience seeks its 'voice' in such works. Each form of these human arts and sciences, of course, is a different 'language' or realm of discourse which exhibits such meaning in its own distinctive way. The specific 'language' (syntax, grammar, semantics) of each realm is quite unique and different from the others.

But if it is true that those works and texts give voice to our mute lives, the contrary is also the case. That is, we have no other way to know or understand that experience than through them. As Gadamer puts it,

> Hermeneutics is the basis for the whole complex of the humanities. Hermeneutics means "theory of interpretation." In a more radical sense, however, interpretation is not just a specialty of the humanities and of our encounter with texts. Because the world is organized by linguistically articulated social patterns, interpretation is the primary access to our experience of the world.[23]

2:4 Disclosive Truth

But do we learn or come to understand anything from art, literature, and the human sciences? If we do, it is certainly not a sort of hypothesis about life, a hypothesis empirically gleaned from matters of fact; nor is it a kind of deductive knowing like geometry. Yet, as we have tried to show, it seems in the face of our experience farfetched to say we learn nothing at all from them as we indicated earlier positivists were driven to claim by their implicit modern assumptions. Furthermore, whatever 'knowing' is going on here does not seem to be a representation 'over here' in the sentences, formed pigment, or narrative text of (or about) life and experience 'over' or 'out there.' What is this human understanding or knowledge so clearly available in significant works of the arts and sciences?

The preceding examples have shown us that we do learn something from those works, but not in the manner of scientific hypothesis or mathematical deduction. Rather, we encounter a sense of what life is sometimes like. We 'see' it through the formed pigment or the narratively shaped vision of nature and human destiny. As we have indicated, learning here isn't so much learning 'about' what it sometimes means to live as it is directly encountering that meaning through the particular text at hand.

In a recent article entitled "Rednecks" in the *New York Review of Books*, V.S. Naipaul reflects on the power of art to make what was for him until this point an alien and unknown world available for the first time. The article discusses how a friend by the name of Campbell leads Naipaul for the first time beyond stereotypes and ignorance into the living world of so-called "rednecks" by very vivid and metaphorical descriptions of their experiences and attitudes. At the end, Naipaul reflects on the experience:

> Art hallows, creates, makes one see. And though other people said other things about rednecks; though one man said that the best way of dealing with them was to have nothing to do with them; that their tempers were too close to the surface, that they were too little educated to cope with what they saw as slights, too little educated to understand human behavior, or to under-stand people who were not like themselves; that their exaggerated sense of slight and honor could make them talk with you and smile even while they were planning to blow your head off; though this was received wisdom, Campbell's description of their mode of living made me see pride and style and a fashion code where I had seen nothing, made me notice what so far I hadn't sufficiently noticed: the pick-up trucks dashingly driven, the baseball caps marked with the name of some company. . . .
>
> For some days Campbell's words and phrases sang in my head; and I spoke them to others. One afternoon I went to a farm just outside Jackson. Someone there, knowing of my new craze, came to me and said, "There are three of your rednecks fishing in the pond." And I hurried to see them, as I might have hurried to see an unusual bird, or a deer. And there indeed they were, bareback, but with the wonderful baseball hats, in a boat among the reeds, on a weekday afternoon—people whom, before Campbell had spoken, I might have seen flatly, but now saw as people with a certain past, living out a certain code, a threatened species.[24]

Understanding here is not something which is 'true' to the degree that it 'corresponds' to the facts of the matter, nor a kind of internal 'coherence' with other parts of the whole system of learnings, nor an 'instrumental' sort of truth which provides utility. Rather, this knowing is an evoking (speaking out), a displaying, a making manifest, an uncovering and revealing of our lived experience, a giving voice to it.

These texts, we have tried to show, let aspects of our lives be seen or uncovered. Their truth is a disclosing or making evident, what Heidegger in *Being and Time* calls "apophansis" or "a-letheia," a making unhidden.[25] This is a knowing and truth, then, which is neither an objective truth based on matters of fact nor an illusion—i.e., a subjective projection upon an essentially meaningless life and experience. On the contrary, that experience is rich with meaning, and to the degree that they are successful, works of the human arts and sciences uncover and permit us to see various aspects of that richness.

In an article on the writing of Flannery O'Connor, Harold Fickett makes the point that for Flannery O'Connor there is learning and truth in literature and that it is tied up with what our lives—both as a whole and in part—mean.

> We do not have to opt for a literature of despair in which man's quest for meaning is seen as absurd, or a literature of gamesmanship in which we are constantly reminded that the symmetry or internal coherence of the work says nothing about the real world but only serves to increase our pleasure in reading. We can aim, O'Connor believed, for the revelation of truth.[26]

As we have seen, a number of different forms of such cognitive disclosure or understanding have been explored in this postmodern period, each with its unique language and grammar. Our immediate interest here lies with the narrative or story mode of such disclosive truth, for such narrative understanding constitutes the primary vehicle for the human perception of an overarching, interpretive disclosure of the meaning of being. In other words, religious stories or founding myths constitute the means whereby human beings see life and human destiny as a meaningful whole, thereby constituting not only the variety of human worlds or cultures, but the religious traditions and philosophical worldviews (such as modernity) which populate those cultures.

2:5 The Turn in Postmodern Philosophy

Modernity developed out of a vision of the historical possibility for human beings to achieve security through the control of nature, a control made possible by scientific and mathematical knowledge. That vision, of course, was not itself a form of empirical or deductive understanding, but a story which made available an interpretive understanding of reality and human destiny—i.e., a myth. Because of this mythological vision of life, the regulative paradigm of philosophy in the modern period was generally to picture (or mirror) scientifically or deductively what is 'out there' as it is in itself. According to Richard Rorty, this embodied

> a desire for constraint—a desire to find "foundations" to which one might cling, frameworks beyond which one must not stray, objects which impose themselves, representations which cannot be gainsaid.[27]

But if that is true, then surely the postmodern awareness that there can be no such sure (inductive or deductive) foundations might be expected to lead to a 'turn' in the very sense of what it means to do philosophy today. Some postmodern thinkers indicate just such a turn by speaking of the end or death of philosophy in the modern sense of the word. At any rate, the postmodern discovery of an interpretive form of understanding beyond induction and deduction—a kind of understanding on which modernity was founded and of which it remained unaware—has led to a revised conception of the nature of understanding in such human sciences as history, literature, sociology, religion, and philosophy itself. Because the present study is basically a philosophical one, it might be helpful for us to pause long enough to briefly explore some of the more important changes that have occurred in our understanding of philosophy in the postmodern context.

1. Philosophy Begins in Wonder

It is by now a venerable tradition in the West that philosophy (and thus intellectual life in general, which developed from it) begins in the experience of wonder. In the words of Plato:

> This sense of wonder is the mark of the philosopher. Philosophy indeed has no other origin. . . .[28]

What did Plato mean by this?

When I was a graduate student in philosophy twenty-five years ago, there was a rather unquestioned set of views about Socrates that it seems to me we can now see were rather narrowly shaped by the modern assumptions we have been discussing. Socrates' philosophy was thought to be either the same as Plato's or merely the 'early' basis for it in the Socratic method of examining issues, a method and philosophical stance which really had to wait for Plato's theory of ideas for its completion. That Socrates claimed in the *Apology* that he "didn't know", that because of this he would not accept payment for what he did, and that the so-called "early dialogues" ended with no final answers or solutions to the questions being addressed was explained away as either a teaching device to leave students the hard task of finishing the dialogues by coming to the truth on their own or a mere rhetorical device to defend Socrates from the wrath of postwar Athens. The picture, then, was that the examination of an issue, although it might begin in wonder, was really aimed at overcoming it by arriving at the end of the dialogue at solid answers—i.e., fully defended and justified definitions of the phenomenon at issue. In other words, Socrates' methodological beginnings needed Plato's theory of ideas (solid truths) to make any sense. Somehow this just does not square with either the claims or the spirit of Socrates.

From the postmodern point of view, I think we can see the Socratic endeavor (and thus the relationship to Plato) in a far different light. It's not that Socrates meant to overcome wonder in favor of a completed truth, or that he intended to firmly and conclusively 'know' at the end of the dialogue. Rather, a dialogue with Socrates on a particular issue was more like what Heidegger calls "the happening of truth." That is, the kind of learning which resulted from the maieutic examination when you were able to enter into it was not objective and final, but rather a dialogic process of question and response through which aspects of reality (e.g., justice, piety, virtue) became more clear, illumined, articulated in much the same way that painting or poetry can reveal elements of our experience not noticed before. The dialogue did not and (from this point of view) could not ever end at some fully justified truth, but would continue as a disclosive process just as long as the discussants were prepared to carry on—i.e., existed in a state of wonder. Far from being a mere intellectual curiosity which is overcome once you 'know,' wonder is in reality a state of being in which you "know you don't know" and in and through which you are capable of entering the process of creative dialogue at all. The Socratic purpose, then, if this is a fair evaluation, was not the Platonic (and modern) one of arriving at solid, final truths but the more humble and modest one of paying attention to and verbally bringing into the light aspects of our experience which we have not previously understood, or for that matter even noticed. The purpose was not so much to overcome wonder by finding answers as it was, from within the sense of wonder itself, to explore and continue to give voice to our mute experience.

But what do we mean by such a 'sense of wonder'? In our ordinary and everyday lives, each of us is willy-nilly involved in a manifold of active experiences. For example, I walk to the store to get a loaf of bread. I remember the day I was married. I shut off the alarm, get out of bed, put on my bathrobe, and then head downstairs to make the coffee. I telephoned my friend to wish him a happy birthday, and then I went back to my study to work on the book. In these typical experiences, I am not reflecting on the experiences—although I can do that—but am simply, immediately, and prereflectively living them through. This worldly and everyday experience which we can become conscious of reflectively is reality (being) for us, the only reality we live and are prereflectively aware of directly and immediately. In such experience, I know my way around and do not face questions concerning the meaning of various words or phenomenon. As Augustine said about 'time' in *The Confessions,* I don't have any problems on this level with such phenomena as 'truth,' 'God,' 'self,' 'cause,' 'justice,' 'revelation,' and 'morality.' It is only when I step back from that experience to reflect upon it that I become perplexed and aware that I don't know what they actually mean.

Wonder, then, is a stepping back from our immediate experience to notice aspects of it which until then were unnoticed because, as we said, we are too busy living them through to reflectively notice them. What is noticed in the state of wonder, first of all, is the astonishing and mysterious, brute factualness of that experience as a whole. As Rudolph Otto puts it in his classic description of the sacred, reality is encountered as *"mysterium tremendum et fascinans."*[29] That is, the experience of wonder entails a shocking and yet fascinating awareness of being itself as a mysterious, inexplicable power-to-be that surges forth in the form of myriad entities and in fact (as we shall see) life as a whole. It is shocking because it is out of the ordinary and it unsettles our ordinary lives. It is fascinating insofar as in the state of wonder we are drawn to notice it. And it is inexplicable because it cannnot be rationally accounted for or even completely understood.

As Kierkegaard was aware, reality or sheer existence is always more than you say about it. There is an unbridgeable gulf between theories about existence and existence itself. When you add to this general picture the insight of quantum physics that nature is indeterminate and that our picture of such reality is not and cannot be objective (in that it is formed and shaped by our senses, minds, and instruments), we are left with a permanent and unavoidable gulf between what is and what we can ever know about it. Reality is radically mysterious and transcendent to any possible theory. Existence is inevitably more than whatever we can say about it and, as such, it is experienced in wonder. In more traditional theological language, Being (God) is transcendent. Although it is only encountered with entities, it is itself not an entity. As Jaspers puts it, "The encompassing always announces itself—in present objects and within the horizon— but it never becomes an object."[30]

In wonder, then, we notice the mysteriousness of existence as a whole. The mysterious fact that the world exists at all is simply not part of our ordinary awareness before we enter the state of wonder. It is only when we step back in wonder that we notice the astonishing fact that there is anything at all. As Leibniz put it: "Why something; why not nothing?" Or as Wittgenstein put it: "It is not how things are in the world that is mystical, but that it exists."[31] In his memoir of Wittgenstein, Norman Malcolm expanded on this.

> Wittgenstein once read a paper on Ethics. . .in which he said that he sometimes had a certain experience which could best be described by saying that when I have it I wonder at the existence of the world. And I am then inclined to use such phrases as "How extraordinary that anything should exist!" or "How extraordinary that the world should exist!"[32]

In a sense, in wonder we notice the fundamental distinction (what Heidegger calls "the ontological difference") between entities and the existence of such entities.[33] In other words, it is through wonder that ontology (and thereby philosophy as a whole) emerges as the primordial intuition of being. This intuition of being is the concrete, encompassing experience of wonder at the astonishing mysteriousness of everything that is insofar as it is.

At the same time, wonder is noticing the mysteriousness of particular aspects (making moral decisions, telling time, claiming truth, etc.) which make up our experience as a whole. Before this, it does not seem strange to pray to an invisible entity, or even that there are such things as invisible entities. We are so at home in our ordinary experience that "drinking the blood and eating the flesh of God" not only does not seem peculiar, it isn't even noticed. Before we begin to reflectively wonder, we find nothing startling or even noteworthy about such astounding and peculiar aspects of our experience. In the words of Ninian Smart:

> Life is both strange and commonplace. But for most of the time it is commonplace, and we are not surprised that the world is

as it is, for we have no experience of any other modes of existence. The surprises that come our way are only surprises within an unsurprising framework. It may astonish us that Henry has suddenly entered a monastery or that the government of France has been overthrown, but Henry and monasteries and governments and France are part of the order of things. Yet every so often the whole set-up may suddenly strikes us as strange. We find ourselves in a universe containing, among other things, France and monasteries: but why should there be a universe at all? Why should it contain conscious, rational beings like ourselves? And what is the world really like? Are the things we see around us really as they seem to be—bathed in colour and light and shade? Or is this only an appearance that our brains and minds foist upon them? Such questions arise from, and themselves also supply, the sense of strangeness that can sometimes afflict us. The universe is our home; and yet now and then we look around uneasily, wondering whether all the time it is a stranger's house. Out of this unease and strangeness and wonder, science and philosophy spring.[34]

Wonder, then, is the experience of mystery. It is a fascinated noticing of a kind of strangeness beyond understanding, an attitude of amazement and perplexity, and sometimes a stunned curiosity in the face of the astonishing and inexplicable.

This noticing of the mysterious at the same time raises the question of 'meaning' both with respect to the parts or aspects of experience as well as the whole. As Socrates emphasized, implicit to the sense of wonder is a recognition that one doesn't know in any final sense what various words, or in reality what various phenomena, in our experience actually 'mean.' To enter into wonder is to be transformed from a state of opinion (*Doxa*) into a recognition of the amazing fact that not only are there various opinions about what such matters as truth, God, and justice mean, but more importantly, there is no demonstrated and absolute understanding of what they actually do mean.

In fact, philosophy itself is one of these mysterious words or phenomena. Thus, philosophy is (notoriously) that intellectual discipline which not only questions its own enterprise but also results in as many understandings of it as there are fundamental philosophical perspectives. Furthermore, the question of philosophical methodology and evidence ultimately is defined within the parameters of the overall philosophical viewpoint being developed. The plain fact of the matter is that there is no agreement among philosophers on a single methodology or understanding of what constitutes valid argument and evidence. That of course means that no philosophical approach or overarching viewpoint can ever be conclusively demonstrated without begging the question, for the very notion of what might constitute such foundational and apodictic demonstration is generated within the viewpoint itself. Philosophy is indeed mysterious.

To experience wonder, then, is to be transformed. As Socrates argued, this transformation in wonder is the condition for the possibility of the philosophical (and intellectual) pursuit of understanding at all. Prior to wonder, as we saw, we live in a state of immediacy, which is to live as if there were such single and secure understanding. There is, then, no impetus or desire to find out. Philosophy (and thus all the sciences and humanities which developed out it) begins in wonder. Wonder is a reflective experience in which a person is transformed by becoming open to the mysterious 'not-knownness' of life and thus made ready for the maiuetic art of actually seeking to better understand it.

In a recent article, Parker Palmer powerfully expresses the centrality of wonder and mystery in the kind of Socratic learning (and teaching) we have been discussing here.

> Mystery is a primal and powerful human experience that can neither be ignored nor reduced to formula. To learn from mystery, we must enter with all our faculties alert, ready to laugh as well as groan, able to 'live the question' rather than demand a final answer. When we enter into mystery this way, we find the mystery entering us, and our lives are challenged and changed.[35]

Wonder, then, is a state of astonished amazement, perplexity and curiosity aroused by the miraculous reality or actuality of life. It is paying attention to it, and is the condition necessary to give meaningful voice to our experiences and lives. One cannot articulate that experience, after all, without paying close attention to it and without recognizing that there are elements of it which have not yet been expressed in, for example, science, literature, or philosophy. It is not just the starting point of philosophy, then, but the *fons et origo* of creative work in any of the sciences and human arts to which it gives birth. As Einstein put it in his autobiography,

> The most beautiful experience we can have is the mysterious. It is the fundamental emotion which stands at the cradle of true art and true science.[36]

It's as if we human beings were a kind of remarkable space in the midst of things in which reality (hitherto a "buzzing and blooming confusion," as William James put it) is given a voice (or voices) through which to meaningfully express and articulate itself to human consciousness. These voices, as we have seen, are the different realms of discourse which constitute the various forms of human understanding—e.g., paintings, poetry, novels, historical studies, religious mythologies, architecture, and (yes) philosophical essays. They bring what was before merely silence and obscurity into the clarity of formed expression.

Wonder, then, lies at the heart of philosophy and the human sciences in at least two senses. First, without it there could be no meaningful disclosure of our lives in any form, for the philosopher, painter, or poet is by that very fact closed to the mysterious reality which calls her to find voice to disclose it. Socrates in fact thought that such a lack of wonder was a kind of ghastly and inhuman trance and the basis of much of the evident social and political terror we visit upon one another. Much later, Sören Kierkegaard called it a "sickness unto death," an attempt to be dead, to be unconscious and have no wonder, while still living.

Second, that wonder at life and everyday experience—both as a whole as well as in its myriad details—is inevitably and lovingly expressed in the great works of philosophy and the other human sciences. Listen, for example, to a comment on himself in a recent poem by the great Polish-American poet, Czeslaw Milosz: "What good are you? In your writing there is nothing except immense amazement."[37]

We should reemphasize here that by 'wonder' we do not mean a kind of mere curiosity which later will be overcome with 'answers'— as if that wonder were just an initial impetus to philosophize and thereby be transcended. On the contrary, to the degree that such wonder is overcome, philosophy itself is overcome in favor of ideology. Wonder is not only the origin of philosophy in particular and human understanding in general, but also the creative condition and constant companion for actually philosophizing

2. Philosophies Embody Hermeneutics

It seems obvious and unexceptional that overarching philosophies or philosophical perspectives are developed by philosophers—that is, real living and breathing human beings. What holds in general for those human beings will likewise hold for philosophers. Philosophers do not philosophize or work out a philosophical perspective by starting with a blank mind (in other words, from the ground up), although of course some have tried to claim that, at least as a regulative ideal of their notion of doing philosophy. On the contrary. Like anyone else, philosophers are historically and culturally situated, and they bring to their lives and activities (including developing a philosophical perspective) a tacit understanding of what life is all about, a way of seeing life as a meaningful whole. That sense of what is most fundamental and significant about living is then brought to life and philosophical creativity and becomes a sort of interpretive framework which structures and permeates the philosophy which ultimately is worked out. We saw earlier that lying behind the typical modern philosophies of the Enlightenment was a mythological dimension which was itself not grounded empirically or deductively—that the story that was to end all stories was itself just another story.

We don't want to throw out the Enlightenment baby with the foundationalist bathwater, but we can no longer philosophize and teach as if there were a reality 'out there' that can simply be mirrored by our empirical and logical propositions. Such a view abstracts from and ignores the way our very interpretation and vision of that reality is shaped by the interplay of knower and known and leads to a kind of teaching which seeks to avoid the sense of wonder and mystery so fundamental to creative reflection by reducing all understanding to presumed 'facts.' On the other hand, this does not mean (as it seems to mean to Richard Rorty at times) that all human understanding is ultimately a subjective illusion projected upon a noumenal nature. On the contrary, I am pointing here to a kind of human understanding which is beyond the dichotomy of objective fact or subjective illusion, a kind of interpretive understanding which is presupposed in the very framing of such a typical modern dilemma.

Philosophies in general, then, are built upon a non- or pre-philosophical, personal interpretation (hermeneutic) of what is fundamental or most basically 'real' and significant about living—a tacit understanding which leads the philosopher involved in particular directions and which conditions and permeates the resultant philosophy as the interpretive point of view from which and through which it has been worked out. Michael Novak puts this very well:

> For the truth is that human experience cannot be interpreted except from a standpoint, except as seen in a certain light, except as assessed in view of certain purposes, except as grasped in the context of experiences and insights and judgments accumulated to that point. The human being in search of his identity cannot stand outside the arena of human life, and he is not infinite in

his perspective: does not incorporate in himself all actual, let alone all possible, perspectives for understanding. In his finiteness, he operates from one standpoint at a time. To grasp the import of what he says, therefore, one must grasp clearly the standpoint from which he says it.[38]

Plato's yearning for true knowledge through the mind's contemplation of the interrelated and harmonious world of ideas is not essentially different from what Mircea Eliade asserts of the religious mind—a nostalgia for Paradise. It is a human interpretation and construal of life in the face of the horror and strife of the Pelloponesian War and the scandal of Athenian political life. It is a vision of an ideal reality in which all is eternal, stable, and harmonious. "If we could only induce our leaders to rise up from the cave of change and mere opinion to 'know' this higher reality," Plato seems to say, "we might be able to make the cave itself a kind of microcosmic and just reflection of the justice and harmony of that other world." A fine dream, but a dream nonetheless. It is an attitude toward life (fundamentally, a religious attitude). It is, in fact, Plato's attitude—an attitude which has not been demonstrated, but which is the interpretive framework he brings to his philosophical task and which undergirds and pervades it as light fills the room and permits us to see the furniture.

Or take Spinoza's dream of a totally clear and deductively certain philosophy based upon apodictic premises. That he should suggest such an approach as an antidote to the horrendous religious and political strife he found around him is human enough. And of course it permeates the *Ethics*. It can be seen between the lines (or behind the text) as his particular passionate vision of what is fundamentally significant about and how best to live life.

The same is true *mutatis mutandis* for all philosophies, I am claiming—including, of course, this one. The British empiricists' appreciation of the power and significance of scientific knowledge is not itself a scientific hypothesis, but a human story and dream through which their actual philosophical explorations are worked out.

As we shall see in Chapters Four and Five (where we will explore in more detail a postmodern view of religious understanding), this means that philosophers bring to their doing of philosophy a pre-philosophical, mythological interpretation of life as a meaningful whole. Philosophies, insofar as they presuppose and presume philosophers to spell them out, rest upon—and in fact are—religious or mythological at their foundations.

The foundationalist project of finding some sure and certain foundation for knowledge, perhaps an ideal mode of discourse to which all other modes of discourse could be reduced, or a self-evident first principle, is a kind of contradiction in terms insofar as the dream itself can never be demonstrated without begging the question. Thus, it is just another human dream, but one which deludes itself by systematically blinding itself to the hermeneutical, interpretive, and mythical foundation on which it truly stands.

3. The Goal of Postmodern Philosophy

We saw earlier that philosophy in the premodern or traditional period was thought to be a kind of allegorical wisdom, the purpose of which was to help us understand and actually come to live more fully and deeply. As Aristotle put it, contemplation was thought to be the highest form of life possible for human beings. Its goals then were existential ones, namely to transform this life in the light of a wisdom or knowledge gained about a transcendent and metaphysical realm beyond it. In other words, this life was interpretively 'seen' in the light of that metaphysical realm beyond. As such, I argued, it was thought to be the allegorical parallel to the spiritual wisdom and insight gained through mythology, holy scripture, or ritual.

In the meantime, of course, modernity did away with this conception of a spiritual or philosophical wisdom in favor of a reduction of all human knowledge to matters of fact or matters of reason, thereby casting us adrift from any spiritual moorings. With the discovery in the postmodern period of the hermeneutical or mythological dimension underlying that modernity, we are in a position to rejoin that earlier tradition of religious and philosophical wisdom, but now at a later and non-allegorical level. Insofar as philosophies presuppose real human philosophers who articulate them, they also presuppose religious understanding or myth—i.e., an interpretive, hermeneutical under-standing of what it means to be. This means that philosophies and religious symbol-traditions share the kind of mythological, interpretive understanding we will be exploring in detail later. Put another way, philosophies are another form of religious expression. The purpose of philosophy in the postmodern period has switched from the foundationalist project of gaining certain and absolute objective knowledge to living life more fully and completely—to what I shall call 'autonomy.'

An autonomous life is one which is self-determined. A heter-onomous life, on the other had, is a life which lacks this self-determination. An autonomous person is aware that any philosophy (including, of course, one's own) is built upon a pre- or extra-philosophical hermeneutic, and thus is never either objectively certain or absolute and exclusively true. That is, the autonomous person owns her philosophy in such a way that she takes responsibility for it. In a way, it is to philosophize while continuing to be aware through wonder of the mystery of existence and the evident fact that we do not know in the sense of 'knowing' certainly and absolutely. That is why we claimed earlier that philosophy doesn't overcome wonder with absolute answers, but rather that wonder is the requisite condition for the possibility of continuing to philosophize at all. When wonder is overcome, philosophy is likewise overcome—in favor of ideology.

From this point of view, what we face in philosophizing is not a dilemma in which our choice is limited to either ignorance or truth, but a third option: living a life of wonder and the search for understanding in which we know we do not know in any certain or final sense and in which we come to better understand particular aspects of our lives. Given the choice of attaining complete truth (an impossibility, we have tried to say) as opposed to infinite striving to reach it, we are agreeing with Lessing and Kierkegaard that the latter way of existing is not only possible but preferable.[39] With the recognition that we bring an interpretive framework and point of view to the doing of philosophy, with an awareness that we are inevitably culturally and historically (and genetically) situated, and with the constant companion of wonder, we can still illumine various aspects of our experience. That is neither knowing nothing nor knowing everything, neither a merely nominal flapping of the mouth nor a universal commensuration to still all doubts and points of view, but a more humble, disciplined striving to give further voice to a reality which remains voiceless until evoked by human consciousness.

This, of course, touches on an ancient and venerable theme in philosophy. The life of wonder is the Socratic examined life beyond mere opinion, an autonomous life in which one takes responsibility for one's hermeneutical standpoint and one's explicit philosophical views. As Martha Nussbaum recently put it: "Since the time of Socrates, philosophy has involved taking your life into your own hands in order to say what you think is true."[40]

If existing autonomously is the goal of postmodern philosophy (as I am claiming), then there must be a way of living and holding a philosophy which falls short of such autonomy. We call that 'heteronomy'—i.e. lacking self-determination. It is a way of existing in which wonder is abolished in favor of holding or simply assuming that one in fact has the answer. It is to deny or at least forget the hermeneutical construal of life which (I've tried to argue) underlies and conditions any philosophy in favor of a dogma which, insofar as it assumes that it is itself objectively true and certain, implies that other (contradictory) philosophies are false. In a way, it is the attempt to live irresponsibly by not taking responsibility for one's own philosophy. It denies such personal and hermeneutical involvement in favor of something beyond oneself—e.g., 'reason,' *Bewustsein Ueberhaupt*, the 'iron hand of history,' *Logos*, God, the Koran, or sacred doctrine. It is, as Kierkegaard put it, an attempt not to be a person, to be dead while living, to avoid decision and responsibility for one's own standpoint and philosophical views.

> Human existence simply is not there until it is established by an act of self-constitution; without it, we merely seem to be persons, but we are in fact empty inside, mere standard "objects" in human form.[41]

From a postmodern point of view, of course, the heteronomous life is naive (unaware of its own hermeneutical roots), childish, dogmatic, and socially dangerous. Certainly Socrates' encounter with the theologian Euthyphro in the Platonic dialogue of the same name illustrates the murderous potential involved in such a heteronomous life. Euthyphro, you will recall, is prosecuting his father for causing the death of a slave boy. In the name of the will of the gods that any kind of murder thwarts that divine will, Euthyphro is about to murder his own father, in spite of the fact that when questioned by Socrates it becomes perfectly clear that he has no idea what he is doing.

Instead of objective and certain knowledge, then, the goal of postmodern philosophy insofar as it is aware of its hermeneutical roots is (as it had been in the premodern or traditional period) a way of existing. What I refer to as the autonomous life of wonder Gadamer calls "*Bildung*" (education or self-formation) and Richard Rorty calls "edification." Edifying philosophy, he claims, takes us "out of ourselves by the powers of strangeness, to aid us in becoming new beings."[42] We become different people than we were before in that we are touched and transformed by the sense of wonder. Far from attempting to overcome the sense of wonder with solid and certain answers, Rorty claims:

> Edifying philosophers want to keep space open for the sense of wonder which poets can sometimes cause—wonder that there is something new under the sun, something which is not an

accurate representation of what was already there, something (at least for the moment) which cannot be explained and can only be described.[43]

Ultimately, of course, postmodern philosophy throws us back on ourselves in that it provides no ultimate standpoint or certainty about what our lives are all about. We find only perspectives and approaches, interpretations of meaning. It throws us back on ourselves, then, and demands that we respond to life by becoming philosophical creators ourselves. It teaches us to own ourselves, to take hold of our own lives, to think for ourselves. We are reminded, here, of those ancient images of waking up, overcoming dogmatic slumbers, emerging from lives of mere opinion (*Doxa*) or ignorance (*avidja*), becoming responsible and autonomous adults. However it is put, it is a sharp and qualitative turn in our lives which is fostered and nourished by wonder.

It happens that the stage sets collapse. Rising, streetcar, four hours in the office or the factory, streetcars, four hours of work, meal, sleep and Monday, Tuesday, Wednesday, Thursday, Friday and Saturday according to the same rhythm—this path is easily followed most of the time. But one day the "why" arises and everything begins in the weariness tinged with amazement. "Begins"—this is important. Weariness inaugurates the impulse of consciousness. It awakens the consciousness and provides what follows. What follows is the gradual return into the chain or it is the definitive awakening.[44]

Philosophy, then, shares the goal and purpose of religious life in general—i.e., to help us live an awakened and responsible life as deeply and fully as possible. As I have indicated, this should not be surprising. Philosophies presuppose philosophers who, to the degree that they are human, share the inevitable human dimension of hermeneutical interpretation and understanding of what it means to be. Exploring that dimension of mythological, interpretive, and narrative understanding is what we will focus upon in the following chapters.

It was Max Weber who reminded us that the world which he thought had once been an "enchanted garden" has become instead flat and disenchanted for far too many of us here at the end of the modern period. As I argued earlier, we are probably in the process of moving beyond that difficult modern worldview, that the great ice sheet has melted into postmodernity. However that may be, if we are to bring about the "reenchantment of the world" (to use Morris Berman's haunting phrase), if we are to find ourselves once again ravished by the world's mystery and wonder and awash in its beauty and worth, postmodern philosophy will play its part.

Part II

The Heart of the Matter

3

The Narrative Self

I know myself immediately only as an ever-changing sequence of occasions of experience, each of which is the present integration of remembered past and anticipated future into a new whole of significance. My life history continually leads through moments of decision in which I must somehow determine what both I and those to whom I am related are to be. Selecting from the heritage of the already actual and the wealth of possibility awaiting realization, I freely fashion myself in creative interaction with a universe of others who also are not dead but alive.

Schubert Ogden

3:1 Exploring the World of Ordinary Experience

We saw in Part One that a kind of interpretive (hermeneutic) understanding underlay and conditioned the modern world, a form of understanding of which modernity remained blissfully and naively unaware. As some have put it, it was a story to end all stories. The recent philosophical consciousness of this nonempirical and nonmathematical form of human understanding, I argued, constitutes the initial step into a postmodern cultural context. My overall purpose here, of course, is to outline a postmodern view of religious knowledge as a form of such interpretive understanding and then to consider the significance of that understanding for our contemporary religious and cultural situation.

In this chapter, I will argue that religious stories or myths are themselves based upon and could not exist without the narrative structure of our actual experience as active agents. But before we turn to the analysis of that narrative structure of experience, we need to clarify and briefly explore the methodological approach used here to get at it.

That approach is existential phenomenology, an approach which I, along with Paul Ricoeur,[1] find not only consistent with hermeneutical studies but a fruitful and indispensable ancillary philosophical tool within them.

Existential phenomenology is a contemporary philosophical movement which can be said to be a synthesis of the two earlier and separate traditions of existentialism and pure phenomenology. As such, it entails an attempt to reflectively lay out or describe various aspects (phenomena) of our concrete experience (existence) from the point of view of the subject(s) or agent(s) involved.

The manifold of concrete experiences is made up of our ordinary and everyday activities: shutting off the alarm clock, walking to the kitchen, making breakfast, designing a building, reading a magazine, telephoning the dentist, driving the car, greeting a loved one, mourning a death, hoping for a letter from a friend, and so on. Experientially, it is not constituted from or reducible to deeper realities (substances) such as an absolute subject or mind (*res cogitans*) separated from what it perceives, imagines, or remembers; or object-things (*res extensa*) which are pictured as existing in themselves apart from and before a mind comes to know them. Rather (and this is the first step in the reflective process of description of concrete experience mentioned above), our experience is always intentional,—i.e., a field in which perceiving, imagining, and remembering subjects exist only over against something perceived, imagined, or remembered, and vice versa. Subjects and objects, far from being primary substances to which experience can be reduced, are in fact correlative moments within an encompassing, actually existing, experiential field in which they are constituted as such.

Our experience is always worldly. We exist in a horizon or field of experiential relationships between ourselves and things, others, the past which lies behind us, and future possibilities which we act toward. This is not the world of object-things floating around in the universe, so to speak, but human worlds of ordinary experience—the world of the Sioux, the world of modern mathematics, the world of fourth century Rome, and so on. These worlds, then, are the horizon or context for our practical and everyday relational experience: a perceptual field, a complex set of social interrelations and behavioral exchanges, and ordinary bodily activity. The body, here, is the 'lived body' as it is experienced by the agent involved rather than the 'objective body' abstracted out of experience as a second-order explanation of it. In such ordinary bodily behavior, I act in a context of the immediate past toward goals which I intend to achieve through that activity, like returning the tennis ball which has just been served to me by running toward it and swinging my racket at just the right moment.

This experience in the world, then, is reality for us, the only reality which we live and know directly. Whatever we come to know about objects present to us, we come to know through a complex perceptual set of experiences which our understanding (or picture) of them presupposes. As Maurice Merleau-Ponty put it, "The world is there before any possible analysis of mine."[2] As Husserl described it, it is

> pregiven to us all quite naturally, as persons within the horizon or our fellow men, i.e., in every actual connection with others, as 'the' world common to us all. Thus it is...the constant ground of validity, an ever-available source of what is taken for granted, to which we, whether as practical men or as scientists, lay claim as a matter of course.[3]

Ordinarily, I pay little reflective attention to worldly experience as such, for I am busy acting in the world: remembering my past, loving my family, trying to live fully, and using things around me to accomplish my tasks. I use the ground to walk on, air to fill my lungs, sunlight to read my book, and the keys of this wordprocessor to transfer thoughts I am struggling with to paper. In this sense, we can say that experience is prereflective and preconceptual—i.e., simply lived through and not ordinarily reflectively thought about. I know my way about this world, as Wittgenstein put it, in the sense of knowing 'how' rather than knowing 'that' or 'what'.

One aspect of this stream of ordinary experience is the astonishing fact that we can become reflectively or conceptually aware of it: we can transform knowing how into knowing that or what. We can turn in upon ourselves to pay attention to the experience(s) we previously simply preconceptually lived through, thereby making it (them) explicitly conscious.

It seems that there is a sort of unthematized or "prereflexive" awareness (as Sartre called it), which goes along with our ordinary experience and which can be consulted in memory and be reflectively and consciously thematized. For example, I was deeply engrossed in reading an essay concerning the growth of the notion of sin in the early Church when my wife said to me, "What are you doing, Paul?" "Oh, I'm reading about Augustine's sense of sin and how that influenced what later was to become the theology of the institutional Church." Clearly, in such ordinary activity as this, reflection is recuperative:

I am able to reflectively recollect an experience which I was having, an experience which I was not explicitly thinking about at the time but of which I was implicitly aware so that later I could identify and describe it. This relationship between ordinary experience in the world and our reflective power to focus upon it and become explicitly conscious of it is, of course, the basis of the present study.

As an aside, we might mention here that several recent commentators have noticed the parallel between, on the one hand, preconceptual experience and a reflective awareness of it and, on the other hand, the premodern, naive experience of God and the modern, critical suspicion of such experience.[4] In these terms, in a kind of historical ontogeny recapitulating human phylogeny, modernity made the premodern, experiential naivete quite impossible, as we have seen. At the same time, the postmodern shift is then seen to be a reflexive understanding of both the premodern and modern worldviews—a "second naivete," as Ricoeur calls it—in which (while maintaining a critical, reflective rigor) an attempt is made to interpretively explore, articulate, and make available in contemporary terms the experiential and first naivete so evident in the premodern or traditional world.

At any rate, existential phenomenology is not interested in objects of experience, but experience as it reflectively is to itself.

> Phenomenology is reflexive description and analysis. It is not description and analysis of any objective aspect of the world, but our experience of the world.[5]

The goal is to evoke and make verbally manifest the sense or meaning of various aspects of experience within the context of that experience itself. For example, what is it like to be an agent involved in acting in the world? For that matter, what is action—not this or that piece of action, but action *per se*? And what do we mean by remembering in its various forms? I remember the date of my marriage, I recall (on my tongue as well as through an image) the taste of dinner, I remember how to ride a bicycle. Or, more to the point of the present essay, what is it to know God—i.e., religiously to know what this life is about, whether it be in the form of a Vedanta conception or that of an Australian bush tribe? In other words, the object is to articulate and make explicit what until then is merely implicit to the experience(s) involved. Paul Ricoeur has said, "Phenomenology wagers that the lived can be understood and said."[6]

From this point of view, argument and fundamental evidence consist of reflectively going back to and exploring the mute world of ordinary experience in order to give voice to various aspects of it, to make conceptual and thematic that which hitherto has been preconceptual and unthematized. Maurice Merleau-Ponty says:

The world is always already there before reflection begins as inalienable presence; and all its [existential phenomenology's] efforts are concentrated upon re-achieving a direct and primitive contact with the world, and endowing that contact with a philosophical status.[7]

Such experiences are not to be pictured as mere facts which somehow lie outside of the linguistic or conceptual worlds in which they occur. On the contrary, from the point of view of existential phenomenology we never just stumble upon facts dissociated from conception and interpretation—or vice versa for that matter. It is impossible (and we know this descriptively) to transcend language in order to discover aspects of experience which are innocent of conceptual assumptions, grammatical practices, or (as we shall see) hermeneutical biases. This means two things.

First, it means that our experience in the world inevitably takes place in a linguistic and hermeneutical context, and that part of the phenomenological description of such experiences must evoke or articulate their sense within such a context of meaning and attitude. In fact, being in a world ultimately means precisely to be linguistically and hermeneutically so contextualized. Richard Rorty puts this very well in his *Philosophy and the Mirror of Nature*:

We shall never be able to avoid the 'hermeneutic circle'—the fact that we cannot understand the parts of a strange culture, practice, theory, language, or whatever, unless we know something about how the whole thing works, whereas we cannot get a grasp on how the whole works until we have some understanding of its parts. This notion of interpretation suggests that coming to understand is more like getting acquainted with a person than like following a demonstration.[8]

Second, it means that phenomenological analysis of ordinary experience in the world is itself an interpretive endeavor with linguistic, conceptual, and hermeneutical constraints upon it. There is—at least for existential phenomenology—no God's-eye point of view.

It is important at this point to understand that these verbal evocations of various aspects of our experience are first-order descriptions of those experiences rather than second-order explanations of them; and that, whatever the pragmatic or utilitarian value of such explanations, neither our experiences nor the first-order descriptions of them are reducible to or replaceable by those second-order explanations.

Mircea Eliade has argued that religion is "first of all, an experience *sui generis*, incited by man's encounter with the sacred."[9] Such an experience can reveal its true meaning only when it is considered as an aspect of or from the point of view of experience itself—i.e., "on its own plane of reference, and not when it is reduced to one of its secondary aspects or its contexts."[10] Eliade, then, sees the task of understanding religion as a hermeneutical one and he urges us to get inside and relive the world of the religious practitioners we are seeking to understand.

Wayne Proudfoot puts this another way in his admirable study, *Religious Experience*:

> Religious experience is the experience of something. It is intentional in that it cannot be described without reference to a grammatical object. Just as fear is always fear of something, and a perceptual act can only be described by reference to its object, a religious experience must be identified under a certain description, and that description must include a reference to the object of the experience. . . . If someone is afraid of a bear, his fear cannot be accurately described without mentioning the bear.[11]

Thus, any adequate or appropriate description of religious activity or experience must be first order,—i.e., from the point of view of the experience of the subject involved. To abstract out of the experiential and intentional context is precisely to lose the experiential sense or meaning of the activity in favor of a second order explanation of it. This is to decontextualize and lose the experiential sense in favor of a covering law to which the experience is reduced—e.g., some social, psychological, or historical theory which is seen as causal and determinative of the experience.

Professor Proudfoot goes on to make a distinction between what he calls "descriptive" and "explanatory reductions." "Descriptive reduction," he tells us, "is the failure to identify an emotion, practice, or experience under the description by which the subject identifies it."[12] This is illicit in that it is a misidentification of the experience which simply reduces it to or replaces it with another. "To describe the experience of a mystic by reference only to alpha waves, altered heart rate, and changes in bodily temperature is to misdescribe it."[13] "Explanatory reduction," on the other hand, "consists in offering an explanation of an experience in terms that are not those of the subject and that might not meet with his approval. This is perfectly justifiable and is, in fact, normal procedure" in, for example, historical, economic, social, or psychological studies.[14] Professor Proudfoot argues that the failure to distinguish these two forms of reduction—one licit and one illicit—has led to a great deal of confusion and misunderstanding.

I agree with that judgment so long as such covering laws or explanatory theories involved are taken pragmatically or as having a merely utilitarian status. But how often is that the case? The usual course, it seems, is that such explanatory theories are implicitly taken in a realistic sense, and that is why they are taken so seriously. That is, they are taken to be mirror reflections in the mind (to use Rorty's metaphor) which are true insofar as they represent reality as it actually is. What is going on in that case is that they are illicitly avoiding showing the experience at hand in favor of replacing it with different, second-order covering laws or explanations. Implicitly, but most often in an unstated fashion, such theories are felt to be valid precisely because it is assumed that they are actually the case (or closer to the case) about reality. As Kierkegaard was wont to put it, they tacitly assume that thought (explanatory theory) is identical to being. One would have to show why, precisely, such an explanation is a more adequate understanding of reality than the phenomenological description and not simply assume it to be the case. Of course, I don't believe that can be done since in fact the only reality we directly live and are reflectively aware of is that experience itself.

In other words, if a hermeneutic can be characterized (as we shall see) as an interpretation of the meaning of being (reality), then evidently we have here a basic hermeneutical dispute concerning the meaning of being. As Kierkegaard put it, to replace existence with a theory—no matter how complete—is not only a result of an "esthetic" form of existence, but a kind of "despair" and "sickness unto death" which is attempting to cover up, forget, and flee that experience in favor of a beautiful ("esthetic") but abstract marble palace where all is in harmony and makes perfect sense. It is an attempt to decontextualize theory by abstracting out of and replacing concrete experience with a second-order explanation. It is an attempt to put the cart before the horse, to replace reality with thoughts about it.

We should emphasize that placing ontological and epistemological priority on our ordinary experience in the world does not do away with second-order explanations as long as they are taken in a pragmatic rather than ontological or realistic sense. It simply makes them second-order understandings which presuppose and depend upon first-order experience and which are validated and justified pragmatically insofar as they help and support us in that ordinary experience in the world.

Because our ordinary experience is what is immediately and primarily real for us, and because that experience is structured narratively, that experience is best perceived through stories rather than abstract concepts. If a person is asked what she has been doing or why she did it, she will normally give an account in terms of a story. She will locate and signify events in terms of humanly understandable projects or goals.

> The temporal, schematic linking of events as narrative is the kind of knowing that is used to understand personal action and autobiography. It is the format people use to organize their understanding of each other as biographies and case histories.[15]

In fact, as I have already indicated, overarching philosophies and metaphysics are themselves stories insofar as they are special forms of mythological narrative.

> Our common *Lebenswelt* contains what appears in 'experience' and deal with in our practical activity, to which narrative locution is our most direct linguistic access. When we speak to or of what is immediately real to us we tell stories and fragments of stories. . . . Narrative locutions remain our primary linguistic sources if we are to concern ourselves with the question of reality at all. . . .The esthetic forms of experience are not abstractions standing between the conscious ego and reality, to be by-passed or beaten down. They are precisely our openings into the flow that encompasses us, the medium, fluid but not amorphous, through which consciousness is carried into that flow.[16]

Having briefly explored the philosophical methodology under-lying this study, let us phenomenologically explore the nature of action and its narrative structure,[17] for the explicit analysis of religious understanding which follows in chapters four and five presupposes and rests upon it.

3:2 Action and Time

If we reflectively pay attention to our ordinary experience, we find that we are in the world not simply as observers and perceivers but as agents who act consciously and purposefully to achieve specific goals. In fact, that experience is really a series of one action after another. ''After breakfast, I made a few business telephone calls that I wanted to get out of the way, and then I walked out to the garage, got in my car, and headed off to the university to teach my first class. . . . '' We are different from other animals, at least in degree, in that we can act toward goals—some proximate (going to the garage) and some more distant (to teach my first class at the university). Reflectively, life as we actually experience it is an active endeavor, or rather a series of such endeavors.

By *'action'* I shall mean specifically human doings rather than natural events. Action involves an intention whereas natural events or happenings refer to other events as their cause. An action is a doing which brings about an end or goal which was intended in the action itself. Getting on an airplane, flying it to ten thousand feet, and then jumping out are all actions. The spin of the propeller, the ability of the air to keep the plane aloft, and falling toward the earth are all events.

Human actions involve temporality, then, not in some abstract way nor in terms of the measurement of time with a clock, but in the sense that action is a present reaching out toward anticipated goals. When I do something such as get on the bus to go downtown, I know in the action itself the difference between the past and future, between what I have already done and what I have yet to do.

Take any action from the reflective point of view of the agent who carries it out—for example, the act of writing this essay this morning.

It's Monday. Last evening, my wife and I returned from a weekend visit with our daughter up in the mountains. All the way back, I thought about what I hoped to accomplish in writing this essay this morning. I woke up early, had my breakfast, said 'goodbye' to my wife as she went off to work, and then went up to my study to begin writing. I promised myself to keep at it until I finished writing the background section on temporal action, narrative identity, and faith.

Phenomenologically, such typical experiential actions are always temporally situated in a context of past and future actions and events. The writing comes after waking up, having breakfast, and saying goodbye. It comes before finishing the section, and so on. Those past actions condition the present activity, and the future ones are intended goals which I seek to achieve by acting toward them. The weekend, my breakfast, and saying goodbye to my wife lie right behind my present action, and finishing this section of the essay is the goal toward which I am presently acting. Each present action retains within it this horizon of retained (past) events which condition it and intended (future) goals which it seeks to achieve. An action makes experiential sense only within such a temporal context. We might call this horizon of retained, past actions which (formerly) intended the present and the goals which we intend and anticipate in our present actions "coreferentiality." That is, each present doing embodies referential ties to what has been and to what is anticipated in the doing itself, and that coreference is retained as such and thus can be explicitly recalled in memory. I recall now that in "going up to my study" I intended to "begin writing," and this "beginning to write" was the result of "going up to my study." Because of this situational coreferentiality of each of my actions, running throughout the series of our experienced actions and available to recall is a unity of coreferentiality which ties the discrete events and doings together into one whole—me and my life. I can more or less recall the significant actions and events in my life, each within its situational coreferentiality and thus each a sort of successive link within a single chain of such actions—my unfolding life.

Actions, then, are a reaching out to bring anticipated goals into being. But beyond acting to make relatively proximate goals present, we also aim our lives at the more distant goal of what we want or intend to become. In other words, we actively seek to be, we strive to make present or bring about some ultimate and encompassing sense of what life is all about, an interpretation of what it means to be. For example, a person might seek nirvana by entering on the Buddhist Eightfold Path. He might seek the power and influence of being a millionaire by going to Harvard Business School. He might seek to bring justice to his people by overthrowing the class enemy. Or he might seek heaven by repenting of his sins. In other words, in our active lives we seek ultimate goals, visions of what we interpret life to be for or about.

This ultimate vision or concern which each of us strives to become and which (as we will see in a moment) configures the series of temporal actions that characterize our ordinary experience into a meaningful plot or story is not a cognitive or philosophical perspective but a personal, preconceptual sense of what it means to exist which precedes and prefigures any explicit philosophy, theology, or set of beliefs. It emerges through our concrete, temporal activity in which we go beyond what has been and is toward intended goals which are not yet but which become present when in fact we actually achieve them. It is a person's sense of what is fundamental and most important about living, then, and it pervades and sleeps within her actions as the very sense of what the actions are ultimately for. Indeed, the action is nothing but the attempt to achieve such a meaningful goal, to become it. Insofar as it is actually achieved, a particular self emerges or is brought into being, just this unique person with his or her unique sense of what life is about. As Karl Jaspers has put it: "The urge to being is an urge to selfhood."[18]

Heidegger calls this living or acting toward an ultimate sense of what life is about "understanding." He tells us that it is a way of "seeing" life "as" this or that, a disclosive interpretation of an ultimate "for-the-sake-of-which" we act. It is a preconceptual interpretation or understanding of the meaning of being which an agent "cares" for by aiming her life toward it.

> In the way in which its Being is projected both upon the "for-the-sake-of-which" and upon significance (the world), there lies the disclosedness of Being in general.[19]

It is through our open-ended and active striving to be, then, that what we have called an interpretive understanding (hermeneutic) of life first emerges. What we do discloses what matters to us, what we sense life is for or what is most basic and focal about it for us. We live beyond ourselves, haunted by memory and yet bedazzled and lured by imagined possibilities which we act toward and seek to make present.

3:3 Narrative Identity

This hermeneutical interpretation of what it means to be which we actively seek to become is a *telos* in the light of which our lives are lived as an unfolding story. As I noted earlier, an action makes sense only insofar as it is situated in a context of past actions which lead to it and future ones toward which it reaches. The hermeneutical goal which a person acts toward and seeks to become is a final way of seeing life as a meaningful whole in terms of which the events of her life become structured as a unique story. Rather than a meaningless series of unrelated events, the vision of life toward which each of us acts permits us to see the interrelated (coreferential) actions of our lives as a meaningful whole—i.e., interpretively to thread those actions together into a particular story. As Paul Ricoeur puts it:

> The plot's configuration superimposes the sense of ending...on the open-endedness of mere succession.[20]

Or, in the words of Donald Polkinghorne:

> Narrative is a scheme by means of which human beings give
> meaning to their experience of temporality and personal actions.
> Narrative meaning functions to give form to the understanding
> of a purpose to life and to join everyday actions and events into
> episodic units. It provides a framework for understanding the past
> events of one's life and for planning future actions. It is the
> primary scheme by means of which human existence is rendered
> meaningful.[21]

There is a temporal syntax about the series of actions which constitute
our ordinary experience. Those events are interrelated with the other
events and the whole by the overarching narrative meaning or outcome
toward which the story is unfolding. Each of our lives is an unfolding
narrative plot, a plot which reveals why the events of our story are
as they are by disclosing what they intend or are for.

Interestingly enough, when a person changes his sense of what
life is for, the former hermeneutic along with its story becomes
integrated into the new story as an ancillary subplot within his life.
Imagine, if you will, the following story.

> Before God took me by the hand and transformed my life through
> a nervous breakdown, I was a violent political activist who wanted
> to change people by changing the conditions in which they live.
> I now see that stage of my life as a painful but necessary way
> for God to lead me to repentance and my present awareness that
> true social change presupposes a transformed heart.

Finally, of course, I am claiming here not only that each of us
has a story, but that each of us is that story. I am both a unity over
time and a series of different *mes* (me at twelve, me at thirty, and so
on). The overarching narrative meaning which is the purpose toward
which I aim my life constitutes a unified theme reaching back into my
past and organizing those separate actions and events (and *mes*) into
a single narrative self. These purposes or visions of life as a meaningful
whole toward which we live and act, temporally embodied in our active
lives as personal narratives or stories we live out, constitute the form
and substance of personal identity.

> A man's sense of his own identity seems largely determined by
> the kind of story which he understands himself to have been
> enacting through the events of his career, the story of his life.[22]

The biography of John Muir, the nineteenth-century wilderness explorer and naturalist, illustrates very well the process through which a person establishes his character and identity by setting out meaningful life goals toward which he acts and which become the focal aim of his life. His decision before he was thirty to become a tramp wandering through the western wilderness of America in search of geological and botanical wisdom—the foundation of his character and ultimate career—did not come easily. His father was something of a religious fanatic who claimed to live only "by the Bible" and who frowned on both geological and botanical studies as either trivial or dangerous to religious life. Pulled this way and that, Muir couldn't seem to discover who he was or was to become. His mother wanted him to be a preacher, but this never appealed to him. He had from rather early in his life displayed a great talent at the invention and construction of novel industrial and agricultural machinery, and he even achieved some success in manufacturing them. But he was also attracted to nature and naturalistic studies. "I was tormented with soul hunger," he says.

> I began to doubt whether I was fully born. . . . I was on the world. But was I in it? . . . A few friends kindly watched my choice of the half-dozen old ways in which all good boys are supposed to walk. "Young man," they said, "choose your profession—doctor, lawyer, minister. . . . You must do your work as part of society."

He was "touched with melancholy and loneliness," he tells us, and "the pressure of time upon life":

> I would like to go to college, but then I have to say to myself, "You will die ere you can do anything else." I should like to invent useful machinery, but it comes, "You do not wish to spend your lifetime among machines." . . . I should like to study medicine that I might do my part in lessening human misery, but again it comes, "You will die ere you are ready."

In early March of 1867, an accident intervened to end his long inner conflict. In his factory, a belt on a machine he was adjusting flew up and pierced his right eye on the edge of the cornea. He was blinded in that eye and his left eye soon became blinded through nerve shock and sympathy. He was left in utter darkness. "I would gladly have died," he tells us.

My days were terrible beyond what I can tell, and my nights were if possible more terrible....My eyes closed forever on all God's beauty!...I am lost!

After a careful examination, however, a specialist indicated that he would eventually see again, imperfectly in the right eye but normally in the left. What he needed to do was to remain for a month in a darkened room. He did that, all the while dreaming of wilderness such as Yosemite Valley in the Sierras. Finally, on an April day one month after the accident, he took his first walk in the woods. When he returned—with the awareness that he could find no happiness apart from wild nature and "that I might be true to myself"—he had made his decision to spend a life of wandering. "This affliction has driven me to the sweet fields," he said. "God has to nearly kill us sometimes to teach us lessons."[23]

He immediately resigned his position in the factory and set out on his own peculiar road to a different kind of character and success—a career from which he never turned back—that of a wandering explorer, naturalist, botanist, geologist, glaciologist, and apostle for wilderness conservation. He had set out to become the real John Muir, the John Muir the world ultimately came to know.

If you want to know 'me,' then, you must learn my personal story, and the story I tell you is a verbalization of the thematic attitude toward life which threads through my everyday life and actions. As Hannah Arendt has put it: "Who somebody is or was we can know only by knowing the story of which he is himself the hero—his biography, in other words."[24]

3:4 Human Stories

Each of our lives—from the reflective point of view of ourselves as active agents—is aimed at an ultimate interpretation of the meaning of being (hermeneutic) which we strive to become and which configures the series of temporal actions that characterize our ordinary experience into a meaningful plot or story. This lived and temporally active story is not only the preverbal story which we can in part verbalize and which characterizes 'me,' but it is the ontological condition for human stories of *any* kind. Without that narrative condition of being an active agent, there could be no literature, history, religion, or even philosophy: These realms of discourse are built upon the human ability to tell and comprehend stories of various kinds, and only a being who in her very nature is acquainted and familiar with narrativity itself could possibly do that. Paul Ricoeur makes just this point.

The composition of...plot is grounded in a pre-understanding of the world of action, its meaningful structures, its symbolic resources, and its temporal character....It is a relation of presupposition and of transformation....In this sense, there is no structural analysis of narrative that does not borrow from an explicit or an implicit phenomenology of 'doing something.'... Upon this preunderstanding, common to both poets and their readers, emplotment is constructed and, with it, textual and literary mimetics...Literature would be incomprehensible if it did not give a configuration to what is already a figure in human action.[25]

Alasdair MacIntyre has made the same point in *After Virtue*.

Surely...human life has a determinate form, the form of a certain kind of story. It is not just that poems and sagas narrate what happens to men and women, but that in their narrative form poems and sagas capture a form that was already present in the lives which they relate.[26]

Not only is the narrativity of ourselves the ontological condition for the possibility of human stories in general (including mythology and historical revelation, of course), but it contributes transcendentally to the form and structure of such stories. Specifically, stories (1) imply goals which the action intends, (2) involve an agent or agents who carry out the action, (3) refer to the motives of such agents in understanding why they act as they do, (4) illuminate character and identity of such agents by displaying their hermeneutical standpoint, (5) take place contextually—i.e., within a temporal horizon of (past) actions which have already been and (future) actions which are not yet, (6) and take place within a horizon of social and natural interaction and involvement.[27] Narrative understanding is not only conditioned and structured by the narrative syntax of our ordinary experience and selves, but it is the form of human understanding most appropriate for expressing and articulating the texture and shape of that ordinary experience—e.g., in literature, history, case studies, and religious mythology.[28]

Human power and supremacy may be the result of science and technology, but they have come about (as we have seen) precisely because of the human ability to catch a glimpse of what is fundamentally significant about life through stories. The human story is the story of story itself. Nothing occurs but the human mind finds a way to fit it into a story. The basic thesis of this essay is that religions are a particular form of such human narrative meaning. They exist to give us an ultimate story to illumine all of creation, human destiny, and life and death—a story to live by.

4

Mythology and the Narrative
Interpretation of Life

I am convinced that narrative is a permanent category for understanding better how the grammar of religious convictions is displayed and how the self is formed by those convictions.

Stanley Hauerwas

4:1 Introduction

The Jataka tales are a vast collection of popular stories in southeast Asia concerning the many incarnations of the Buddha. One of the most famous concerns the miraculous conception and birth of Siddhartha. It is a story not untypical of the various religious traditions. One might compare it, for example, to the birth stories of Jesus in the gospels of Matthew and Luke.

One night Mahamaya, chief queen of Suddhodhana, king of the Sakyas, dreamt that she was carried away to the divine lake Anavatapta in the Himalayas, where she was bathed by the heavenly guardians of the four quarters of the universe. A great white elephant with a lotus flower in his trunk approached her, and entered her side. Next day the dream was interpreted for her by wise men—she had conceived a wonderful son, who would be either a Universal Emperor or a Universal Teacher. The child was born in a grove of Sal trees called Lumbini, near the capital of the Sakyas, Kapilavastu, while his mother was on the way to her parents' home for her confinement. At birth, he stood upright, took seven strides and spoke: ''This is my last birth—henceforth there is no more birth for me.''[1]

As soon as we hear that Gotama's mother is bathed by "heavenly guardians of the four quarters of the universe" in the waters of a "divine lake" and approached by a white elephant carrying a lotus flower in his trunk who "entered her side," we know that we are entering the realm of story as opposed to that of actual history. This all gets confirmed when we are told of "wise men" who interpret the dream, and when the just-born Buddha miraculously walks and predicts his own liberation from the cycle of birth and suffering which, interestingly enough, might be said to constitute the very essence of his later teaching.

What are we to do with such a story? We are all aware that babies are not conceived this way, nor do newborns walk and talk. Perhaps we should follow our modern instincts and simply dismiss these tales as pious poetry or enchanting dreams—popular and ignorant ramblings fit only for children or to establish holidays—and having no epistemic bearing or weight at all. But if we enter onto that slippery slope, how do we get off, and just where does it end? What will happen to *Genesis*, the birth stories of Jesus, the stories of Isis and Osiris, the miracle of Exodus, Mohammed's reception of the Koran, or resurrection from the dead, not to mention the seeming infinity of myths which found the myriad religious traditions and cultures? Do we dismiss them all as fairy tales? If we do, we not only swallow whole the modern view that knowledge is limited to matters of verifiable fact (itself based upon a view of life and human destiny which was mythical, as we have seen), but we also imprison ourselves in a painful world from which genuine spiritual life seems eternally banished in favor of technical power and control with its attendant environmental degradation. Furthermore, by doing that we simply overlook the kind of understanding that is actually involved in such myths and stories. Are our choices when facing mythologies and religious stories limited to skepticism or some sort of fanatical leap in the dark? Is it possible that there is another kind of knowing involved in the religious dimension, a nonconceptual way of coming to terms with life by understanding what it demands of us?. Our thesis, of course, is precisely that there is such a nonempirical, mythological and hermeneutical understanding which our present cultural movement beyond modernity permits us to discern. In other words, contrary to the assumptions of modernity, religious life does involve understanding, albeit in neither empirical nor deductive form.

The point of such stories (it seems to me) is not that they be reconciled with modern science, but that they express the significance of Gotama's birth to those whose lives have been transformed by his life and teaching. It is not the facts of the matter that count here, but how Gotama's (or Jesus's or Mohammed's) birth and life make possible a vision of how we ought to live our lives. Ever since Gotama was born, there have been countless people in countless lands who have lived the way they have because of his teaching concerning the Middle Way, and of course much the same can be said of other religious founders and scriptures.

My claim here is that religious traditions and cultures are not founded on 'fact,' but on different narratively expressed interpretations of what it means to be. As we have seen, the modern world itself was founded on such a nonfactual interpretive story about reality and human destiny. What the Jataka tales are expressing in the story of Gotama's birth is a truth about life, a truth which can transform our lives and which no language is too poetic or miraculous to capture. It is a hermeneutical and existential truth, then, a truth about how to genuinely and fully live life that such stories narratively make available to us. The elephant, divine lake, wise men, guardians of the four quarters, and the gods themselves are but personages in the story which point to and manifest that truth.

In the following chapters, I will attempt to flesh out such a conception of spiritual understanding. In particular, I want to spell out phenomenologically in some detail (in what I called in the previous chapter "first-order description" as opposed to "second-order explanation") what is experientially going on in such interpretive understanding and to raise the question of whether there are criteria for evaluating such visions of life and destiny.

My claim here is that religious life entails understanding in two ways: (1) the narrative disclosure of ways of seeing life as a meaningful whole, especially in founding myths (this chapter); and (2) actually coming to live-out such an interpretation of life as a personal story (the following chapter). That is, stories which inform us about how we *ought* to live can lead us to transform and deepen the way we actually *do* live. Put another way, there is no mythology without concrete ways of being which reflect it. And there are no concrete ways of living without a mythological vision to inform and support them. These are not two different kinds of religious understanding, then, so much as different aspects or steps in the total process of actively living a narrative vision of what reality demands of us. Because both of these aspects are forms of narrative, I will ultimately argue in Chapter Six that religious truth involves evaluative criteria commonly associated with stories in general.

4:2 Mythological Understanding

By *narrative* I shall mean a temporal series of actions in which—like the notes in a melody—those actions are individually significant only in so far as they are interrelated as parts of a meaningful whole.

> Narrative is a meaning structure that organizes events and human actions into a whole, thereby attributing significance to individual actions and events according to their effect on the whole. . . . The organizing theme that identifies the significance and the role of the individual events is normally called the "plot" of the narrative. The plot functions to transform a chronicle or listing of events into a schematic whole by highlighting and recognizing the contribution that certain events make to the development and outcome of the story.[2]

As indicated earlier, the form of understanding which such stories embody is not just an attractive way of coming to know someone or something. Rather, it is the form of understanding which is most appropriate for actual historical experience, for it discloses that experience as a whole—that is, intact with its diachronic events which are held together in a synchronic plot aimed at and structured by its meaningful end.

Roland Barthes has recognized that narrative comes in many shapes and forms.

> The narrative may incorporate articulate language, spoken or written; pictures, still or moving; gestures and the ordered arrangement of all the ingredients: it is present in myth, legend, fable, short story, epic, glass windows, cinema, comic strips, journalism, conversation.[3]

As we have seen, human life is a process and an endeavor, the active pursuit of intended ends—including, of course, ultimate ways of seeing life as a meaningful whole. In our lives, we strive to live fully, to come to be as fully and deeply as possible. In the face of mystery and mortality, each of us seeks to maximize the quality of living. It is the *leitmotif* to the question we often ask ourselves: "Is this all there is?" But that seeking of fullness in life implies some sense of what might constitute such a full and successful life. In short, it implies some overarching interpretation of what life and destiny are all about, what we have called a hermeneutic. Discussing his latest book, *The Spiritual*

Life of Children, Robert Coles points to the ubiquity and importance of this spiritual aspect of our lives.

> I think that what we have to learn is that [spirituality] is a big part of ourselves. These questions about the meaning of life and these efforts on the part of children—and all of us—to understand what the world means. . .where we're headed, and why we're here are the fundamental existentialist questions of humanity.[4]

It is that hermeneutic construal of what life is for which we seek to become that organizes the events of our lives into a story. As the psychologist George Howard has put it recently,

> We are in the process of creating value in our lives—of finding the meaning of our lives. A life becomes meaningful when one sees himself or herself as an actor within the context of a story—be it a cultural tale, a religious narrative, a family saga, the march of science, a political movement, and so forth."[5]

But how do such ultimate hermeneutic goals become available to us? They don't simply emerge from blind and arbitrary acts which just happen to bump into them. Although not necessarily consciously, when we act we understand what we are doing or acting for. My claim, here, is a simple one. It is through mythology (including its varying forms of historical revelation and philosophical perspective) that such interpretive visions of what life is for are made available to us. Rather than factual error, then, myth in this context means *the narrative disclosure of an interpretive understanding of what life is about.* The great founding myths have offered meaning and guidance to people all over the world and in all periods of history. Take the founding myth of Christianity, for example, as described by Ninian Smart.

> The myth was something like this. Man was made by God, but he was disobedient, and so could only partly be reconciled to God. This partial reconciliation came through the covenant or contract which God offered to the people of Israel. The people were miraculously helped by God; he also inspired certain prophets who maintained, on balance, the fidelity of the people. But the people came to see that salvation must lie in the future, with the coming of the Anointed One. The Hebrew scriptures authorize us to seek such a Messiah. And he came, in the form of Jesus. Jesus saved man, for he was actually God, son of God.

Only God could offer the perfect sacrifice which could atone for man's disobedience. This sacrifice happened at Calvary, where Christ, the prototype of martyrs, was rejected both by Jews and the imperial power. But Jesus showed his victory through the fact that he got up from the dead and appeared to the disciples. We, likewise, can in Christ conquer death. Christ was the new man, the second Adam, and he will come again to make a final judgment, at the end of the world as we know it. Thus will be created a new heaven and a new earth.[6]

Here is a vision of life and human destiny narratively displayed as a meaningful whole. Of course, the number of alternative religious interpretations of life which have emerged in history seems endless. Modernity itself, we argued, rested on a mythical story in which the fundamental purpose of human life was to progress toward power and liberation from fear and superstition by means of scientific and mathematical knowledge.

These founding religious myths not only provide a vision of life as a whole, but a means whereby the particular events of history and life can be seen as significant (steps) within that larger, unfolding, narrative meaning. Along this line, Clifford Geertz writes that

A Christian sees the Nazi movement against the background of the Fall which, though it does not, in a causal sense, explain it, places it in a moral, cognitive, even an affective sense. An Azande sees the collapse of a granary upon a friend or relative against the background of a concrete and rather special notion of witchcraft....A synopsis of cosmic order, a set of religious beliefs, is also a gloss upon the mundane world of social relationships and psychological events. It renders them graspable.[7]

Michael Barnes points out a more contemporary and yet equally fabulous example within Scientology. Notice how the narrativity of the myth lays out and connects primordial and divine beginnings with an equally divine destiny.

The system of thought known as Scientology makes...impressive claims, according to one report. L. Ron Hubbard, founder of Scientology, says that we are Thetans, members of a race of superbeings who have lived for millions of years. By the power of our minds alone, we could leap small galaxies at a single bound, travel faster than a speeding photon. But it was all too easy for us, he goes on, so we began to set limitations on our powers in order to make our existence more challenging. The greatest limitation we chose was loss of memory that we are Thetan. All the frustrating limitations we now experience in life, therefore, are self-imposed, artificial. With the proper training, we can become 'clear,' our memories restored and with them our superpowers.[8]

Furthermore, to the degree that they become socially shared, these mythical overarching visions of life constitute a kind of template or blueprint of the various human cultures or lifeworlds to which they are attached. In other words, mythologies—especially cosmogonic or creation myths—found and structure overarching worlds of oriented meaning in which we live and know our way about. By 'world' I do not mean the totality of things, but the horizon of human consciousness and oriented activity—i.e., what I called earlier "the world of ordinary experience." "Understanding people's mythologies and theologies," Mircea Eliade claimed, "is understanding their mode of being in the world."[9] In other words, for people generally the story of how the universe came to be and what the human role within it is is the fundamental source of how they see what life ultimately means. It is for this reason that we can talk about the Zoroastrian world, the Byzantine world, the Mayan world, or—as we have seen—the modern world. And it is also for this reason that we will discuss in the following pages a new story of creation, a cosmological story seemingly shared by both science and religion which may help to define and delimit the postmodern world. Interpretive understanding is not so much a set of conceptual convictions (beliefs), then, as it is an attitude toward life which is behaved and which structures a world of ordinary experience.

Finally, the great foundational myths not only ward off chaos and meaninglessness by providing a guiding outline of what life is about, but by that means provide a framework in which to actively strive to live that life fully. In that sense, mythology can be said to disclose or make available to active agents possible ways of plumbing life to its depths.

> Religions reveal various possibilities for human freedom. . . . To interpret the religious classics is to allow them to challenge what we presently consider possible.[10]

It seems that human beings need this narrative display of possible modes of existence found in mythology for the formation of character:

myths present us with meaningful modes of behavior which we can appropriate or become. They have to do with personal identity, then— who we are and who we will become. As such, they are not so much vehicles to escape reality as ways to display it so powerfully that we return to our everyday worlds reoriented to life's real—albeit forgotten or sometimes never even imagined—possibilities. They open our hearts and minds to new possibilities of meaningful being in life. They help me discover who I am:

> We learn who we are through the stories we embrace as our own—the story of my life is structured by the larger stories (social, political, mythic) in which I understand my personal story to take place.[11]

We dismiss such stories, then, at the risk of impoverishing ourselves. Insofar as a person can enter into the mythological world (in the same sense that we can enter into the fictional world of a novel or drama), those possible modes of being can convict her and transform her life.

> What it means to be 'I myself' is already manifest in the tradition to which I belong. Myth, poetic symbol, ritual, narrative, philosophy, and theology present me with figures of a potentiality to be myself. They do not say 'let me take the burden of existence from you.' Images of authentic selfhood say, 'let me disclose your own authentic selfhood. This is something you can be on your own, within your own situation.' In our Western tradition, the images of Jesus as Christ and Socrates are root symbols of authentic selfhood from which a multiplicity of expressions and interpretations have grown.[12]

We might ask at this point precisely how mythology accomplishes this, how they make such a way of seeing life as a meaningful whole narratively available.

As we have seen, mythologies manifest a haunting awareness of transcendent reality reflected in the lesser (because merely reflected) visible universe. We can define mythology as stories which relate the ordinary world of life with a transcendent, divine world beyond it. The sacred level is considered to be eternal, unchanging, holy, all-important, and (above all) 'real,' whereas the level of ordinary life (what Eliade calls "the profane") is thought of as a temporal, changing, lesser (fallen and a sort of inferior, reflective image) reality dependent upon the sacred for its existence, order, success, and meaning. This world is a 'sacred cosmos'—that is, a meaningful and ordered universe—to the degree that it reflects that deeper, sacred reality.

> Sacred myths speak of the acts of divine beings in setting the goals for human beings, the meaning of human suffering and trials, and the sequence of life stages through which every individual must pass. Myths intend the integration of individual and collective life within the sacred order of being. Individuals and cults internalize the mythological narrative, allowing it to shape their lives. The meanings of dreams, death, transitions in life from youth to adulthood, or the range of practices of the community (farming, hunting, crafts of all kinds, customs, names of things, and so on) are intelligible either directly through the mythical narratives or indirectly in their light. Ritual reenactment of myth ensures the public, social status of the myth and enables the internalization of meaning. Because of public ritual, myths are not just stories, but are scripts for performance. We learn through ritual performance that myth guides human action in the world.[13]

The sacred level, then, acts as a hierophany or epiphany which breaks into ordinary space and time to found the human world of systematically interrelated meaningfulness. That is, mythologies tell the story of the relationship of the ordinary and the sacred level beyond it and thereby transform a mute and meaningless nature into a symbolic, human world which is meaningful insofar as it is 'seen as' being centered on an absolute reality beyond it. Such myths, I have indicated, lay out the divine origins of this life, explain or otherwise rationalize the existence of suffering and evil by placing it within a larger mythic picture, and provide an overarching vision of human destiny.

By disclosing a deep level of sacred reality, mythology frames ordinary life with an interpretive vision of what it and human destiny are all about, a vision which informs and structures how we actually live. It does this by 'seeing' that ordinary world 'as' a dependent reflection of the sacred other.

> The 'as' makes up the structure of the explicitness of something that is understood. It constitutes the interpretation.[14]

In other words, this life is interpretively 'seen as' a dependent reflection of the sacred or being itself. That means that a major aspect of founding mythologies is the imperative to live this life focused and centered upon that which is alone ultimately meaningful—the sacred.

Thus, the various mythologically founded religious traditions are worlds or cultural contexts in which life is not only 'seen' in the light of a deep dimension of interpretive meaning, but in which there is an appeal and demand to go beyond self-centeredness to God-centeredness. As the famous Hindu prayer says, "Lead me from the unreal to the Real."

Clearly, what makes this interpretive 'seeing. . .as' possible at all is the human ability to utilize metaphor. Mythology enables us to see this life in the light of a "surplus of meaning" (to use Ricoeur's splendid expression) which is disclosed in the myth. We have here another example—this time in the religious dimension—of the wondrous human ability in different realms of discourse to extend human insight and meaning by seeing one thing 'through' another or 'like' another. As I said earlier, "Metaphor is nothing but applying to one thing or experience characteristics or descriptions conventionally applied to another on the grounds of an implicit similarity between the two." For example, a reorientation and renewal of life becomes a 'rebirth.' The metaphorical extension of meaning occurs precisely when an ordinary experience is made to serve as a frame or set of glasses through which to see another. Mythology, then, displays overarching interpretations of human life and destiny by metaphorically 'seeing' our ordinary experience in the light of a deep level of significance, like a figure against a background. Of course, insofar as that sacred deep level is itself narratively manifest in the myth by being 'seen' in terms of familiar images drawn from ordinary experience, it can thereby act as the background against which this life is seen as a dependent reflection. The prophet Hosea, for example, sees Yahweh as a patient, loving, and at the same time righteously demanding husband to an errant Israel, thereby interpretively understanding (seeing) Israel as a headstrong and disloyal wife who must be brought to see her covenantal duty to her husband.

In a very real sense, mythology shapes and structures people's concrete behavior by helping them to notice the difference between what their ordinary lives are like and what they might or ought to be like, thereby helping them to see or interpret those lives over against that spiritual imperative. Having discovered that mythological interpretation of the meaning of being, human beings then live in 'worlds' or cultures configured by it, like octopi inside their inky effusion.

In their religious practices, institutions, and rituals humans have found orientation in life, have found an interpretation of what human existence is all about and how it is to be lived. Or rather, we should say it was in their search for orientation in life, in their attempt to come to an understanding of what human existence is all about and how it is to be lived, that humans created and developed the various religious traditions, thus giving life the variant meanings it has come to have.[15]

These founding myths are above all overarching and synthesizing narrative interpretations of what it means to be. As John Hick puts it:

The primary locus of religious significance is the believer's experience as a whole. The basic act of interpretation which reveals to him the religious significance of life is uniquely a total interpretation.[16]

Mythological narratives are uniquely qualified to provide a vehicle for seeing life as such a meaningful whole because, as we have seen, stories integrate separate episodic events into an inclusive plot. They permit us, then, to 'see together' the events of our ordinary lives into a single, overarching, interpretive whole.

It's not that the narrative myth over 'here,' so to speak, merely represents or stands in for a hermeneutical interpretation of what life is about 'out there.' Rather (as we saw in our earlier discussion of the kind of understanding involved in the arts and humanities), that interpretation of life is seen *through* the metaphorical expression. Rather than inferring it, we directly encounter that meaning, see it through the myth as if through a pair of glasses. In this sense, mythology is like art. It's not as if Willy Loman in *Death of a Salesman* merely 'represents' what life is sometimes like. On the contrary, we directly 'see' what it's like through his voice and behavior, at least insofar as we enter the world of the drama. So, too, when we are able to let go and enter into the visionary world of myth.

Narrative mythology, then, does provide a kind of understanding—albeit in neither empirical nor deductive form. It is not something which is 'true' to the degree that it 'corresponds' to the facts of the matter because, as we have seen, it not a hypothesis 'over here' which can be said to represent or correspond to facts 'out there.' The understanding available through mythology is neither objective fact nor subjective illusion, but rather an interpretive display. It is an understanding that is true to the degree that it evokes (speaks out), makes manifest, or uncovers and reveals an interpretation of life as a whole. Truth, here, is what Heidegger called "apophansis" or "a-letheia," a disclosing, noticing, or bringing into the light so that it can be seen.[17]

As Heidegger himself has pointed out, any such disclosive truth at one and the same time covers up and hides other elements of the reality it is evoking, precisely because it can't bring everything about that reality into the open all at once. This means that no such truth can be absolute, exclusively true, or adequate (in Locke's sense) to the reality it is bringing into the light. Reality is always more than you can say about it, and none of the illuminative 'sayings' about it is true to the exclusion of others that are equally disclosive. To use an analogy from painting, all of the self portraits by Rembrandt are true in this sense, and none of them is either absolutely or exclusively true. The same point, can be made *mutatis mutandis* about founding mythologies. Although they are (or can be if one can enter their worlds) disclosively true, none of them is absolutely or exclusively so. As Gandhi remarked about absolute truth, it is beyond human capacity to hear or tell.[18] Naturally, this will have important bearing upon our understanding of religious truth in a world in which there are both many and conflicting claims of such truth.

4:3 The Act of Interpretation

It would seem that both myths and interpreters aware of their meaning are indissolubly linked together. I mean that there are no authoritative religious myths or scriptures without intimate interpreters open to their meaning, and there are no interpreters of human life and destiny without actual stories, scripture, or philosophical systems which make such meaning manifest. Phenomenologically, a meaningful myth neither stands alone in and of itself nor can it be constructed from or reduced to the intending subject. Likewise, the religiously receptive and understanding subject who comes to see life as a meaningful whole can neither stand apart from meaningful myths nor simply be reduced to them. Myths and someone's (or some group's) interpretive understanding, we might say, are but correlative moments in a process which involves both and which we might call the dialogical act of interpretation.[19] There can be no Christians, for example, without meaningful gospels which in fact 'speak' to and for them. And there can be no classical or canonical Christian gospels without Christian interpreters who materialize them as canon by 'seeing' (in their various ways) their meaning. Religious understanding entails a dialogical act of interpretation. Obviously, this is the case in any act of interpretation whether it be the mythological interpretation of life as a whole or the interpretation of specific myths, historical revelations, or canonical texts of various sorts.

As with interpretation in general, interpreters can never be empty and neutral observers who simply wait for the meaning of the myth (or reality) to be released to them. They inevitably bring with them a set of historical, cultural, linguistic, class, and gender conditions which—although they may not determine the interpretation involved—surely form and shape it. Furthermore, such interpreters are inevitably living persons who bring to the mythological text at hand some already established point of view or sense of life. A person, precisely insofar as he or she has an identity, is an active and temporal agent 'in the world,' located in just this cultural and human situation, coming from somewhere and going somewhere. Any mythological text, then, emerges within the temporal flow of someone's experience: someone is reading it for a reason, and inevitably responds to it or 'sees' it in terms of the basic values and goals in life which she is trying to achieve. As Heidegger put it:

> Dasein has, as Dasein, already projected itself; and as long as it is, it is projecting....[Thus] an interpretation is never a presuppositionless apprehending of something presented to us. If, when one is engaged in a particular textual interpretation, one likes to appeal to what 'stands there,' then one finds that what 'stands there' in the first instance is nothing other than the obvious undiscussed assumption (Vormeinung) of the person who does the interpreting.[20]

A set of assumptions is always in force in the act of interpretively understanding. It would seem, then, that we have been unceremoniously thrust into yet another version of the notorious 'hermeneutical circle': we are forced to recognize that any mythological interpretation of life (or reality itself) must be interpreted by a reader in the light of the particular mythological sense of life she happens to carry with her at the moment and which, I have argued, is fundamental to her identity. It seems that what you get out of a myth is nothing but what you bring to it.

Heidegger recognized that the act of interpreting a myth involves an inevitable influence on the part of the responsive subject(s). The myth is 'seen...as' this or that in the light of the story or faith which the interpreter is already living. David Klemm, in discussing the postmodern and Heideggerian notion that reality is always an interpreted reality, puts this very well.

> Everything that we understand, in word, text, gesture, or action, is approached through anticipation (or preunderstanding). These

anticipations direct our questions to the other. They make understanding the other possible. They situate understanding within the horizon of anticipations that are historically effective here and now.[21]

There is an inevitable tilt toward the reader(s) in the act of interpretation insofar as the interpreter emerges from a human world and insofar as he responds to the myth. But how far does this go?

Reception theory within literary criticism—a recent movement initiated by such scholars as Wolfgang Iser, Hans Jauss, and Stanley Fish—emphasizes the importance of the reader in any act of interpretation. The reader, from this point of view, materializes the text which, until then, is in itself meaningless marks on paper or sounds in the air. The text (or reality), then, is like a skeleton which calls upon a reader to concretize it in an act of receptive interpretation which puts flesh upon it. Indeed, Stanley Fish would go further and straightforwardly deny that there is any meaningful text there at all. For him, the reader's act of interpretation produces meaning:

> Interpretation is not the art of construing, but the art of constructing. Interpreters do not decode poems. They make them.[22]

This leaves us with a question which constitutes one of the fundamental philosophical *aporias* involved in interpretation in general in the postmodern context. Does the inevitable response of the interpreter of the mythological text or reality so distort it that we are left with nothing but illusion projected upon it? Is it constructed from whole cloth by the subject(s) doing the interpreting? If so, it would seem that we are fated to reduce any newly encountered mythology to the one we have always held. Genuine religious conversion would thereby become impossible and the question of precisely how we (or anyone) has arrived at the mythological attitude we presently hold would become moot. I think such a view is too extreme.

Although I think that Heidegger has overstated the case, it seems quite evident that he is right. There is no avoiding the fact that the interpreter brings to the myth or reality at hand a set of glasses through which he or she sees it. This seems inevitable and in fact necessary for 'seeing' the mythological text at all. Such lenses are certainly necessary insofar as we are never without them in the act of interpretive understanding and, in fact, would be blind without them. In that sense, they are neither disposable nor dispensable. The reader or interpreter, then, as Ricoeur has put it, has certain 'rights' when it comes to interpreting the text or the myth. Because of this there will in principle inevitably be a plurality of interpretations of any myth, historical revelation or metaphysical system.

On the other hand, the mythological text (or reality) also has 'rights': it resists being interpreted in any which way that an interpreter just happens to want to impose upon it. First of all, such myths are socially rather than individually constructed: each of us learns from others how to 'see' things. Furthermore, myths belong to societies and language as a whole rather than to the individual. We are not free to do anything we like with language because, if we are to communicate at all, that language cannot be unique to you or me. Language is a social force which shapes each of us and all of us. Language preexists each of us. It is the condition and constraint for all that we are or can be— including, of course reception theorists and their particular perspective. Because of this, mythological texts limit and constrain our interpretive understanding of them.

I argued earlier that what is required is a dialogue rather than a metaphysical and evaluative reduction of the meaning of the text either to the active subject or the static text alone. In fact, part of my claim is that such a reduction of the meaning of the mythological text to this dichotomy is precisely a result of modernity, a position which I am trying to go beyond by spelling out a dialogical alternative. A valid act of interpretation entails both an openness to the very myth at hand as well as a human sense of life through which it can be 'seen' to be meaningful. Ricoeur writes:

> It is the semantic autonomy of the text which opens up the range of potential readers and, so to speak, creates the audience of the text. On the other hand, it is the response of the audience which makes the text important and therefore significant.[23]

In the dialogical encounter of text and reader which is the act of interpretation, the reader responds to the text with both a set of conditions (history, culture, language, gender, class) and an attitudinal set of glasses. Those glasses do not create the meaning of the text. Rather, they frame it with significance so that it (or aspects of it unnoticed through other glasses) can be seen.

> The historicity of our existence entails that prejudices, in the literal sense of the word, constitute the initial directedness of our whole ability to experience. Prejudices are biases of our openness to the

world. They are simply conditions whereby we experience something—whereby what we encounter says something to us.[24]

Both the text as it is in itself as well as the interpretive reader who frames it with significance are indispensable to the interpretive act— the former to display or disclose a meaningful presentation of experience and the latter to permit it to be seen (interpreted) as this or that by framing it within her interpretive understanding of life. The meaning of the myth is there in a raw form which demands interpretation in order to become manifest. We interpretively make available a narrative vision of life and a possible way of being by encompassing it within our own ongoing stories. As opposed to the dilemma imposed on interpretation by the modern bias in which religious understanding was reduced willy-nilly to either objective fact or subjective illusion, we are claiming that it involves a dialogical act of interpretive disclosure which is neither objectively 'there' nor subjectively projected upon reality.

Put another way, we might say that both the myth or reality and the responsive interpreter are necessary for the act of interpretation to take place. As we said earlier, there can be no overarching mythological vision of life without interpreters who care about it or respond to it, and there can be no interpretive, religious tradition without a founding myth (or reality) around which it is formed. It is a two-way street in which a paradigmatic vision of life is applied as a measure and demand to everyday life, and in which that everyday life in turn is responsively used to frame that founding vision in such a way that it permits it to be interpretively 'seen.' The ideal life which scripture shows us becomes the basis for living our everyday lives, and those lives in turn become an ongoing interpretive commentary through which that scripture is understood. If it is true that we modify the myth in interpretation (and I think it is), then I think it is equally true that we are modified by it insofar as we genuinely encounter it.

Let us emphasize here a point which will have great bearing on our later analysis of whether it is possible to have a conception of religious truth which is compatible with religious pluralism and tolerance. As we have seen, both the acts of interpreting life mythologically as well as interpreting already established myths, historical revelations, and canonical texts such as the *New Testament* or the *Dhammapada* necessarily involve a response of an interpreter who brings to that which is being interpreted a set of anticipatory understandings through which it is framed and interpretively 'seen.' This does not mean that the resulting interpretation is simply a subjective projection upon reality. Rather, it means that all interpretations involve a finite and human point of view which makes available and illuminates the reality or text at hand so that it manifests itself. Wolfhart Pannenberg writes:

> Life's moments have a significance (Bedeutung) in themselves, but we can only grasp their significance through the medium of an interpretation (Deutung) which itself is conditioned by the perspective of a particular historical standpoint. This insight is valid for the life experience of the individual just as much as for history at large.[25]

These interpretations or points of view, of course, are clothed in and metaphorically made available to consciousness by what John Hick calls 'images'—i.e., the concrete metaphors and meaningful characteristics which constitute the substance of the interpretation. Hick argues that we can never know historical figures like Lincoln, Gandhi, or Napoleon as they were in themselves, but only through various selective images of them which have evolved through the creative imaginations of our historians. In precisely the same way, he argues, we can never grasp reality (or any particular mythological text) in itself, but only through culturally and historically generated images of it. Hick's *'images'* are what I have called *'interpretations.'* That is, we inevitably see Reality from a particular point of view and that interpretive framework becomes embodied in the selective metaphors and images with which we imaginatively clothe and express our interpretations and through which (as through a window) we encounter (or see) the interpretive meaning involved. Words and images are all we consciously know of reality. Gordon Kaufman puts this point very well in reflecting on the need to reinterpret (or reimagine) God in this nuclear age.

> The symbol *God* is given its specific content and meaning, and thus enabled to provide actual guidance and orientation in the decisions and actions of everyday life, by the concrete metaphors and images which we use in constructing it. . . . Obviously if God is conceived as a dominating kingly being, who is working in the world in a domineering all-powerful fashion, and who demands of worshipers that they 'subdue' the earth and all its creatures (Gen. 1:28) and that they destroy without remainder all their enemies and God's (Deut. 25:19, 1 Sam. 15: 1–33; Rev. 17–18, and so forth), a very powerful motivation toward a disciplined

and authoritarian pattern of life will be engendered in the minds and hearts of believers. Corresponding character structures, social institutions, and styles of life will be shaped, as believers seek to respond obediently to the almighty God and King who is their ruler and lord. . . . This piety was focussed by a mythic conception of God as a quasi-person, a conception fashioned with the aid of anthropomorphic images of lordship, parenthood, and the making of artifacts.[26]

Hick's and my conclusion, then, is that there is not and never can be one single, objectively true interpretation, for the human condition imposes on us culturally and historically contingent understandings (metaphors and images) which are an inevitable and unavoidable aspect of any such interpretation. Putting the same thing another way, no particular set of historically generated images of reality (God) can ever by identified with that reality. There is an inevitable gulf between those images and the reality they frame and make available. They are not the reality itself, but merely the contingent framework through which we come to see it. Thus, no particular religious tradition (which is itself a whole history of such interpretive images) can claim absolute or exclusive truth, for its fabric is stitched together from finite cloth. As Hick puts it:

God as experienced by this or that individual or group is real, not illusory; and yet the experience of God is partial and is adapted to our human spiritual capacities. God as humanly known is not God *an sich* but God in relation to mankind, thought and experienced in terms of some particular limited tradition of religious awareness and response. . . . God is to be thought of as the divine noumenon, experienced by mankind as a range of divine phenomena which take both theistic and non-theistic forms.[27]

4:4 A New Cosmological Story for Our Time

So far, we have seen that the Enlightenment developed a new, nontraditional story about the nature of reality and human destiny, a myth on which the modern world or era was founded. That modern world, then, like any other human world, was based on a narrative disclosure of an overarching interpretive understanding of life metaphorically 'seen as' a meaningful whole. It was a vision of human historical destiny in which nature would be progressively dominated and controlled through science and technology. In the name of the transformation of nature into useful products for human life, then, the industrial-consumer societies emerged and increasingly assaulted nature in the name of human progress and security. It was a vision of reality which was beneficial to human life in many respects, which is certainly one of the reasons that it has lasted so long and became so pervasive around the globe. Yet, as we noted in Chapter One, it led to a number of painful spiritual difficulties.

I argued, in fact, that it was ultimately dysfunctional for spiritual life. It rendered spiritual life increasingly impossible at the same time that it fostered a sense of disorientation and meaninglessness. And while that was taking place, of course, rampant industrial growth sustained by the fundamental modern vision exploded into the present worldwide ecological crisis in which our voracious hunger for nonrenewable resources may not only exhaust those resources but may actually lead to the destruction of the ecosystem itself. These painful spiritual aspects of modernity are powerful forces presently pushing us toward a new and hopefully more adequate and effective spiritual story and world.

In the meantime, we noted that the recognition of a kind of narrative, interpretive understanding on which modernity rested and of which it remained until recently unaware constituted the initial step into a new, postmodern world. We became aware that human beings necessarily live within worlds or cultures which are pervaded by overarching visions of life's purpose and meaning. These visions are made available not by philosophies, which I argued are themselves based upon such preconceptual interpretive understandings of life, but by mythological stories about the sacred reality and our relation to it. Especially in the form of creation stories, such mythologies found and structure the panoply of human worlds which are manifest in history.

The mechanics of this interpretive, mythological understanding consist of 'seeing' life 'as' meaning this or that by metaphorically 'seeing' this life in the reflective light of the other, sacred level. In the widened sense of interpretive understanding, then, spiritual or religious understanding and truth are central to and unavoidable in human life. *The* spiritual issue in human life in general is not *whether* to be spiritual (i.e., theism versus atheism), but *how* to be spiritual, how to live meaningfully and deeply.

It's all a matter of story. Since the beginning of human consciousness, story has been the fundamental instrument and vehicle for communicating human insight and meaning. Listen to a psychologist on the importance of stories for human life.

Stories are habitations. We live in and through stories. They conjure worlds. We do not know the world other than as story world. Stories inform life. They hold us together and keep us apart. We inhabit the great stories of our culture. We live through stories. We are *lived* by the stories of our race and place. It is this enveloping and constituting function of stories that is especially important to sense more fully. We are, each of us, locations where the stories of our place and time become partially tellable.[28]

Through story, then, humans have been able to step back and stitch together the myriad elements of nature and their own lives into significant wholes. Through story, they are able to see reality all together. Through story, they have found hope in the face of the deadly limits and realities of nature by narratively framing it with an ultimate significance beyond life and death itself. Narrative mythology (especially creation mythology) is crucial to our lives, for it is the way we answer the questions we have asked ever since fresh from the womb: *What's going on? Where did we come from? What are we doing here? Where are we headed? How ought we to live?* Without narrative mythology, human beings would not live in their various worlds, for there could be no such worlds without the metaphorical disclosure of ultimate meaning embodied in such founding stories. Put another way, interpretive understanding is the human way of being in a world. We are, as Peter Berger has noted, "world-building animals" born into ongoing stories about what counts and is most significant in life. These stories, then, sustain us. They shape our lives and behavior by enveloping us in a sense of purpose in the light of which we act and interrelate with one another. They synoptically integrate the various events and aspects of life into a vision of the sacred whole which provides meaning, orientation and significant space in which to live. To be human is to take part in an overarching and ultimate cosmic story.

One of the most interesting developments in the past few years is not merely the postmodern awareness of the narrative, spiritual dimension of life, but *the actual emergence of a new cosmological story.* Scientific advances and a global concern for the environment have led to the articulation of a new ecologically oriented theology variously called "ecological spirituality," "environmental theology," "process theology," "creation spirituality," "eco-feminism," or simply "reverence for life." John Cobb, Carolyn Merchant, Thomas Berry, David Ray Griffin, Mathew Fox, Jay McDaniel, and the physicist Brian Swimme are just a few of the thinkers who have in the past ten years helped to give voice to this new view. A new, cosmological story has been developed, then—a sacred story about the nature and value of creation and our role and destiny within it.

A major premise underlying this new story is that the anthropocentric character of human beings in the modern age is the underlying reason for the increasing despoliation of the global environment. In the consumer-industrial societies, it seems that human concerns, needs, and desires are what really count and that nature can take care of itself: "I've got mine, Jack; you take care of yours!" Rabbi Ismar Schorsch, Chancellor of the Jewish Theological Seminary of America, puts it this way:

> The fact that society has made of consumption a commonplace and of distraction a fiendish art shows humanity has installed itself at the center of the universe and is engaged in self-worship to the detriment of the rest of creation.[29]

That attitude might not have been so costly to nature in an earlier period of industrial development, but we have learned recently that nature can't "take care of itself" in the usual manner when the number of humans and the amount of industrial development needed to support them has grown so enormously. What has been discovered and documented is that the natural ecological systems of the globe have been massively impacted at an expanding and extremely dangerous rate. What is being suggested is that to halt this process we must first overcome our anthropocentric attitude in favor of caring for nature sufficiently to become loyal stewards of it. Wendell Berry says:

> The fowls of the air and the lilies of the field can be preserved only by true religion, by the *practice* of a proper love and respect for them as creatures of God.[30]

The major question we face, then, is how this can be accomplished, how those long-ingrained habits can be replaced with a sense of respect or even reverence and piety for the entire family of creation. How can we come to 'see' ourselves 'as' a part of the interrelated and unfolding larger reality, a part which feels intimately and familialy connected to the rest, a part which has an important role to play and destiny to fulfill in the further creative development of the universe? Some argue that, in order to do that, we must come to 'see' the whole of unfolding reality (including ourselves) 'as' holy, fundamentally real, that originating mystery from which every galaxy and summer flower has emerged, that of which none greater can be conceived, the basis and foundation of all that is—in short—God. "If we can develop such a reverence for nature, however we name it, if we can experience that larger reality as the body of God or Mother Nature or Gaia," they seem to say, "perhaps we can develop a technology and industry which are life-enhancing rather than life-destroying." We need a framework of meaning, an ultimate story which might help us revere life and develop technologies which respect and support the Earth rather than plunder it.

As you might expect, this new vision is laid out in a creation story, a new cosmology which has emerged within science in the past twenty-five years, but which, insofar as it induces a sense of wonder in us, is at the same time implicitly a religious or spiritual vehicle. In fact, as with the traditional creation mythologies of earlier times, this life is 'seen as' meaningful to the degree that it reflects the sacred level peeking out through the cracks of the whole unfolding universe as the miraculous and mysterious creativity permeating it. The myth helps us to 'see' the present painful spiritual and ecological situation 'as' due to a turning away within modern industrial society from the natural human state of wonder and reverence for that creative reality in favor of human power and control. Finally, the story helps us to understand that the ultimate destiny of humankind is to awaken from this sorry state of self-concern to care for the incredible unfolding whole which is the body or face of God. The fact that this new story is both scientific and religious is one of the most startling and remarkable aspects of it. It is so startling, in fact, that we ought to pause for a moment to reflect upon it. How is it that a natural cosmology which brings together both science and religion has not been available for over three hundred years? And why has it emerged at just this time? I find Stephen Toulmin, the eminent contemporary philosopher of science, most helpful in exploring these issues.

Cosmology or natural theology (as it had been called earlier), the human attempt to understand (or see) the natural world in its entirety, has not really been possible since the seventeenth century for two reasons. First, Descartes and the modern worldview in general divided reality into two aspects, mind and matter. Theology was limited to the former and mechanics and the new science in general were assigned to the latter. That meant that theology was simply *a priori* excluded from any commerce with nature: nature was desacralized and a natural theology or cosmology was thereby rendered impossible. Stephen Toulmin puts it this way:

Any reintegration of humanity into nature...needs to be considered as holding out the possibility of healing the emotional and even the religious wounds that were created when the Cartesian surgery of the seventeenth century natural philosophers separated the two halves of their bifurcated world and, by doing so, set the mental lives of human beings apart from and in opposition to the natural phenomena and the natural processes of the natural realm.[31]

Second, as Toulmin has further argued, by 1860 the natural sciences had become fragmented into separate disciplines, each with its own terminology, interests, and particular preoccupations. It was no longer the business of science as a whole or any science in particular to think about the whole of nature and the interrelations of various aspects of it.[32] If it is true that the answers we get in science depend on the questions we ask, it ought to be no surprise that a science which is divided into a host of separate and relatively insulated disciplines—each with its own set of questions—should arrive at no overarching answer concerning the whole of nature. At any rate, cosmology fell between the cracks, because neither theology nor science was in any position to deal with it.

As opposed to this modern absence of an overarching cosmological understanding of nature, Toulmin argues that the new, postmodern intellectual situation has not only led to, but is forcing upon us, the remarkable possibility of a genuine cosmology which is both scientific and theological in content:

There is [now] indeed room for scientists, philosophers, and theologians to sit down together and to reexamine in detail the scientific, ethical, and theological issues that arise about such ideas as 'natural status' and 'the larger scheme of things' (cosmos).[33]

There seem to be at least three reasons for this remarkable shift. First, Toulmin argues that science has come up against its own theoretical and discipline-bound limits. That is, contemporary science increasingly recognizes that there is no purely objective knowledge of reality, that as scientists we bring to our endeavor a sense of what life is about (a narrative interpretive understanding of life, as I have argued), and our senses, minds, and instruments condition and shape whatever we come to 'know.' This is the essential message of Heisenberg's Principle of Indeterminacy and Bohr's Principle of Complementarity (Quantum Physics).

Second, there is no pure 'spectator'. Whatever we do influences the reality we are observing. Contemporary science is so powerful that it necessarily impacts that nature it is observing and thereby raises deeply significant ethical and religious questions concerning its ends and purposes. That is, postmodern scientists are being forced to see themselves not just as spectators and theorists with no constraints whatever but as participants and ethical and religious agents whose scientific endeavors have practical impact and implications. A good example of this is the presently evident impact of science and technology on the entire environment. In facing these practical limits, postmodern science is being forced to come to terms with the moral and spiritual ends of human life. In other words, the power of science and technology are pushing scientists to take responsibility for their actions as complete human beings. That means that they are increasingly recognizing that their professional concerns have to be evaluated in the overall light of human concerns—that is, within an overarching sense of purpose and human destiny. That recognition of ethical and spiritual constraints on scientific endeavors—the acknowledgement that scientists are after all human agents who must face *all* the issues human beings in general have always faced (and not just scientific and technical ones)—is in part precisely what defines the 'postmodern' cultural situation as such.

Third, there now seems in fact to be a science of the whole beyond the fragmented fields within it: *ecology*. Ecology is the study of different forms of reality within their enveloping 'home,' that is within the interconnected physical and life systems which constitute the cosmos as a whole.

This ecological understanding of the interconnected whole is fundamentally a grasp of reality as a historical or temporal unfolding, an evolutionary story of emergence and integration over billions of years. It turns out, then, to be a cosmology, a scientific and theological *story* through which we can see the entirety of nature as a meaningful whole as well as the peculiar role and destiny of human beings within it. A breathtaking new possibility has emerged—the possibility of a cosmogonic story which may afford our postmodern world a vision of reality as a whole, a vision which at the same time might help us find our way back to our spiritual home.

We can do our best to build up a conception of the 'overall scheme of things' which draws as heavily as it can on the results of scientific study, informed by a genuine piety in all its attitudes toward creatures of other kinds: a piety that goes beyond the consideration of their usefulness to Humanity as intruments for the fulfillment of human ends. That is an alternative within which human beings can both *feel*, and also *be*, at home.... Scientists, theologians and philosophers will have to sit down together and follow their joint discussion where it leads.[34]

The barest outline of this incredibly complex story of the evolution of the universe will have to suffice here.[35] This is the story. About 18 billion years ago being (and with it time and space, of course) emerged in an immense explosion of light. Here, of course, in contemplating the very first moment, we are struck dumb with wonder at the miraculous and incomprehensible existence of something rather than nothing. Out of the originating mystery, everything emerged and continues to emerge. In other words, reality is still explosively transcending itself into a fantasy of new forms. Reality is creative. It manifests a process of self-transcendence toward creative differentiation and novelty, an evolution through differentiation into the infinity of kinds that people the universe. Sara Maitland expressed this sense of the miraculous creativity of God and her own consequent wonder in the face of it in an interview. She had just been asked if she thought God was female, to which she replied that she certainly did not. In fact, she indicated that traditionally God ought not to be considered either male or female. Then she was asked:

"What sort of God do you believe in?"

She paused for a long time, her head thrown back, her eyes shut tight.

"A God who is wild, not tamed... I have tried to read recently some new physics. A god who can work out quarks inside atoms does not need gender, and rule books and stuff."

The pace of her voice quickened.

"I feel we are all trying to pin God down and make him manageable: 'You must say "he," and you mustn't say "she"; you must define the trinity in this particular way. You must have dogmas for this, that and the other.'... There's a wonderful, wonderful book by a woman called Annie Dillard, called *Pilgrim at Tinker's Creek*. At one point, she says, 'If I were God, and had dreamed up the brilliant idea of creating something, I'd have made do with a tiny little glob of matter.' That, in itself would have been such a brilliant notion. Instead, what do we get? A kind of God who seems perfectly happy to have three million five hundred different forms of insect life.

"The whole thing is so abandoned..." she said, making a big sweep with her arms. "I believe in this enormously generous God, so enormous that the whole universe can be contained within the Godness of God...I am awestruck by God...That's the sort of God I believe in."[36]

At the same time, of course, this evolving reality manifests a convergence and communion: differentiated reality collects itself together into communities and sets of things (quanta, nuclei, galaxies, solar systems, the earth, etc.) and ultimately a single, interrelated and interdependent whole. Every part of reality is integral to itself as such a unique and differentiated community while at the same time integrated within the systemic and interactive whole.

There are four chapters in this cosmological story. First is the cosmic stage, in which stars emerged from the dust of the original explosion, and then trillions of communities of solar systems called galaxies formed. Dead stars exploded, spewing all the metals we know into the expanding universe. New second-generation stars emerged and out of these our Milky Way developed, our particular neighborhood in the seemingly infinite spaces of the universe. Our own sun and solar system were formed from a once-dead star. The molten earth emerged, and thus began the second chapter of the story—the geological stage.

During this stage, the sun got hotter, the moon cooled, a crust was formed over the molten core of the earth, and an atmosphere gradually came to envelop it. The earth formed a unique, integrated, and self-regulating whole, what some have called "Gaia." Various kinds of complex molecules emerged, including carbon.

After about 10 to 15 billion years, a new level of creative differentiation and integration called "life" emerged in the form of single-cell creatures called "prokaryotes." These creatures transformed the atmosphere and prepared it for the next stage of creative emergence. At first, life reproduced by cell-division, but ultimately cells grouped into new kinds of communities which ultimately could swim, fly, walk, and reproduce sexually. Plants, insects, and reptiles emerged. And in this period reptiles transcended themselves by becoming birds, plants and trees spread around the world, and the various forms of animals and ultimately mammals came into being.

Finally, a scant few million years ago, there emerged in Africa a particular kind of mammal primate who was aware of the mystery and drama of creation and who carried out religious rituals (e.g., the burial of the dead) in order to remain oriented around it—the human species. Thus began the final chapter of the story, the cultural stage of creation.

These human beings were not only an integral part of the creative whole that is nature, but were themselves the unique, culturally evolving entities through which that wider reality became conscious of itself in a variety of ways. This final chapter (so far) was itself broken into at least four stages—the Paleolithic, Neolithic, classical, and modern stages. Each of these cultural periods was characterized not only by unique forms of human survival and social organization, but also by evolving forms of religious expression and practice. At least until the modern stage, the religious myths and rituals which characterized the culture were vehicles through which humans became aware of the encompassing creative mystery of life and continued to relate and integrate themselves to every natural manifestation within it. Black Elk, the Lakota (Sioux) shaman of recent and deserved fame, has put it well:

> We should understand well that all things are the works of the Great Spirit. We should know that He is within all things: the trees, the grasses, the rivers, the mountains, and all the four-legged animals, and the winged peoples; and even more important, we should understand that He is also above all these things and peoples. When we do understand all this deeply in our hearts, then we will fear, and love, and know the Great Spirit, and then we will be and act and live as He intends.[37]

The modern stage, however, was a powerful new human vision and cultural self-definition which not only attenuated spiritual life but also reduced nature to raw material significant only insofar as it could provide the resources for human production and use. It was, then, a break in the traditional reverence for life in all its forms, a break which ultimately led to our present ecological crisis and to flattened, weakened, and disoriented spiritual lives.

We presently find ourselves at a critical cultural and ecological turning point. It is a turning point at which either we will continue on the modern, industrial path toward possible suicide or we will create a new age in which we become aware once again of the holiness of nature and our special role of caring for and sustaining it, just as it ultimately sustains us.

We have in this story a vast vision which, like other creation myths, narratively reveals both a sense of what reality is all about and what the uniquely human role and destiny is within it. The universe is at one and the same time wondrously expanding and evolving toward greater differentiation (novelty) and wider, overarching integration. It is in fact a single, ongoing, complex energy event over time. The fracture from the original whole (the "Fall," if you will) which occurred when the modern world turned away from nature merely to fulfill its own desire for control and security was (the story tells us) a temporary lapse in a sense of reverence for life. The ultimate destiny of human life is to return to the awareness of that divine reality (or its reflexive awareness of itself through us) expressed in myth, story, poetry, art, and philosophy. To do this, we must ourselves creatively (differentiation and integration) determine our own cultural future by narratively 'seeing' it in the light of the holiness of being, thereby bringing into being a new, 'ecological' world or age in which there will be a reverence for all of the family that is the Earth and in which new technologies will be developed to sustain it.

We can and certainly do argue about how the complex whole which is nature actually evolved and works. We can and do argue about where we ought to be headed—in other words, what we'd like to see human society become. But we cannot argue seriously about the *existence* of the universe, that it evolved, and that evolution displays a wondrous creative drive toward both novelty and integration. 'God' is just another name for this miraculous creative activity which characterizes the universe, this flowering of reality into the myriad levels and forms which it displays. Sallie McFague says, "God is in, with and under the entire evolutionary process, and that process is unfinished and continuing."[38] If you don't like the word *God*, then call it 'reality,' 'life,' 'nature,' 'the whole,' 'the originating mystery,' or whatever. The name is not important. From this point of view, God (or whatever) is not so much this galaxy or that molecule, this flower or that wooly mammoth, this insect or that primate, but the constant creative coming into being in those myriad forms, the constant *that-ing* or *is-ing* of everything, the explosive process transcending toward the existence of new and hitherto unimagined forms. Meister Eckhart caught this sense when he defined God as being: "God is like nothing so much as being [*Esse*]. . . .everything that God is is being."[39] More recently, Erazim Kohak has described this experience of being in *The Embers and the Stars*, which is his account of his Thoreau-like spiritual return to nature in the woods of New Hampshire.

The forest enfolds you in a profound peace and there is the same feeling, the sense of unity and the fullness of life. It is not the experience of the darkened forest, the boulders, the path, or the solitary walker. All that has receded and a different reality has moved into its place, that of the fullness of Being. In such moments you sense it is always there just beneath the surface of the insistent individuality of subjects and objects, ready to rise up when the clamor subsides. You must not insist, you must not impose yourself upon it. But if you are willing to listen, it is there, the fullness and unity of life, the presence of Being—and it is one and good.[40]

In Chapter Two we saw that wonder is the human experience of the transcendence or indefinability of such beingness, an awareness that being itself cannot be reduced to whatever happens to be, that there is a difference between being and beings that are. It is a sense of reverence and awe in the face of the mystery of being, or (as we put it) "a fascinated noticing of a kind of strangeness beyond understanding, an attitude of amazement and perplexity, and a sometimes stunned curiosity in the face of the astonishing and inexplicable" fact that the seemingly endless forms of reality continue to come into being. The American astronaut Edgar Mitchell experienced such wonder on his return to Earth from the moon:

Instead of an intellectual search, there was suddenly a very deep gut feeling that something was different. It occurred when looking at Earth and seeing this blue-and-white planet floating there, and knowing it was orbiting the Sun, seeing that Sun, seeing it set in the background of the very deep black and velvety cosmos, seeing—rather, knowing for sure—that there was a purpose-fulness of flow, of energy, of time, of space in the cosmos—that it was beyond man's rational ability to understand, that suddenly there was a nonrational way of understanding that had been beyond my previous experience.

There seems to be more to the universe than random, chaotic, purposeless movement of a collection of molecular particles.

On the return trip home, gazing through 240,000 miles of space toward the stars and the planet from which I had come, I suddenly experienced the universe as intelligent, loving, harmonious.[41]

We shall return to this story in Chapter Seven when we attempt to reflect upon and evaluate the postmodern narrative understanding of religious truth we are still in the midst of articulating.

5

Faith: Living the Story

Of all the worn, smudged, dog-eared words in our vocabulary, 'love' is surely the grubbiest, smelliest, slimiest. Bawled from a million pulpits, lasciviously crooned through hundreds of millions of loudspeakers, it has become an outrage to good taste and decent feeling, an obscenity which one hesitates to pronounce. And yet it has to be pronounced, for, after all, Love is the last word.

Aldous Huxley

5:1 Reasons of the Heart

Pascal's distinction between "*L'esprit de geometrie*" and "*L'esprit de finesse*" in the *Pensees* highlights a fundamental difference and divide between theoretical understanding on the one hand and faith on the other. Faith has its own, nonconceptual and conative form of understanding, an understanding (if you will) which involves the heart as opposed to the mind, a knowing-how-to-live in the face of mystery and mortality rather than an empirical or mathematical knowing-this-or-that about it, a real doing rather than an hypothesis about such doing. As Pascal put it, "The heart has its reasons, which reason does not know."[1] Who, for instance, would be content with a theory about love if in fact he never could actually love? All the theory in the world is neither the same as nor equal to just one, emaciated, confused, but real experience of love. I can know of infinite numbers of possible worlds, but the whole lot is not worth just one moment of experiencing this actual one. I will argue in this chapter that the same is true of faith. To have an interpretive understanding of life is not the same as actually living it. Or, in Kierkegaard's way of putting it, subjective truth is not the same as objective truth; existential understanding is not the same as pure thought; living a religious faith is not the same as thinking about it.

The title of this book, *The Inside Story*, is of course a double entendre. The first aspect of its double meaning is the well-known journalistic practice announcing hidden elements behind public events or the lives of famous people—in this essay, the unfolding story behind our present spiritual and environmental situation. The second aspect of the double meaning has to do with the word *inside*. The meaning intended here is that narrative religious understanding—the way we see life as meaningful—founds a horizon or world which we live 'inside' of as opposed to an objective, physical reality in the world of object-things known exclusively by scientific hypothesis. In fact, I argued earlier that the attempt to locate religious understanding and faith in the world of things known (and dominated) by science and technology is a category mistake. It is like trying to generate moral value in a scientific laboratory or empirical hypothesis by legal argument and court trial. What is not intended by the word *inside* is the Cartesian sense that religious understanding is limited to the mind, which all too often is pictured as inside the body. On the contrary, I have tried to show that narrative religious understanding pervades and shapes our concrete behavior as the intentional purpose toward which it is directed. That means that such understanding takes place out in the world of ordinary experience. In fact, narrative mythology provides an interpretive understanding which founds and structures such experiential worlds. As we saw, that understanding is not something which temporally precedes living in the world, as if we first envision how to live life and then fashion a world to match it. Rather, mythological understanding is congruent with 'world'; being in a world is how we interpretively understand the vision of possible life laid out in the myth.

The purpose of this chapter, then, is to show precisely how such founding myths lead to and structure actual behavior within the various, human lifeworlds. Put another way (and reiterating what we have already expressed in the preceding chapter), narrative religious understanding involves two complementary moments. First there is the mythological story which makes available a vision of a possible meaningful way to be (the preceding chapter). And second, there is the actual embodying and living out of such an inclusive understanding of life in faith (this chapter). They are not temporal moments apart from one another so much as distinguishable aspects of a single interpretive understanding. Neither the mythological understanding of life nor actually living out such a vision in faith can stand by itself, because (as I argued earlier) both depend upon and imply one another. Mythology that is not responded to and brought into existence isn't living myth, and there can be no faith or concrete way of being which does not rest upon and find its origin in a mythological vision of life. In other words, there can be no mythological understanding except to those who strive in their own lives to make it be, and there can be no oriented world of meaningful behavior without a disclosive, mythological vision of reality which founds it. Myth, as many scholars have noted, latently contains within it performance as religious ritual, and such religious performance is inevitably an acting out of a founding myth. Myth, it might be said, is the script for the meaningful and narratively shaped world of active performance and behavior which is the context of our ordinary lives.

The second stage or step involved in religious understanding, then, is an existential one. It is a way of actually living by responding to and taking on a possible way of being disclosed in and through myth.

5:2 The Pursuit of Being

Kierkegaard tells a wonderfully revealing story about himself in the *Concluding Unscientific Postscript*. He had already graduated from the seminary and was, he says, "of riper years." On a Sunday afternoon, he was seated out-of-doors in the Frederiksberg Garden, smoking his cigar and contemplating what he should do with his life. For several years, he had been living an indolent life of a student—reading a great deal, writing very little, and all in all engaged in a sort of "glittering inactivity" (an occupation he says for which he still has a great partiality and no little genius). But where was his life headed? What could he do with himself?

So there I sat and smoked my cigar until I lapsed into thought. Among other thoughts I remember these: 'You are going on', I said to myself, 'to become an old man, without being anything, and without really undertaking to do anything. On the other hand, wherever you look about you, in literature and in life, you see the celebrated names of figures, the precious and much heralded men who are coming into prominence and are much talked about, the many benefactors of the age who know how to benefit mankind by making life easier and easier, some by railways, some by omnibusses and steamboats, others by the telegraph, others by easily apprehended compendiums and short recitals of everything worth knowing, and finally the true benefactors of the age who make spiritual existence in virtue of thought easier and easier, yet more and more significant. And what are you doing?' Here my soliloquy was interrupted, for my cigar was smoked out and a new one had to be lit. So I smoked again, and then suddenly this throught flashed through my mind: 'You must do something, but inasmuch as with your limited capacities it will be impossible to make anything easier than it has become, you must, with the same humanitarian enthusiasm as the others, undertake to make something *harder*.'[2]

Kierkegaard meant this seriously, I believe, in two ways. First of all, he did in fact make life "harder" because he recognized that there is an unavoidable, nonfactual and nontheoretical dimension of our lives, what we have called interpretive understanding. Even philosophies, as we saw, insofar as they presuppose real human philosophers to develop and articulate them, rest upon a tacit, hermeneutical interpretation or vision of what it means to be, a way of 'seeing' life 'as' a meaningful whole. The fact is, human life can be seen or interpreted only from a particular standpoint, from a point of view about what is fundamentally meaningful about living. Hegel's notorious view that "the rational is real and the real is rational"—a view which underlies and pervades his entire philosophical corpus— is not itself rationally demonstrated or, for that matter, even demonstrable. It is in fact Hegel's own passionate and mythological sense of what it means to be, and it is, as Kierkegaard put it, "70,000 fathoms over the deep!" It is what Hegel the man brings to the doing of philosophy, that which he cares enough about to actually do. That Hegel in his philosophy then absent-mindedly forgets that personal involvement in favor of having 'reason' or 'the Spirit' speak through and for him endlessly delights Kierkegaard. He has to remind Hegel continuously to speak to him as a person rather than an 'over-earthly' or 'underearthly' being, and to cease trying to die to himself in favor of an abstraction.[3] He has to keep nagging the absent-minded and comical Hegel (it's comical to forget yourself) to acknowledge honestly his personal, hermeneutical, nonrational involvement in both life and his own philosophy. That doesn't seem like too much to ask.

Kierkegaard thinks that subsuming faith under the category of objective understanding makes it nearly impossible to actually be a Christian. He has made things harder, then, just as he said.

Suppose Christianity is not a matter of knowledge, so that the increased knowledge is of no avail, except to make it easier to fall into the confusion of considering Christianity as a matter of knowledge...[that] means a sum of doctrinal propositions. But suppose Christianity were nothing of the kind; suppose on the contrary it were inwardness, and hence also the paradox, so as to thrust the individual away objectively, in order to obtain significance for the existing individual in the inwardness of his existence. . . . Verily, if it was once difficult to become a Christian, now I believe it becomes increasingly difficult year by year, because it has now become so easy that the only ambition which stirs any competition is that of becoming a speculative philosopher. . . . The realm of faith is thus not a class for numskulls in the sphere of the intellectual, or an asylum for the feeble-minded. Faith constitutes a sphere all by itself, and every misunderstanding of Christianity may at once be recognized by its transforming it into a doctrine, transferring it to the sphere of the intellectual.[4]

He has made life harder, then. Beneath the modern pursuit of reason lies an ill-disguised mythological vision or construal of what life is all about. The heady optimism and belief in rational progress of the Enlightenment and nineteenth century turn out to be a kind of naive self-deception, or (as we put it earlier) "a myth to end all myths."

But he also made life harder in another sense. We can no longer claim an objective foundation or basis for life, but must step up and take responsibility for it ourselves. Rather than a merely theoretical answer to life, religious life involves a risk and a commitment to carry out and actually live the kind of life made available in the mythical vision of things, a personal decision to appropriate and make it real. This is a matter of existential understanding and truth, a question of how to *live* most fully and completely. Such an existential issue cannot be resolved theoretically—whether in the laboratory, mathematics and logic, or just plain foundationalist philosophy—because it involves not only a person's (or people's) sense of how best to live, but a decisive coming to actually live that way. As Kierkegaard wrote in his *Journals*:

what I really lack is to be clear about *what I am to do,* not what I am to know. . . . What good would it do me to be able to explain the meaning of Christianity if it had *no* deeper significance *for me and for my life.*[5]

Kierkegaard calls this existential aspect of our lives "subjective truth" or faith. It is, he says, "an objective uncertainty [it can't be demonstrated and is in no sense a doctrine or objective truth] held fast in an appropriation process [we actively seek to become it] of the most passionate inwardness.'"[6] Faith, then, is a becoming, a way of existing meaningfully, an attempt to be, an active commitment and venture toward living as fully and deeply as possible. Life confronts us with the question of who we are and what we think we are doing, what our lives mean to us, and then demands that we actually become it. Faith entails an overarching vision of life as a whole which is existentialized in a real life of action and behavior. Faith is a doing, a restless striving or coming to be.

> Faith does not result simply from scientific inquiry; it does not come directly at all. On the contrary, in this objectivity one tends to lose that infinite personal interestedness in passion which is the condition of faith, the *ubique et nusquam* in which faith can come into being.[7]

As we saw earlier, life is fundamentally an active endeavor or series of such endeavors. In actively living toward an overarching vision of what life is about, we seek to make it be, to become it. We strive for spiritual illumination and contentment, seeking to be as much as possible. By that process, we transform the events of our lives into a story. Faith is nothing but the living of this existential story centered on a mythologically disclosed interpretive understanding of life 'seen as' a meaningful whole. H. Richard Niebuhr, in his early classic, *The Meaning of Revelation*, wrote:

> An inner history, life's flow as regarded from the point of view of living selves, is always an affair of faith. As long as a man lives he must believe in something for the sake of which he lives; without belief in something that makes life worth living man cannot exist....Man as a practical, living being never exists without a god or gods; there are some things to which he must cling as the sources and goals of his activity....[8]

Our ordinary lives, then, are pervaded by a profound will to live, by a sense that we have not yet gotten the most out of life. In fact, the very striving to make our lives qualitatively richer and better implies an existential assumption that there is a right way to be. I don't mean this objectively, but existentially. At the same time, of course, such striving loudly proclaims that 'I' have not yet achieved it, that there remains a gap between who I am and who I desire to be, between the appetite and its fulfillment. As Paul Ricoeur has put it:

The sacred calls upon man and in this call manifests itself as that which commands his existence because it posits this existence absolutely, as effort and as desire to be.[9]

In other words, the call of the sacred takes place and makes sense only within the human condition in which the future is open (merely possible) and must be brought into being. Existence is posited absolutely by the sacred call because there is no other way for human existence to come to be except by being desired and (through an effort) pursued and made to be. Wayne Booth has admirably caught this sense of life's existential demands upon us in the following description. Religious faiths, he tells us, are responses to

> some sort of cosmic demand—that is, to a demand made to us by the *way things are*....Life as we meet it and live it is not all that it *should be;* the world does not work as it should. Something is radically wrong. Everybody agrees to *that*. Religion enters when I add *"and I ought* to help put it right, first by righting myself."[10]

We do that by making the vision of life manifest in a mythological interpretation real. That is, we strive to live it by 'righting' ourselves in the light of it. One of the spiritual crises in the life of Leo Tolstoy, and the manner in which he ultimately resolved it by actually *changing his way of living,* dramatically illustrates this sometimes painful process. In his *Confession* of 1879, he tells us that about five years earlier he had begun to enter a deep depression in which life seemed meaningless:

> At first I experienced moments of perplexity and arrest of life, as though I did not know what to do or how to live and I felt lost and became dejected....these moments of perplexity began to recur oftener and oftener, and always in the same form. They were always expressed by the questions: What is it for? What does it lead to?

His suffering increased, he tells us, and he could not find his way free of the power which seemed to turn him against life.

> All my strength drew me away from life. The thought of self destruction now came to me as naturally as thoughts of how to improve my life had come formerly....My mental condition presented itself to me in this way: my life is a stupid and spiteful joke someone has played on me.

In his earlier life, he had had a simple faith and hope in life which now seemed crushed and lost forever.

My question—that which at the age of fifty brought me to the verge of suicide—was the simplest of questions. . . . It was: 'What will come of what I am doing today or shall do tomorrow? What will come of my whole life?' . . . Why should I live? . . . Is there any meaning in my life that the inevitable death awaiting me does not destroy?

He tried to think his way out of his misery, to argue himself into the essence of living, to rationally cross over from the finite to the infinite. That failed, of course, and he was left, if anything, more stranded and alone with his sense of meaninglessness than before.

Gradually he came to see in his painful situation his heart's yearning for God.

That search for God was not reasoning, but a feeling, because that search proceeded not from the course of my thoughts . . . but proceeded from the heart. It was a feeling of fear, orphanage, isolation in a strange land, and a hope of help from someone.

Finally recognizing that 'reason' was inadequate to the task of finding meaning which he could actually live and be, he came to see faith in a different light:

Looking again at people of other lands, at my contemporaries and at their predecessors, I saw the same thing. Where there is life, there since man began faith has made life possible for him . . . every such answer gives to the finite existence of man an infinite meaning, a meaning not destroyed by sufferings, deprivations, or death. . . . Faith is a knowledge of the meaning of human life in consequence of which man does not destroy himself but lives. Faith is the strength of life.

In the light of that, Tolstoy soon became aware that for him it was the ordinary and long-suffering Russian peasants who most embodied this faith-energy and force for living, and that if he himself was ever to overcome his despair he must live differently. He must live the down-to-earth life of common men and give up the vain, artificial, cerebral life of the upper classes. It was his living wrongly that had led to his present state. To overcome his malaise, he tells us, he had to live differently!

I began to draw near to the believers among the poor, simple, unlettered folk: pilgrims, monks, sectarians, and peasants...the whole life of the working-folk believers was a confirmation of the meaning of life which their faith gave them....I had erred not so much because I thought incorrectly as because I lived badly.

I remember that it was in early spring: I was alone in the wood listening to its sounds. I listened and thought ever of the same thing, as I had constantly done during those long three years. I was again seeking God....I remembered that I only lived at those times in which I believed in God. As it was before, so it was now; I need only be aware of God to live; I need only forget Him, or disbelieve Him, and I died....I live, really live, only when I feel Him and seek Him. "What more do you seek?" exclaimed a voice within me. "This is He. He is that without which one cannot live. To know God and to live is one and the same thing. God is life. Live seeking God, and then you will not live without God." And more than ever before, all within me and around me lit up, and the light did not again abandon me. And I was saved from suicide.[11]

The sacred, then, is experienced as the unconditional demand to transform ourselves and to live righteously or truly. Mythological interpretations of life imply, according to Mircea Eliade, "a transmutation of the person who receives, interprets and assimilates the revelation."[12] Clearly this is an existential truth rather than a conceptual one. Thomas á Kempis put this powerfully when he noted:

Truly, at the day of judgment we shall not be examined as to what we have read, but as to what we have done; not as to how well we have spoken, but as to how religiously we have lived.[13]

Nelson Pike, in a very interesting analysis of the writings of St. John of the Cross, concludes that John thought that mystical understanding of God is not a kind of propositional or cognitive knowing in which information is conveyed, but rather a kind of illumination or "spiritual growth" which "comes in the form of a cognitive wallop." For John of the Cross, mystic states

Work on the soul as a dose of vitamins might work on the body. They effect a kind of spiritual tune-up that results in easy commerce between the visionary and God. *Question:* Why does God confer mystic apprehensions? *Answer:* In spite of the danger of error and confusion, they are given in order to enhance the 'spiritual growth' of the individual receiver.[14]

Whatever else it may be, faith is the attempt to live truly by appropriating and actualizing what has been recognized as God's demands concerning how we ought to live disclosed in myth. It is a 'knowing how' as opposed to a 'knowing that,' an ability to trust and act in terms of what has been discovered to be the right way to live. In *The Sacred Pipe*, Black Elk put this very forcefully:

> *O Wakan-Tanka*, You are the truth. The two-legged peoples who put their mouths to this pipe will become the truth itself; there will be in them nothing impure. Help us to walk the sacred path of life without difficulty, with our minds and hearts continually fixed on you!...May we who are Your people stand in a *wakan* manner, pleasing to you!...Because You have made your will known to us, we will walk the path of life in holiness, bearing the love and knowledge of You in our hearts![15]

Notice that they "will become the truth" and that—just as Pascal claimed—such knowledge lies within "our hearts" rather than our minds.

> *The typical conclusion to genuine religious thinking is not more thought but action.* What is sought are not more beautiful thoughts on love and justice but just and loving lives.[16]

In fact, my claim here that religious understanding and truth entails how one actually behaves and exists is supported by Hendrik Vroom in his recent comparative study of the notion of religious truth across a number of different traditions. Hinduism, Buddhism, Judaism, Christianity, and Islam, he claims, all emphasize that religious truth requires commitment and obedience, living differently than before. The goal of living truly in the light of the demands of the sacred, he claims, is indispensable to their understanding of such religious truth.[17]

Faith is living in the light of an interpretive understanding of life made manifest narratively or mythologically. It is not primarily 'beliefs' about an absent (transcendent) entity called God, not propositional assertions considered true or false in some matter-of-fact way, but a mode of being, actively living out a personal story centered on such an interpretive understanding of what it means to be, a way of existing in a world. It has more to do with who we are than what we think. Put another way, the moral and religious gravity of the human situation is inherent in the temporal reach toward possibility which structures our ordinary behavior. Spiritual demand makes sense precisely insofar as it becomes the goal of the human passion to bring a better, more meaningful, more real life into being. To actually pursue some purpose or goal in life, to choose it, to commit some part of life to achieving it is to create value. It is to go beyond all actual and possible factual knowledge to a kind of wisdom or understanding which is both a vision of how life ought to be lived and a reaching out to actually live it. Our reach exceeds our grasp: the phenomenon of a transcendent and holy dimension beyond or before nature and ordinary life results from the human necessity of living and behaving in the light of possibility.

Faith is a quality of living, then, a quality which obviously takes a variety of forms. As such, it is an ortho*praxis* rather than an ortho*doxy*. Sometimes a person's faith is such that he or she is serene, accepting, compassionate, patient, and caring. In other instances, faith renders a life meager, stunted, distracted, narcissistic, and narrow-minded. In any case, such narrative faith seems to be a necessary and essential aspect of human life and behavior. In fact, it may be *the* essential human quality. That is why, perhaps, we know of no human beings from the paleolithic period until now who have not or do not live in some mythologically construed world or culture. It would seem, then, that the history of religion lies at the core of human history in general, for without that history there could be no social, political, technological, institutional, intellectual, or national histories which presuppose it.

There you have it. Religious understanding involves two interrelated aspects or, as we put it, 'moments': (1) the narrative disclosure of ways of seeing life as a meaningful whole which at the same time are 'possible' ways of existing, and (2) actually coming to live out narratively such a vision of life and human destiny in response to the demand present in the myth. Such religious understanding is neither inductive nor deductive. As we have seen, it involves acts of interpretation which are neither objectively and exclusively true nor merely subjective illusion. Although it would be unreasonable (as we have seen) for any religious tradition to claim that its particular vision of life is alone authentic and that all others are false, the possibility remains that some interpretations may be more or less adequate than others. By what criteria and through what procedures can we make such evaluations of religious truth claims? Because both aspects of religious understanding involve narrative, it would seem to follow that whatever criteria for evaluating the truth of religious understanding there may be will be tied up with the kinds of assessment procedures appropriate to stories in general.

Narrative Knowledge and Religious Truth

The tragedy is that most intelligent, educated Western men and women see no way out of the materialistic maze....However, a clear understanding of the process of how we know (known philosophically as epistemology) can lift us out of the flatland of disbelief.

Morton T. Kelsey

6:1 Religious Conviction

It is traditional in philosophical analyses of epistemology to indicate procedures for verifying or falsifying hypothetical truth claims or—as they are called in the religious sphere—beliefs. Indeed, the positivism of the 1930s, 1940s, and 1950s held that because religious beliefs are operationally unverifiable or unfalsifiable, they were not only not true but actually nonsensical and meaningless, like the incoherent (to us) babblings of a monkey or the rustling of the wind in the trees. I have argued, however, that this very view of religious knowledge as empirical-like hypotheses to be confirmed or disconfirmed by the 'facts' was the result of the Enlightenment and led to the present painful spiritual situation in which we find ourselves.

In fact, Wilfred Cantwell Smith has pointed out that the names by which we now know the various religious traditions were for the most part invented in the eighteenth century. (We are reminded here of Foucault's famous dictum that "modern man was invented in the eighteenth century.") Before then, the notion of a number of competing belief systems all claiming truth was unknown. In fact, Smith claims that

it is a surprising modern aberration for anyone to think Christianity is true or that Islam is—since the Enlightenment, basically,

when Europe began to postulate religions as intellectualistic systems, patterns of doctrine, so that they could for the first time be labeled 'Christianity' or 'Buddhism,' and could be called true or false.[1]

In order to avoid this difficulty, R.B. Braithwaite has argued that religious belief is not a form of propositional or information-bearing knowledge at all, but rather more like moral beliefs or assertions.

A moral belief is an intention to behave in a certain way: a religious belief is an intention to behave in a certain way (a moral belief) together with the entertainment of certain stories associated with the intention in the mind of the believer.[2]

In spite of significant differences in other respects between Braithwaite's position and mine, I think this is a view which is very close to the position I have outlined above. Like mine, Braithwaite's position involves stories or myths which unite the will and behavior by means of the cement of imagination—what we have called "myth." That is: "People...resolve upon and...carry through a course of action" by imagining a possible mode of life in the lively form of stories. Second, religious beliefs (what I have called "faith") are not so much hypotheses about an external divine entity as commitments to or expressions of an intention to behave in a certain way or to live a particular way of life.[3] They are a 'knowing-how' that is carried out in actual behavior. And, as Merold Westphal has put it recently, this

doing is rather a self-transformative activity intended to bring me (us) into conformity with God's ends....Biblically understood, truth is not reducible to correct beliefs, even correct beliefs about God, because truth is something to be done.[4]

6:2 Evaluating Religious Conviction

Religious knowledge, then, is neither an objective nor a deductive kind of understanding. To think of it as such is not only to fall into a category mistake but to let loose in the world a swarm of spiritual difficulties which seem to go along with the view. Rather, religious knowledge is a separate and unique narrative and interpretive kind of understanding having to do with the overall nature of reality and human destiny. We might expect that its kind of evaluative criteria and procedures, then, will also be unique to it. It is not a question here of objective truth and falsehood with its implicit claims for absoluteness (such truths can't be both true and false) and exclusivity (contradictory claims can't both be true). Religious knowledge entails a different kind of truth, a disclosive truth in which particular claims can be both true and false in the sense that in the (true) disclosure they cover up or hide other aspects of reality not attended to. And such different and seemingly contradictory religious truths can *all* be true insofar as none of them can reach or be either identified with or fully adequate to the reality being disclosed. So, finally, religious understanding, I am claiming, should be evaluated in less absolute and exclusive terms. It can be assessed in softer terms more appropriate to the religious dimension—that is, in terms of the degree of the special kind of truth which it embodies. Evaluating the truth of a religious understanding and way of life is less a matter of judgment than a way of appraising its plausibility—i.e., estimating how true or false it is in terms of the degree of its success in achieving its particular task of transforming and living life more effectively and fully. In this sense, it is a procedure which is closer to the way we assess the truthfulness of stories of various kinds than it is to judging the truthfulness of an empirical hypothesis or the validity and truth of a syllogism. Terrence Tilley puts it this way:

> To call a story 'true' is to evaluate it, grade it or assess it as 'not exaggerated, not too rough, not misleading, not too general,' etc....People have to evaluate the religious stories they are told as part of their accepting those religious stories as their own.[5]

Furthermore, assessing the 'truth' of a story is made more complicated and delicate (softer) by an additional element. To evaluate the plausibility of a story means to weigh it within its total context. How we evaluate it is contingent to a large degree on what kind of story it is, who is telling it, what his or her intentions are, who the audience for it is, and what the particular social situation is in which it is being told. The same story, in fact, may be more or less true in different contexts. The truth of the resurrection stories about Jesus, for example, are liable to be less true (in terms of the criteria we will be outlining in just a moment) if they are being told by Madeleine Murray or Antony Flew at a meeting of the Ethical Culture Society than if such stories were being told by Stanley Hauerwas or Terrence Tilley at a meeting of the Theological Society of America.

Both Frederick Ferré and, more recently, David Wolfe have suggested that criteria for effectiveness and success of particular activities depend on the particular endeavor or task one has set out to accomplish. In David Wolfe's words, such criteria are

> simply a clarification of the project we or someone else sets for us. In such cases the criteria are not arbitrary with respect to the given project, *they are the project*. More precisely, they are the project formulated as a set of standards by which we can test the outcome of attempts to carry out the project...the giving reasons [or justifications for evaluative estimations] is possible only in the context of the project.[6]

By clarifying the goals of a task or project, we can in fact determine when and whether or not that task or project has been successfully accomplished. In other words, baking can be evaluated in terms of the degree to which the goals of the baking project are in fact achieved. The same goes for painting, bicycle riding, city planning, automotive maintenance, or whatever. All of this might remind the reader of the ancient Greek conception of *arete* (virtue), which is very similar. Such virtue (*arete*) was defined precisely as 'practical success' or the achievement of the goals (a *telos* or good) implicit to the particular activity at hand.

At any rate, I want to argue that this picture of the appraisal of projects in terms of criteria derived from their implicit goals can be helpful to us in establishing specific standards for the evaluation of religious understanding. If we could clarify or make explicit the particular goals which are implicit to that understanding, we would have in hand a set of specific evaluative criteria appropriate to it and available for sorting out various religious truth claims.

Rather than a propositional knowledge concerning the 'facts' of the world, it is finally in action and doing that we find religious understanding, and it is there ultimately that we shall seek to find its particular kind of validity. Stated generally, the religious task is *to live as deeply and fully as possible in the light of a sacred or ontological demand disclosed narratively in mythology*. In the light of this project of religious understanding, we might expect that the evaluative criteria in terms of which we are to ascertain how successfully it is accomplished hinge on the degree to which the double task is actually achieved. My claim, of course, is that the validity of religious understanding can be 'tested' in two ways which flow from this double task: (1) the degree to which a particular person (or group) is open to and responsively transformed by the demand to live the ideal life revealed by the myth (or, to put it another way, actually carries out her intentions to live in a certain way); and (2) the degree to which the promise of that life is achieved in living a fuller and richer life than before or than other interpretations of life hold out as possible. This twofold task of religious understanding can in turn be broken down into a number of subordinate goals in terms of which we might be able to generate specific criteria for appraising the truth or falsity of various claims to religious understanding and truth.

Perhaps we can best express those goals in a kind of formula. Religious understanding involves (1) a disclosive mythological (or historically revelatory or metaphysical) interpretation of life or experience which makes available to us (2) a vision of that life as an overarching and meaningful whole. Furthermore, these mythological interpretations, (3) insofar as they are forceful and we are open to them, (4) make demands on us (5) to overcome our false (sinful or ignorant or self-centered) ways of living in favor of (6) transforming ourselves and living authentically by centering our lives on the sacred meaning which they reveal to us. It seems to me that these goals or ends involved in the task of religious understanding point to the kinds of specific evaluative criteria we shall be discussing in just a moment. I am claiming, of course, that it is in terms of these criteria that we can assess the plausibility of particular religious claims, that is the degree to which those goals are or can be actually achieved.

It is important before laying out the specifics of these evaluative criteria to keep in mind several important points. First, since I have argued that the modern worldview as well as the many philosophies which have emerged historically rest on interpretive understanding (myth), they are by that fact to be fundamentally evaluated and assessed as religious convictions—i.e., in terms of these criteria. That, of course, includes this philosophy.

But second, I argued earlier that interpretive understanding is necessarily 'seen' through and shaped by the interpretive glasses which an interpreter(s) brings to life and the evaluation of other views. That means, of course, that we should maintain a healthy scepticism and vigilance in actually evaluating religious understanding. We need to be suspicious of the degree to which our own biases enter into such assessments. This suspicion is powerfully reinforced when we recall such masters of the 'hermeneutics of suspicion' as Nietzsche, Marx, and Freud, who have taught us to be aware that we often carry not only biases of perspective with us, but also hidden (from our conscious selves) biases of desire. They have made us (sometimes painfully) conscious that self-interest and self-deception may condition and determine our interpretive understandings. In other words, in assessing religious understanding, we must be on guard against our own possible perversity as well as our own points of view, our own self-interests and self-deception as well as our own situation and perspective. The evaluative assessment of religious understanding, then, is difficult enough insofar as it is not an obvious (or even subtle) matter of fact. When you add to that a sense of the ubiquity of perspectival bias and hidden desire, you become aware of the depth of the dangers and difficulties in such assessment. Because of this and because, after all, it is our lives that are at stake in this matter, we need to assess the truth of these matters with some "fear and trembling" (to use Kierkegaard's beautiful phrase).

We have seen that the modern worldview was constituted by such a narrative, interpretive understanding of life. We have also summarily outlined a new cosmological story which may provide a postmodern vision of reality and human destiny. In laying out these evaluative criteria, it might be helpful at the same time to briefly weigh each of these basic myths in the light of them. Not only might this help us clarify our understanding of those evaluative measures, but it might also sharpen our understanding of the kinds of subtle difficulties and ambiguities involved in the process of assessing serious religious attitudes toward life. In other words, life is interpreted from a variety of standpoints, and none of them is demonstrable in some easy, factual or deductive manner. That just happens to be the way it is.

6:3 Some Specific Evaluative Criteria

Given the difficulty, ambiguity, and 'softness' involved in assessing religious understanding, it still seems to me that the following evaluative criteria follow from what we have indicated are the goals of religious understanding. I am claiming, then, that—in spite of those difficulties and qualifications—these are in fact some of the ways through which we actually do weigh and assess the degree of truth which a particular religious understanding of life embodies.

1. *Disclosiveness.* Religious understandings may be evaluated in terms of the degree to which they make available an interpretive vision of how to live life which was unnoticed beforehand. They must represent our experience to us in such a way that we are led to see it differently—that is, uncover or make noticeable an interpretive understanding of it which had hitherto remained hidden or unconscious.

It has certainly been the case that modernity manifested such a disclosive nature. In fact, the very fact that it was considered 'modern'—and thus both new and critical of the traditional vision of life against which it defined itself—seems to me to indicate that it did strongly re-present life to many people in a startlingly new way. Whether or not it continues to do so, I think, can be doubted, for it has become so engrained in human consciousness and culture around the world that there seems to be no new, disclosive re-presentation of life going on.

The new cosmological story, on the other hand, makes available a new and different interpretive understanding of the evolution of the universe and our place within. It narratively re-presents life to us in such a way that interpretive aspects of reality are disclosed which hitherto have been covered over and lost to consciousness by some of the assumptions and biases that are part and parcel of the modern point of view.

2. *Adequacy.* An acceptable religious understanding is one which fits our experience and in illuminating it remains faithful to it. To be adequate, it must be plausible or ring true to that experience and not run counter or be false to it.

I believe that modernity does not fit our actual spiritual experience. In fact, I have argued that it loses sight of our ordinary lived experience in the world in favor of a technical knowledge which transforms reality into the world of physical, object-things. Such an interpretive framework, I argued, simply filters out the possibility of spiritual life based upon the experience of narrative interpretive understanding because it filters out and blinds us to that experience in general. It also does away with the human sense of wonder in the face of the mystery of being in favor of foundational, solid 'answers' and 'truths' that reduce life to a manageable order.

The new cosmological story, on the other hand, seems to me to fit our experience better. First of all, there is a recognition within it that our experience in the world is real and significant and not to be dismissed out of hand. But second, it opens up and makes available genuine spiritual experience (especially vis-a-vis nature) which—due to the perverse vision of modernity—was increasingly marginalized and attenuated.

3. *Comprehensiveness.* Since one distinctive task of religious understanding is to 'see' life 'as' a meaningful whole, then a measure by which it may be assessed is the degree to which it is genuinely overarching and comprehensive of the entirety of human experience. It must, then, 'see together' the entirety of our experience from birth to death, with all of its joy as well as its suffering, with some indication

of how it all has come about, and with a vision of our role and destiny as human beings within it.

In many ways, modernity was genuinely more comprehensive than the traditional worldview which preceded it, especially insofar as its vision encompassed the new view of the universe made possible by the Copernican revolution and the discovery of the telescope. It also provided human beings with a unique and pivotal role in history— indeed perhaps too much so. Yet, having encouraged the separation of mind and matter, value and truth, theology and science, it then all but did away with 'mind' in favor of a mechanistic and lifeless matter known by science. In a word, having separated religious understanding from nature, it then simply did away with it by drying up the reality to which it had been assigned (mind), thereby leaving religion nowhere to go and an increasingly powerful science and technology cut off from religious and moral understanding and value.

Furthermore, modernity seems less comprehensive than the new cosmological story insofar as it does not (and of course could not) include an understanding of the whole, remarkable, twenty-billion-year evolution of nature as the rich, comprehensive whole which encompasses everything, including human desires and understanding. In fact, it reduced nature to being merely the occasion for the imposition of strictly human desires and needs upon it.

4. *Ultimacy.* But to the degree that it is actually comprehensive, genuine religious understanding must point beyond all that is finite and limited to that which is not finite, to that which is ultimate. As Paul Tillich put it, faith is "ultimate concern." Such ultimate concern must be evaluated in terms of whether it is genuinely ultimate or merely a proximate concern posing as ultimate. The first criterion of the truth of faith, he tells us, is whether or not the symbols or images which interpretively express it are alive or—as I shall put it with respect to the next evaluative criterion—demanding.

> The other criterion of the truth of a symbol of faith is that it expresses the ultimate which is really ultimate. In other words, that it is not idolatrous. . . . Every type of faith has the tendency to elevate its concrete symbols to absolute validity. The criterion of the truth of faith, therefore, is that it implies an element of self-negation. That symbol is most adequate which expresses not only the ultimate but also its own lack of ultimacy.[7]

We can put this another way. To be genuinely comprehensive, religious understanding must involve a sacred meaning which is not "part of the furniture of the universe" (as Tillich used to put it). The sacred must be ultimate to be genuinely comprehensive. It must be transcendent, empty, apophatic, indefinable, nonfinite. Listen, for example, to a conversation between Robert Coles and a ten-year-old Hopi girl concerning what she considered a typical Anglo misunderstanding of such ultimate reality.

"The sky watches us and listens to us. It talks to us, and it hopes we are ready to talk back. The sky is where the God of the Anglos lives, a teacher told us. She asked where our God lives. I said, 'I don't know.' I was telling the truth! Our God is the sky, and lives wherever the sky is. Our God is the sun and the moon, too; and our God is our [the Hopi] people, if we remember to stay here [on the consecrated land]. This is where we're supposed to be, and if we leave, we lose God."

Did she explain the above to the teacher?

"No"

"Why?"

"Because—she thinks God is a person. If I'd told her, she'd give us that smile."

"What smile?"

"The smile that says to us, 'You kids are cute, but you're dumb; you're different — and you're all wrong!"

"Perhaps you could have explained to her what you've just tried to explain to me."

"We tried that a long time ago; our people spoke to the Anglos and told them what we think, but they don't listen to hear *us*; they listen to hear themselves, my dad says, and he hears them all day....My Grandmother says they live to conquer the sky, and we live to pray to it, and you can't explain yourself to people who conquer—just pray for them, too. So we smile and say yes to them all the time, and we pray for them."[8]

The degree of valid religious understanding, then, is proportional to the degree that it protects the transcendence or ultimacy of God by insisting that human understandings are merely analogical or metaphorical hints which are never adequate to that which they are trying to manifest. God transcends any form of finitude. As has often been noted by scholars of religion, a pervasive characteristic of genuine religious understanding is that it takes back in one breath what it has just stated in another in order (on the one hand) to make available an overarching interpretation of life while (on the other) safeguarding the ultimacy of that vision.

Here the modern worldview has failed rather miserably. It either pushes God off into a causal hypothesis as a deist creator unavailable to and for experience, or it replaces God with the finite idol of matter as understood by our human sciences. Either horn of the dilemma, it seems to me, leads precisely to the reduction of the *infinity* and *trans*cendence of reality (its mystery) to finite terms and understandings.

The postmodern, cosmological story, on the other hand, embodies a specific and yet ultimate sense of reality or God as the mysterious, creative, and wonderful ground of all finite realties which emerge from it. God is not only available to human experience once again, but is precisely *ultimate* insofar as 'it' is experienced in wonder apophatically—that is, as the reality which is not and cannot be reduced to factual (finite) explanations or hypotheses. Rather, that reality (Being itself) is experienced in wonder as transcendent only at the boundaries or limits of rational explanation and understandings—i.e., as that nonfinite mystery beyond all possible explanation.

5. *Demand.* A religious understanding is true to the degree that it is 'alive' and makes demands on people, to the degree that it stands out and forcefully draws them to the possible mode of existence exhibited in the mythological story. In fact, forcefulness is one of the characteristics of a well-wrought story and is probably one of the reasons why religious understanding is so tied up with such mythological narratives. As Stanley Hauerwas puts it:

> We all love a good story. For example, if I had begun this essay with the phrase, ''I would like to begin by telling you a story,'' I would have your attention much more than a lecture about stories....The power of stories to command our attention has opened up a fruitful line of investigation for theological reflection. For it is obvious that whatever else it is the message that appears central to the Christian faith is in the form of a story.[9]

The modern story has certainly been a powerful one that has provided an interpretive vision of life which has affected human culture around the globe. I doubt that anyone today could doubt that. Whether or not it will remain as 'alive' and demanding in the future as it has been over the past few centuries—especially with its spiritual and ecological limitations—remains to be seen.

The obverse of that comment might be said of the new cosmological story. It remains to be seen whether or not this story will be experienced as a forcefully refreshing and renewing vision which demands the attention of people in the particular historical and spiritual situation in which they find themselves at the end of the twentieth century.

6. *Existential effectiveness.* Since religious understanding aims at transforming us and helping us to live more deeply and fully, then its truth can be assessed in part in terms of the degree to which that actually happens—i.e., the degree to which its adherents can be said to be living 'truly.' Religious understanding needs to be weighed in terms of its existential fruits: the degree to which a person (or group) actually carries out his or her intention to live differently in the light of the demands of a particular mythical understanding. John Hick puts this well in his essay entitled "On Grading Religions":

> The test of the veridical character of such an experience must thus be the test of the larger religious totality which has been built around it. And such a test can only be pragmatic: is this complex of religious experience, belief, and behavior soteriologically effective? Does it make possible the transformation of human existence from self-centeredness to Reality-centeredness?[10]

To understand religiously is not just to intend to go on in life, but actually to find a way to do so by finding a mode of being in the world that is pragmatically possible in a particular historical and cultural situation. Once again, Stanley Hauerwas expresses this powerfully:

> I am suggesting that a true story must be one that helps me to go on. For when we do not understand, we are afraid, and we tell ourselves stories that protect ourselves from the unknown and foreign—indeed, stories that even deny that there is an unknown or foreign. Thus a true story is one that helps me to uncover the true path that is also the path for me through the unknown and foreign.[11]

The very fact that religious understanding is embodied in how a person actually behaves and lives her life, I believe, is one reason why so many of us are actually drawn to a faith through example— e.g., a parent, a teacher, a relative, a friend. Far from arguments leading to faith, it seems more often that we become convicted by what appear to us to be truthful lives of, for example, courage and guts, simplicity, serenity, or reverence for life.

On the one hand, modernity in its 'critical' aspect and in its vision of transforming human life through the power of science and technology has certainly been existentially effective. On the other hand, I have argued that genuine spiritual life has become increasingly difficult if not impossible in the modern industrial-consumer society. If that is true, then it appears that modernity is existentially ineffective, that it has led to existentially alienated and barren lives (what I called earlier "heteronomy") instead of effective lives of wonder and autonomy.

The postmodern cosmological story, it seems to me, aims precisely at existentially transforming how we actually live by making us aware of our creativity. The claim is that we can live such creative (autonomous) lives by experiencing through a reverential wonder the mysterious creativity which permeates all of nature. From this point of view, to become autonomous is to step into our creative destiny within the unfolding of nature by bringing forth the 'ecological age'. Through wonder we can 'see' all of reality 'as' a single, creative, divine (transcendent) family. We have a new vision here which intends, at any rate, to transform us in order to call us back to our primary and genuine destiny within the whole, unfolding nature of which we are a part. That it intends such an existential transformation, of course, is no guarantee that it will actually achieve it. Who knows? It could be that we humans will inadvertently commit environmental suicide. That remains to be seen.

7. *Interpretive utility.* Certainly, one important criteria for evaluating religious understanding in its various forms is the degree to which it helps us come to grips more adequately with the spiritual issues and difficulties which face us in the particular cultural situation in which we find ourselves. For example, I have argued that modernity has led to "the spiritual blues." Specifically, modernity: (1) led to the obliteration of the traditional notion of a perennial wisdom having to do with how to live life most fully; (2) lost sight of the 'world of ordinary experience' in which religious understanding and practice make sense; (3) introduced the twin specter of meaninglessness and fanaticism; (4) made the pursuit of religious life almost impossible, especially for the educated; (5) reduced the notion of interpretation to factual truth;

(6) attenuated and flattened the notion of religious renewal; (7) brought us to the brink of ecological disaster; (8) blinded us to the real spiritual idolatry and danger of our time—the pursuit of technological power and progress; and (9) fostered a world fragmented into antagonistic and highly armed religious traditions all too often bitterly at war with one another. Any religious understanding (including, of course, the present philosophical interpretation) which can help us honestly face and to whatever degree ameliorate these issues can be said to be more adequate and true than those which fail to do so.

As I have tried to show, not only does the modern worldview not help us to deal with these spiritual maladies seemingly innundating our global culture(s), but—if my argument is at all true—it has actually been the primary cause of them.

Certainly one of the basic intentions of the postmodern cosmological story (indeed, I think its raison d'être) has been precisely to help us come to grips with these spiritual issues. In fact, I argued earlier that these spiritual difficulties are one of the forces powerfully pushing us toward that new story and the postmodern worldview which it makes available. I shall return to this theme in the concluding chapter.

8. *Coherence.* To be true, religious understanding must constitute a consistent whole free from internal and self-destructive contradictions. Obvious or even subtle inconsistencies within the entire understanding (the mythological act of interpretation plus the existential response to it) may lead to an assessment that it lacks integrity and thereby credibility. Terrence Tilley, for example, points out the obvious inconsistency of some fundamentalists who interpret the Bible as literally and exhaustively true while denying that they are in fact interpreting at all.[12]

In its attempt to limit its ontology, epistemology, and vision of life to those elements intrumental to the control and domination of nature for purely human ends, modernity simply contradicted itself. As we have seen, underlying the view that matters of fact and matters of reason were the only forms of understanding available was an obvious (from the postmodern point of view, at any rate) hidden form of narrative interpretive understanding on which it was founded and of which it was unaware. From the vantage point of postmodernity, this seems to be an obvious inconsistency, if not an outright self-contradiction, at the heart of modernity—an incoherence which has already contributed toward pushing us beyond it.

Is the new cosmological story coherent and free of inconsistencies and contradictions? It certainly would be difficult to claim that with any finality, and yet at the present historical juncture I am not aware of any obvious incoherence within it.

9. *Survivability.* Ultimately, of course, the truth of any religious understanding must be tested by time and broad critical scrutiny. The variety of myths and historical revelations should be and are sifted through and evaluated by many people who confront them with the total context of human experience. Those religious truths which have survived such a test of time have been judged by the human faculty of practical reason to be, over the long haul, effective or successful and, in that respect at least, true. Because such truths are not in any case matters of fact, then obviously they are neither infallible nor absolute, but at best (as we have seen) humanly efficacious or spiritually effective in living life. In other words, the truth of religious understanding comes out in the wash. Those religious truth claims which do not pragmatically contribute to life in all the ways we are outlining here might not be expected to survive very long. Equally, one might expect that those which remain humanly and existentially effective in living life might survive for that very reason. The great New Testament scholar, Norman Perrin, put this beautifully when discussing the kind of truth involved in the New Testament:

> One way to make our point is to claim that a myth cannot be true or false; it can only be effective or ineffective. Another way is to state, as Eliade has done orally, that no one can self-consciously create a myth. A myth has to arise spontaneously out of the consciousness of the people; it has to correspond to reality as they experience it; and it has to make sense for them of that reality, or a significant part of it. If it does these things, then it is "true," or "effective"; if it does not, it is false and ineffective. . . . They [myths] also operate at a more primal level as they are accepted without conscious thought as expressing the way things are, or can be, or should be.[13]

It was the right-wing Hegelians, you'll recall, who claimed that the historical longevity of Christianity was evidence for its truth. That raises some obvious questions. Is a religious understanding or tradition more true the longer it survives? Is it less true the shorter time it survives? In a way, yes. But we must keep in mind here that we are not talking about factual truth and that, in any case, survival is only one of the measures (criteria) in terms of which religious understanding is weighed.

In the light of this, what can we say about modernity and the new cosmological story? Certainly it is true that modernity has survived for over three hundred years. That must be some indication of its human effectiveness, at least until now. Will it continue? Obviously, how long each of these stories will continue to survive historically remains to be seen.

10. *An ethical and critical sense.* Surely, we are all aware that such myths as absolute power, racisms of various kinds, some forms of nationalism, some varieties of 'liberation,' and even the constant demand for 'progess' at the cost of members of the larger family of nature cannot and should not be taken on their own terms. At the end of the twentieth century, most of us are painfully aware that such human myths are not only unethical but humanly ineffective precisely because they are so thoroughly unethical. We need to step back from such myths, then, to critically unmask them for what they are and to insist that they live up to serious ethical standards. In other words, we can neither ignore myth nor take it at face value. Not only must we approach it with suspicion, but one of the primary criteria in terms of which we assess its effective truth must be the degree to which it lives up to the fundamental standards of ethical and social behavior which we all demand of ourselves. Those visions of human reality which marginalize or even victimize other peoples, classes, or races not only should be ethically judged as morally and spiritually inadequate, but precisely to that degree should be rejected as 'untrue' visions of human life and history. Put in a more positive manner, we can demand that, to be 'true,' religious interpretive understandings must seek to integrate and incorporate different cultures and cultures of difference into their vision of life. Our time has surely taught us that, to the best of our ability, we must be ready to apply standards of ethics as best we see them. Narrowness, victimization, exclusivism, and intolerance simply do not fit ethically into the present economic, political, and spiritual situation because—among other things—that situation increasingly demands interconnection and interaction between different cultures.

Is it ethical to spiritually flatten and narrow our lives in the pursuit of greater production and control? Is it ethical to sacrifice quality of life for quantity of material goods? Is it ethical to simply declare that another human vision of life is factually false and thus not to be tolerated, never mind accepted? Is it ethical to rule other religious myths and forms of life out of order because they are different from ours? For that matter, is it ethical to sacrifice nature in general or even particular entities within nature for the (possibly) myopic human goals of comfort and security? I don't know. But I do know that these kinds of questions are (or should be) part of the way we assess different religious understandings of life.

These ten evaluative criteria, then, constitute the informal procedures which we can and do use to measure the unique kind of truth involved in narrative religious understanding. They help us weigh the degree to which such religious truth claims fulfill the task or purpose of such understanding.

6:4 Objections

Some might object to these evaluative criteria on at least two grounds. First, it might be argued that the very criteria—along with the whole philosophical perspective in which they are embedded—are the result of a particular interpretive way of 'seeing' reality, and therefore are incommensurate and inapplicable to other philosophical interpretations with their own sets of evaluative or evidential criteria. Second, a critic might claim that the very application of these evaluative criteria—the assessment of the degree to which a religious truth claim meets those criteria—is tied up with the evaluator's own particular interpretive framework. Both of these criticisms, it seems to me, are to a large degree quite well taken.

I argued earlier that any philosophical perspective is a kind of interpretive, mythological expression and that, as such, it defines not only what philosophy is but what constitutes adequate philosophical argumentation and evidence. Clearly, then, as R.M. Hare has put it, the various mythological interpretations of life (philosophies, historical revelations, and mythologies) are like 'bliks.' They are points of view which cannot be rationally justified outside their own interpretive framework because the very notion and criteria of justification are internally generated within them.

> With a *blik* there can be no explanation; for it is by our *bliks* that we decide what is and what is not an explanation.[14]

I also claimed that the very act of mythological interpretation necessarily involves framing or seeing reality (including other points of view) through the interpreter's pre-existing set of interpretive or mythological glasses. What this comes down to, then, is that none of us can escape or pretend to stand outside a hermeneutical position. As we said earlier, *there is and can be no God's eye point of view.* On the other hand, that does not mean that such interpretations—along with the evaluative criteria or standards of truth they entail—are merely subjective illusions projected upon reality or that all we have and can have is a host of mutually exclusive universes of discourse in closed and hostile contact with one another. On the contrary, I argued that that view of things is caught in the assumptions of modernity. From the point of view of modernity, you will recall, fundamental interpretive truth claims must be either objectively true or subjectively false, but not both. As opposed to that vicious dilemma, I suggested that interpretation is a "dialogical act" which involves both the evaluator's interpretive glasses as well as the very reality (or text) which is being interpreted. We necessarily see the world and other interpretations from a particular standpoint, yes, but in such seeing we also disclose and make available aspects of it hitherto unseen. Beyond objective truth and subjective illusion there lies a third kind of understanding— interpretive or mythological understanding—with its own unique evaluative procedures. On the one hand, none of these visions of life is absolute or exclusively true for they are not factual or objective claims at all. On the other hand, each of these religious visions is true as an interpretive understanding of life. We are fated by the human condition, then, to weigh and assess different interpretive religious traditions when we encounter them. Surely we ought to do so with a recognition that we are not only finitely situated within an interpretive perspective but also liable within it to be influenced by self-interest and even self-deception. Although such mutual evaluations of different religious perspectives are not mere subjective illusion, still the possibilities of distortion and dismissal are so humanly real that we need to maintain as tolerant and open an attitude toward other perspectives as possible.

In response to the second criticism that all evaluations of religious truth claims are tainted with hermeneutical constraints, I would say, "Of course." All forms of religious evaluation contain interpretive elements and thereby take sides. That means that there can be no such thing as religious certainty about the evaluation of various religious claims. It's a tough life, a life in which there is no certainty about how best to live or who 'I' or 'we' are to become. We live in a world of ambiguity, as Maurice Merleau-Ponty might have put it, a spiritual world in which nothing is certain except the fact that there is no certainty in such matters. Furthermore, since it is a world in which religious truth involves the actual bringing of a vision of how best to live life into being, then such religious interpretive understanding necessarily involves risk and commitment beyond theory and fact.

Finally, it is a world in which we find ourselves in increasing contact with different points of view and in which the very plurality of religious traditions and views forces us to make evaluations for our own lives. It seems to me that all we can do in such a world is acknowledge the differences and strive to maintain dialogue with those other views while remaining aware of and taking responsibility for our own fundamental attitudes.

Part III

Denouement

Surveying the Promised Land

The erosion of meaning and coherence in our lives is not something Americans desire. Indeed, the profound yearning for the idealized small town that we found among most of the people we talked to is a yearning for just such meaning and coherence. But although the yearning for the small town is nostalgia for the irretrievably lost, it is worth considering whether the biblical and republican traditions that small town once embodied can be reappropriated in ways that respond to our present need. Indeed, we would argue that if we are ever to enter that new world that so far has been powerless to be born, it will be through reversing modernity's tendency to obliterate all previous culture. We need to learn again from the cultural riches of the human species and to reappropriate and revitalize those riches so that they can speak to our condition today.

Robert Bellah, *Habits of the Heart*

7:1 To Reiterate

That's the story. Religious understanding, which began as mythology and historical revelation but soon developed into an inclusive, allegorical 'wisdom' during the pre-modern or traditional period, was simply set aside during the Enlightenment in favor of the modern worldview's limitation of knowledge to matters of fact and matters of reason. That reduction of human understanding, as we saw, not only eliminated the traditional conception of religious understanding or wisdom, but at the same time was a Pandora's box which, when opened, released a swarm of spiritual issues or difficulties which have characterized the modern period until our own time. This not only made genuine religious life and understanding increasingly difficult, but it led to the possible annihilation of nature (and ourselves) at the hands of an omnivorous and all-powerful industrial-consumer culture fostered by it.

This modern overview was in turn part of a larger story, namely the claim to do away with mythology entirely in favor of a worldview solidly founded (foundationalism) on empirical or mathematical knowledge. That, of course, has turned out to be an illusion. Although it claimed otherwise and had blinded itself to this factor until recently, modernity itself rested upon a nonempirical interpretive understanding of the nature of reality (being) and the human role and destiny within it. It was just another story—this time "the story to end all stories."

Like other such worlds of oriented meaning and behavior, then, the modern world was itself based on a story—a founding mythology which narratively manifested and made available to human consciousness an overarching vision of nature and human historical purpose. The story was that human beings had always sought control over nature as a secure refuge from her viscissitudes, but they did not properly or adequately understand the working of that nature because they did not understand the nature of scientific knowledge. Now, the story goes on, we have learned how to know, we have discovered that knowledge proper is limited to matters of fact and matters of reason. Such scientific understanding *is* power since it leads rather directly to our ability to control nature and thereby opens the future to the industrial and technological domination and manipulation of reality (nature). By this means, we are told, a bountiful future of 'progress' has become possible for humans, a future in which there is no need for other forms of human knowledge (e.g., myth) and in which we will witness the progessive and unending domination of nature through science and industry for strictly human ends. Nature, it seemed to be assumed, is so vast and self-sustaining that it is virtually inexhaustable.

This extraordinary and powerful myth is a vision of life which (along with the industrial-consumer society that emerged from it) has spread around the world and either altered or obliterated the more traditional worldviews with which it has come in touch. But its influence has been far from all bad. On the contrary, as we noted earlier, it was deeply and broadly beneficial to human beings in many ways. Yet it also led to a narrowing of—if not an outright demise of—serious spiritual understanding and life, as well as the evident environmental difficulties of which we are just now becoming aware.

As we saw, the discovery of the mythological or hermeneutical dimension underlying modernity led to what has been termed 'postmodernity.' More specifically, it led not only to a criticism of modernity but also to an altered conception of knowledge or understanding in the human arts and sciences. This conception of interpretive and narrative understanding, I claimed, changes the very way we conceive of science, the arts and humanities, the human sciences, and philosophy. In a way, it returns us to the more down-to-earth, modest, situated and contextualized intellectual attitude that existed before the Enlightenment decontextualized matters in its haste to reduce reality to the clean but abstract certainty of logic and mathematics. Stephen Toulmin has put it this way.

> Since the 1960s, then, both philosophy and science are back in the intellectual postures of the last generation *before* Descartes. In natural science, the imperial dominion of physics over all other fields has come to an end: ecologists and anthropologists can now look astronomers and physicists straight in the eye. In philosophy, Descartes' formalist wish—to refute the skepticism of the Renaissance humanists, by substituting the abstract demands of logical certainty for their concrete reliance on human experience—is now seen to have led the enterprise of philosophy into a dead end. Scientifically and philosophically, that is, we are freed from the exclusively theoretical agenda of rationalism, and can take up again the practical issues sidelined by Descartes' *coup d'etat* some 300 years ago.[1]

It changed the very picture of what is involved in human understanding in general, then, and in the process significantly shaped a postmodern conception of religious understanding.

We went on to develop that postmodern model of religious knowledge and truth as an alternative and antidote to the constricted and spiritually destructive modern view. From this postmodern perspective, religious understanding—whether in the form of mythology, historical revelation, or philosophical system—is a kind of responsive interpretive act which makes available an overarching vision of what life is for. Insofar as a people respond to the demand disclosed within it, they constitute different cultural 'worlds' in which they live out (behave) the hermeneutical understanding it contains—e.g., the apocalyptic world of the Dead Sea sects, the Confucian world of Sung Dynasty China, or the modern world of Europe since the Enlightenment.

We have seen that narrative interpretive understanding founds human worlds or cultures and that it is an inevitable and necessary form of human understanding. We are all born into a story about reality and human destiny, and the changing of such stories entails spiritual pain. At the same time, we discussed a recently articulated cosmological story which narratively makes available a new, postmodern vision of reality and human destiny in relationship to it. Suddenly, a new kind of contemporary creation myth has emerged which is not only consistent with present science but in fact a development of it. It may help us renew ourselves spiritually while at the same time starting the difficult process of healing the earth from the devastating assaults of industrialism.

We have here, then, new possibilities of and for religious understanding. Indeed, I have argued that a whole shift of worldview has occurred from modernity to postmodernity, a shift which not only entails a new understanding of religious knowledge and truth but the possibility for the first time of seriously addressing some of the spiritual maladies and issues which we have inherited from modernity and which in effect constitute our spiritual situation. Many commentators think so. Brian Swimme, for example, has put it this way:

> We are in the midst of a revelatory experience of the universe that must be compared in magnitude with those of the great religious revelations. And we need only wander about [like the early Christians] telling this story to ignite a transformation of humanity.[2]

It seems to be a time of great promise, then. Indeed, if the metaphor is not too farfetched, we seem poised like the ancient Israelites before a promised land, a land in which we might not only be able to *think* about our religious lives differently, but might also be able to *live* them differently and more genuinely than before.

We need to ask ourselves at this point exactly what the 'promise' is of that new world which seems to lie before us. We need to survey the promised land, if you will, to take its measure before we fully enter it. I think we can best accomplish that here by outlining what I believe are some of the implications of our postmodern model of religious understanding for our present spiritual situation. Since that situation is defined and circumscribed by the issues we have inherited from modernity, we need to bring this model of religious knowledge to bear upon those issues.

7:2 Rejoining the Tradition of Religious Understanding

Insofar as modernity reduced all knowledge to matters of fact and matters of reason, it made the by-then traditional perennial wisdom (mythology, historical revelation, and allegorical metaphysical systems) quite impossible. We argued that this left any possible form of religious understanding during the modern period in hopeless confusion and disarray.

Our postmodern interpretation of religious understanding, on the other hand, rejoins that earlier tradition. It does this by renewing in a different form the premodern tradition in which religious and philosophical knowledge were seen to be aspects of a single perennial wisdom. This perennial wisdom—or religious understanding as we have termed it—includes mythology, historical revelation, and philosophical system. But rather than being understood as it had been earlier as literally true myths or revelations which can then be allegorically interpreted as metaphysics, religious understanding is now seen to be narrative interpretive understanding which manifests itself in a variety of (at least three) different forms.

Put another way, we can say that this postmodern model of interpretive understanding is a sort of postcritical naivete. That is, while critically going beyond the traditional naivete of literalness as had modernity, it also transcends the myth of critical rationality underlying modernity itself to make available a postmodern form of interpretive understanding which uncovers the traditional stories at a higher (later) level.

Our strategy here has not been to deny the cognitive aspect of faith in order to make room for it in a world of scientific reason. Rather, it has been to claim for such faith its own unique form of understanding outside and beyond science. The final step in our strategy has been to argue that modernity itself (in which the scientific endeavor came into its own) is also a worldview or faith beyond scientific fact and logical deduction. John Smith expresses the point I am trying to make very clearly in a recent article:

> It belongs to man as man in the world to raise the religious question of the ground and goal of his own existence, so that some form of religious concern is inescapable. . . . Instead of establishing some standard of rationality on the basis of science and common sense, and then asking whether religious belief is "rational" in that sense, we must attempt to make critical comparisons between beliefs within the universe of discourse established by the religions themselves and their secular counterparts.[3]

7:3 Regaining the World of Ordinary Experience

Modernity lost sight of the world of ordinary experience insofar as it reduced reality to either 'things in themselves' or 'minds' which cognize them. I argued that to suppress and lose sight of that world of ordinary experience in favor, ultimately, of the world of object-things was to take away the only context in which religious understanding and religious behavior make sense.

Clearly, this postmodern interpretation of religious understanding is only possible because we can now see it (and religious activity in general) in the context of the experiential world from which it had been so violently and disastrously separated in the modern period. The rediscovery of that world of ordinary experience not only makes a more adequate understanding of religious behavior possible, but at the same time makes possible (hitherto an impossibility) an articulation in drama, philosophy, literature, art, and religious studies of the whole experiential complex of our lives, including most especially the religious phenomena it entails.

But this rediscovery of the world of ordinary experience has yet another benefit: it overcomes the old and very vicious dichotomy between science and mathematics on the one hand and the human arts and sciences (including religion) on the other. In other words, it fosters a healing of the breach between what C.P. Snow called the "two cultures." Both science and the arts and humanities, of course, take place in that world, and thus can be seen to be fragments or aspects of that encompassing, experiential whole.

> We are not to suppose that the world is made up of two different kinds of individuals—men of science and men of faith, each dwelling in a separate sphere. There is simply man confronting himself, other persons, the world, and whatever other realities there may be, and life in the world requires *both* knowledge about it and some resolution of the problem to which religion speaks, namely who we are, why we are, and what the whole thing means.[4]

Furthermore, both the natural and human arts and sciences presuppose what we have termed interpretive mythological understanding. By illuminating the narrative interpretive understanding tied up with myth and philosophy, and by noticing that modernity itself was based upon such a mythological understanding of human history and destiny, we now have the breathtaking opportunity to see life as whole once again. Needless to say, such a unified vision of life has clearly been a goal of both philosophy and religion from their very beginnings, and the glaring lack of such a comprehensive vision in the modern period constituted a painful and all-too-evident scandal to both.

7:4 Overcoming Spiritual Schizophrenia

Until recently, much intellectual analysis of religion was sidetracked by the modern assumption that religious beliefs were much the same as scientific hypotheses. That, of course, ultimately led to the positivist notion that if such beliefs were not verifiable or falsifiable, then they must in fact be meaningless. It also led some religious apologists such as the creationists to take the Biblical stories of creation as literally true, as if those stories were in the same family of propositions as admittedly scientific hypotheses. All of this seems to be a giant category mistake in which science and religion, empirical matters of fact and mythology, are simply run together and confused. We have claimed, of course, that religiously 'seeing' the world 'as' hospitable and life-sustaining is a different order of discourse from empirical hypotheses such as the rate of descent of falling bodies or genetic factors involved in some forms of human disease. Put another way, we have argued that religious understanding is simply a different form of human understanding than either inductive hypotheses or deductive syllogisms.

Because it had reduced all knowledge to the paradigm of either empirical induction or logical deduction, modernity simply obliterated the traditional understanding of religious knowledge. At the same time, it interpreted religious understanding (in the light of its underlying mythology) as either subjective illusion or objective and increasingly exclusivistic truth. This led in turn to what we called earlier ''the twin specter of meaninglessness and dogmatism'' which seems so characteristic of our modern culture.

Whereas modernity led to a schizoid spiritual situation in which the only possible religious choices were limited to either a religious dogmatism and exclusivism or skeptical relativity, our postmodern view of religious understanding suggests a third alternative. Religious knowledge is neither objective nor subjective, but rather a narrative act which makes available an interpretation (hermeneutic) of life as a meaningful whole, a vision of life within which we then concretely live and act, not unlike the way fish live in water or birds in air. 'Truth' from this point of view is not a matter of correspondence so much as it is degree of disclosure.

That there is such a thing as religious truth, I argued, permits genuine spiritual commitment and exploration, for it is only if a religious view is in some sense or other 'true' that someone will pursue it. On the other hand, we have here a kind of understanding and truth which, as we saw earlier, can never be absolute or exclusively true.

With the support of John Hick and Paul Tillich, we claimed that no concrete interpretive understanding can ever be 'ultimate' or adequate to that reality (God) which it expresses, and that therefore no religious truth claim can ever be absolute or exclusively true. In the words of Tillich:

> Must the encounter of faith with faith lead either to tolerance without criteria or to an intolerance without self-criticism? If faith is understood as the state of being ultimately concerned, this alternative is overcome. The criterion of every faith is the ultimacy of the ultimate which it tries to express. The self-criticism of every faith is the insight into the relative validity of the concrete symbols in which it appears.[5]

It seems to me, then, that we have in this postmodern conception of religious understanding the possibility of genuine religious truth which at the same time permits real pluralism and toleration. Surely this is no small matter in a shrinking (and yet increasingly violent) world in which various religious traditions are in head-on collision with one another.

7:5 New Possibilities for Religious Life

Modernity, then, forced on our culture a disastrous spiritual choice between skeptical meaninglessness and exclusivistic and increasingly fanatical dogmatism. I argued earlier that this constricted choice made religious life almost impossible, certainly for the more educated of our population. On the one hand, the educated can see the foundationlessness as well as the danger involved in the fanatical horn of the dilemma. On the other hand, no one would willingly choose meaninglessness and pure relativity in life. Thus, the modern religious situation is one in which we daily witness the simultaneous growth of both fanaticism and meaninglessness. As each grows, it is hauntingly and painfully mirrored by the other: the more a sense of skepticism and meaninglessness stalks the world, the more we see the development of absolutistic and fanatical religious claims. And the more such dogmatic sects spread, the more the educated and cultured are pushed into lives of painful skepticism and meaninglessness.

I think our postmodern paradigm of religious understanding, on the other hand, is an alternative which permits intelligent, informed, and genuine spiritual commitment and growth. It avoids both skeptical relativism and historicism as well as a narrow dogmatism. Rather, it sees faith and religious understanding as an interpretive understanding (beyond empirical hypotheses and mathematics) of how best to live our lives. Such understanding is both a necessary aspect of human life as well as an inevitably limited and finite vision which can never claim absolute and exclusive truth.

7:6 The Interpretation of Myth and Revelation

To the degree that modernity lost the sense of interpretive, metaphorical discourse, it came to view the interpretation of life, mythology, and historical revelation as either a factual matter that is literally the case or merely human illusion. I argued that this is a naive understanding of interpretation which has simply never looked at what goes on in the act of interpretation whether it be of some sort of text or reality itself. Furthermore, it myopically ignores the fact that the view that interpretation is either fact or human concoction is itself not a fact but a kind of unillumined interpretation.

But, more importantly, this has led to the disastrous modern phenomenon of treating mythology and revelation (e.g., scripture) as either literally true or merely a human invention, thereby (I think) missing the metaphorical and hermeneutical point of such mythology and scripture. To limit interpretation to this sorry choice is really to miss the religious point. For example, to limit our understanding of Buddha's birth as disclosed in the *Jataka* tales to a matter of its literal truth is, I claimed, simply to overlook the interpretive and very human dimension it is loudly and narratively proclaiming in favor of a modern obsession with factual knowledge. In other words, it says more about that modern interpreter than it does about the *Jataka* stories or, for that matter, Gotama Buddha. Obviously, the same is true of such other important religious stories (myths or historical revelations) as the Garden of Eden, Exodus, the virgin birth of Jesus, the resurrection of Jesus (as we shall see in a moment), or even the dream of a perfect communist society which will arrive as a kingdom of heaven on earth.

Our postmodern view, on the other hand, is a conception of metaphorical interpretation which permits an alternative understanding of myth, revelation, and scripture. From this point of view, such matters have nothing to do with scientific truth. Rather, they are the symbolic means by which human cultures articulate an overarching interpretation of what it means to be, thereby spelling out for themselves ideal or possible ways of being unknowable in any other way. Myth and revelation in this case are neither scientific facts nor scientific lies, and neither the meaning of Marduk's slaying of the monster Tiamat in the Babylonian *Enuma Elish* nor the empty tomb of Jesus can be fit into such a constricted interpretive framework. On the contrary, they are mythological and historical stories, which insofar as they are effective, give voice to a people's vision of life by making manifest a sacred dimension in terms of which they can 'see' this life 'as' a meaningful whole.

A good example of the difficulty of being unaware or misunderstanding this alternative form of interpretive understanding recently emerged in Thomas Sheehan's otherwise interesting and sophisticated analysis of the resurrection stories in his recent book, *The First Coming: How the Kingdom of God Became Christianity*. By using the tools of recent scholarly critical analysis of the New Testament sources concerning the resurrection of Jesus after his crucifixion, Sheehan claims to demonstrate that both the traditional (conservative) and liberal interpretations of the resurrection events are quite impossible. The former (the traditional) is simply a naive, literalist, top-down view that is not confirmed by either the letters of Paul (the earliest evidence) or the various (and contradictory) gospel accounts. The liberal view, on the other hand, is that Easter did not constitute a literal, physical resurrection at all but the resurrection of Jesus into the Christ of faith. But if that resurrection is not literally true, he seems to say, then it must be a merely subjective belief on the part of the early Church, a belief which ultimately led the church to confuse the message of Jesus concerning the imminent arrival of the kingdom of heaven with the messenger—i.e., Jesus himself.

Sheehan himself rejects either view in favor of declaring that the stories of the resurrection are—beneath all the accretions and additions by the New Testament community—about the "absolute absence of Jesus."[6] He seems to be claiming that, if the resurrection can't be accepted as physically and factually true then it must be simply the subjective desire of faith that has created the illusion that it is.[7] That's in effect what Sheehan thinks underlay the early church's confusion of the proclamation of Jesus with Jesus the proclaimer. This view, it appears to me, has fallen into the typical modern dialectic: either a claim is factually true or it must be a subjective illusion based on the human desire for it. From Sheehan's point of view, Jesus died and that's that. The messenger is dead and all that remains is his message about the possibility of an ideal kingdom of heaven on earth, a kingdom suffused with justice, equity, and love.

It is noteworthy that Sheehan claims that the symbolism of the empty tomb really means that at the core of human life is a restless yearning and "desire for that which can never be met," a desire for more, a desire which endlessly seeks an unrealizable being. It is this desire which makes us (in the words of Sartre) "a futile passion": without it we would be either God or another kind of entity lacking this desire "that exceeds the possibility of being fulfilled."[8]

I believe that the view of interpretive understanding which I have tried to explore in this essay is (in spite of Sheehan's experience and sophistication with respect to hermeneutics) an alternative position. First of all, from my point of view, the question of the resurrection is neither factual truth nor factual error (mere subjective illusion or desire). That means that when Sheehan (and New Testament scholars) show that the resurrection stories not only do not verify such a factual claim but actually raise questions about it by contradicting one another, that does not lead to the conclusion that they are therefore merely subjective desires and projections by Jesus' broken-hearted followers in an emotionally intolerable situation. His view—to put it plainly—is pervaded not only by modern biases but by a sort of (Sartrian) humanism which is, of course, an absolutely alternative (to Christianity) faith or interpretive understanding. In other words, Sheehan acts as if he is free of such interpretive perspective and that his view just happens to be the case. On the contrary, I believe that the view is deeply shaped by modernity and a resultant humanism. Surprisingly, he does not take the radicality of hermeneutics quite seriously enough.

From the postmodern perspective we have been outlining, on the other hand, the resurrection stories (like the *Jataka* tales) are symbolic narratives which interpretively make available a Christian vision of reality and human destiny which—as the New Testament makes clear—transformed the lives of those who were touched by them. And, rather than operations useful in testing claims to factual truth, of course, the truth of such interpretive religious understandings is more appropriatly weighed and measured in terms of the evaluative criteria peculiar to it.

In my opinion, Sheehan is closer to the nub of the matter when he tells us that after we realize that Jesus was not (factually) resurrected we will realize that "we remain, fundamentally, an act of questioning to which there is no answer."[9] This is closer insofar as he realizes that there can be no factual answers to religious questions in our lives. On the other hand, his way of expressing it seems (remarkably) still deeply infected with modern interpretive biases. He calls the object of such awareness, for example, "absolute absence," "the absurd", "that which is absolutely deaf (*surdus*) to our desire to render it present in any way," and he claims that it leads to "*the end of religion.*"[10] Notice in what follows that he discusses 'God' as if that were a special kind of all-powerful object-entity which might be present to human consciousness, a *Deus Abscondicus* which as a matter of fact has withdrawn into transcendence and which therefore remains hidden from us. What sort of peculiar picture is it that he has of God that can lead him to say of God that He "is an unsurpassable absence that cannot be changed into any form of presence"?

> There is no Jesus to be found anywhere anymore, neither here nor elsewhere. The women who went to the tomb and found absolutely nothing—and we too who observe their pilgrimage— may leave the grave with the awareness that, as regards Jesus and his God, there is nothing to be found and therefore nothing to be searched for. The meaning of the dead prophet is an unsurpassable absence that cannot be changed into any form of presence.[11]

All of this seems to be a sort of contemporary form of deconstruction with a variety of modern biases intact. The assumption that the only alternative to factual truth must be nominalist error ("the end of religion") is the first of these biases. In fact, as I have tried to argue, religious understanding is neither. But secondly, it seems extraordinary to me to treat God as a sort of entity that is "hidden" and that could be "present" if only He existed. Rather, from my point of view, 'God' is not a thing at all, but a symbol for the mysterious, indefinable, transcendence of reality (being). As such, God is not an onto-theological thing that might be present, that can be conceived not to exist, and that we can (or could if we could penetrate his hiddenness to find him) contain in a definition, concept, or particular set of predicates. It is not a 'something' in any case which is hidden (like Dorothy's uncle in the *Wizard of Oz*) behind a curtain of transcendence and which, if that curtain could be pushed aside, would be present 'there' for consciousness to grasp. Such a God would be simply another finite something or other and thus not ultimate at all. Rather, this transcendent Being is made available to the experience of wonder precisely *as mystery* at the boundaries of reason. Wonder, as we saw earlier, is not something to be overcome and thus replaced with solid answers, for there is no answer here in the usual sense. In fact, it is not propositional at all, but an experience of the amazing and miraculous existence of anything at all which we then display and represent to ourselves and others in founding narratives or myths. Annie Dillard captures something of this miraculous effervescence of being in the following:

If the landscape reveals one certainty, it is that the extravagant gesture is the very stuff of creation. After the one extravagant gesture of creation in the first place, the universe has continued to deal exclusively in extravagances, flinging intricacies and colossi down aeons of emptiness, heaping profusions on profligacies with ever-fresh vigor. The whole show has been on fire from the word go. I come down to the water to cool my eyes. But everywhere I look I see fire; that which isn't flint is tinder, and the whole world sparks and flames.[12]

7:7 Religious Renewal

From a modern point of view, religious renewal has been interpreted for the most part as either denial of present conditions in favor of a fixed and settled past or a dismissal of past interpretations in favor of completely present demands. Thus, renewal has typically been construed to be either conservative or liberal, but not both, and not some third alternative. On the one hand, we are urged to return to some particular interpretation within a tradition which is considered by someone or other to be orthodox: for example, the letters of Paul as opposed to the theology of St. Augustine, or Theravadin as opposed to Mahdyamika Buddhism. By this means we simply deny and close ourselves to the interpretive demands of the present as well as other points of view in favor of our own myopic vision. On the other hand, liberal modernists urge us to demythologize or otherwise reduce the interpretation of a scripture or historical revelation to contemporary understanding, language and concerns, thereby casting us adrift in a sea of complete relativity. This ultimately leads, as we have seen, to the kind of skeptical disorientation which seems so much a part of our modern situation.

From the perspective of our postmodern conception of interpretive religious understanding, that vicious dichotomy between conservative or liberal interpretations seems naive and much too simple. From this point of view, genuine religious renewal consists of an interpretive act which is *both* a renewal of the past *and* at the same time a responsive translation of it which meets the conditions and needs of the present interpreter(s). Thus, the term *renewal* here does not signify either a reduction of the present to the past or an obliteration of the past in favor of now, but rather a genuine responsive understanding which finds in the tradition hermeneutical demands helpful to us in our particular situation here and now.

We can put this another way. Following Paul Ricoeur, we might characterize premodern or traditional religious life as a kind of uncritical 'first naivete' which ultimately was transcended by the reflective and critical gaze of modernity which then made such naive living quite impossible. Postmodernity, on the other hand, critically scrutinized the assumptions of that modern period and thereby brought into the open the hitherto unnoticed mythological or hermeneutical understanding underlying it. The postmodern period, then, has been conditioned by both the traditional naivete as well as the modern criticism of it. But at the same time it has discovered, if you will, a new level of hermeneutical understanding beyond but underlying and conditioning both. What that means (again in the words of Ricoeur) is that the postmodern stage is a kind of 'second naivete' which critically reflects on both the traditional and modern periods from a hermeneutical standpoint. It is a second naivete in that it cannot 'believe' in the same naive sense as seemed to be the case in the traditional period because critical modernity has made us too aware of the empirical and historical limitations of such a literalist posture. On the other hand, as opposed to modernity, it is a second naivete which can reflectively recover on the postmodern and hermeneutical level what the traditional faith was all about.[13] Religious renewal here means going back to or renewing the traditional religious life, but now with the critical insights of modernity intact and in the light of our present postmodern awareness of the inevitability of religious interpretive understanding within the human condition. In other words, religious myths and revelations are neither facts nor mere illusions, but articulations of what it means to be, interpretive visions of how we ought to live. Renewal means interpretively to respond to and take up the tradition, but now from a postcritical perspective and in the face of our present needs and awareness. Robert Bellah puts this beautifully in the final words of his book, *Habits of the Heart*:

> Such a vision is neither conservative nor liberal in terms of the truncated spectrum of present American political discourse. It does not seek to return to the harmony of a 'traditional' society, though it is open to learning from the wisdom of such societies. It does not reject the modern criticism of all traditions, but it insists in turn on the criticism of criticism, that human life is lived in the balance between faith and doubt.[14]

7:8 Rumors of Reverence in Industrial Society

As we have seen, the human drive for security in a sometimes hostile and inevitably niggardly nature was reinforced and at least initially enhanced by the modern discovery that we can control and dominate nature by properly and appropriately understanding it. That is, we learned how to know in precisely the sense of mastering nature for human ends. That discovery of scientific and mathematical knowledge, then, constituted a vision of human destiny as the widening and progressive control and transformation of nature into products useful for human comfort and health. Of course, it was a vision which simply assumed (as we have since learned not to assume) that nature is so vast—so infinite and inexhaustible—that we need not be concerned for her welfare. It was by this means, I argued, that industrial, consumer societies have come to characterize modern life. And that industrial technology in turn brought us to the present environmental crisis in which we are literally befouling and poisoning the earth and air while depleting (and in fact devastating) the natural environment which sustains us all. The explosive growth of human population along with the equally explosive assault on the environment in order to support that population cannot go on for it turns out that this earth is actually a finite, interactive, and interdependent ecological system with real limits.

In response to this, a new, postmodern cosmological story has emerged which may help us forestall what seems to be the seemingly inevitable, suicidal result of all that 'progress.' Like other such cosmological myths, this story displays not only an interpretive understanding of what is most significant about life (how to live most fully and deeply) but the human role and destiny within it. It began twenty billion years ago, and from the very beginning it has been characterized by both a creative, effervescent eruption into life of myriad forms of being and an equally creative integration of new levels of existence into systematic wholes.

Ultimately (after billions of years of this fecund eruption of being, and only a few million years ago) human cultures emerged in which a reverential awareness of the incredible creative core of reality was displayed in their myths and rituals (especially death rituals). This human, cultural level was a sudden and astonishing 'higher' order of existence, a new and creative plane of existence hitherto unknown. Through human consciousness, reality had now achieved an explicit consciousness of itself. At the same time, after those billions of years of unfolding creativity, human beings had reached a point at which they were free to creatively define and determine themselves by envisaging in myth a future being which they actively sought to actualize.

After the Paleolithic, Neolithic, and Classical stages of culture, the modern age emerged as one more such human self-determination.

It was, as we have seen, a culture founded on the myth of human power and the progressive domination and management of nature. In terms of the larger, encompassing story of the evolution of nature, of course, that modern culture constituted an alienation of human culture and life from its proper role (as defined by the myth) of being reverentially aware of the mysterious transcendence and creativity at the heart of nature. At the same time, of course, it was an alienation in which human culture—by 'seeing' life 'as' an opportunity merely to assure human security through industrial technology—assaulted and threatened that encompassing reality with destruction. Human beings had lost their spiritual way. They had lost themselves and, in the process, threatened to destroy everything else as well.

All of this constitutes an overarching cosmological myth which makes available an interpretive vision of human life within the larger context of reality itself. The human role, from this point of view, is to become conscious of the sacred nature of creation through the sense of wonder. The story makes clear that human culture lost its way and (instead) reduced reality to a mere material occasion for the fulfillment of anthropocentric desires and dreams. This self-centered and alienated life, the story goes on, is not only the cause of our spiritual poverty but the fundamental reason for the suicidal devastation of the environment we are presently witnessing.

It may be that this new cosmological story will provide a founding interpretive vision of a postmodern and ecological culture. That remains to be seen. At any rate, it may contribute to such an understanding insofar as it makes the experience of God possible once again and insofar as it helps us to restrain—or should I say redirect—our industrial power toward environmental responsibility.

First of all, it seems to me that this story embodies a more coherent sense of God and transcendence than the traditional theistic perspective. From this point of view, God is not some sort of entity (how could God be an entity and still be nonfinite and ultimate?) who is apart (what in the world could 'apart' mean?) from creation and hidden (transcendent) from us by that separation. Rather, God is the name for reality itself—that mysterious, indefinable, nonfinite, creative effervescence which permeates nature as the astonishing and remarkable *beingness* of things. This is, of course, a panentheistic view which envisages God as available within nature but as *more* than any (or all) of the entities which constitute it and *more* than any possible conception of it. It makes God available to experience within nature once again through the sense of wonder rather than being simply hypothesized to exist. Finally, it overcomes the disastrous split between mind and matter, value and fact, religion and science which, as we saw, characterized the modern view. That view desacralized and emptied experience and nature of the divine and left it to become the raw material for industrial power.

But second, insofar as it actually helps us to experience wonder, it may to that degree transform our lives so that we can experience a reverence for nature instead of the present disdain for it which seems so characteristic of our industrial attitude. And, to the degree that happens, perhaps we can alter those industrial practices enough to heal and sustain the environment. In other words, this story may help us develop a more sane industrial technology by helping us become aware of our responsibility to and for the whole earth.

7:9 New Possibilities for Religious Dialogue

We saw earlier that modernity fostered a plethora of fragmented and apparently irreconcilable religious cultures and traditions, all claiming truth. To make matters worse, modern technological progress brought these often antagonistic traditions into close economic and political proximity and interdependence and at the same time armed them to the teeth. All of this is destablizing and dangerous, to say the least, doubly so to the degree that the modern world's fixation on factual knowledge has all too often led those traditions to dogmatism, absolutism, and (even) exclusivism with respect to their claims to understanding and truth.

In the meantime, I have argued for an alternative model of religious understanding and truth which, while certainly permitting those different spiritual traditions to claim truth, also recognizes that no tradition or religious perspective can claim that its views and practices are absolutely or exclusively true. This view of narrative religious truth, I have claimed, might help to ameliorate the dangerous confrontation of these different traditions and in fact soften their dialogue in the direction of mutual understanding and tolerance. Needless to say, that is the profound hope of all of us.

But there is something else in this emerging postmodern context which might stimulate such interreligious dialogue and understanding: the new cosmological story we have discussed above. This is an overarching story, as we saw, which is not only shared by postmodern science and theology, but a story which is being told around the world and to one degree or another across the whole spectrum of religious traditions. Because of this, it may serve as a basis for dialogue between those differing traditions. Of course, the story will be absorbed into those traditions by being interpreted and clothed in the images and metaphors which lie at their heart. Because of this, many commentators do not expect that a single spiritual perspective will replace them; but perhaps they will be interpretively modified by the new story in such a way that they can more easily move into dialogue with one another.

Put another way, it may be that the new cosmological story will help each of the different traditions rediscover its own form of wonder and gratitude for the mysterious gift of life in the light of the vision disclosed within it. That vision, after all, spells out that we are all earthlings—not just we human beings with our varying cultural perspectives—but the entire, astonishing panoply of beings which make up this one, integrated earth (*Gaia*). Thus, it may be a way to overcome those common, very dangerous, and truly painful 'isms' which are part of the fabric of the modern world: exclusivism, absolutism, dogmatism, ethnocentrism, and anthropomorphism. In the light of this new cosmic story, our destiny seems to be to acknowledge mystery, celebrate existence, and create a communal bond beyond these divisive 'isms,' not just with our fellow human beings but with all that is.

7:10 Yes, But is This Essay 'True'?

The question will surely arise: what about this essay? Is it true? In what sense? I argued earlier that no overarching philosophical perspective has been demonstrated to be true, and that in fact such an attempt would be circular in any case since the very definition of what constitutes a 'demonstration' is internally generated within the system. Furthermore, I claimed that for that reason the very notion of a 'founded' philosophy is farfetched, and that each philosophical perspective actually rests on an interpretive myth or hermeneutic. Insofar as a philosophy is the product of a human philosopher, I tried to show, it is necessarily founded on a narrative, religious interpretation of what it means to be. The entire articulated philosophy can be thought of as a peculiar alternative (to mythology and historical revelation) expression of that overarching interpretation. John Caputo makes this point very clearly in a recent article on hermeneutics and religious truth:

> Faith itself is a kind of hermeneutics, a way we have of reading the traces in the sand of human existence. That is true not only of faith, but a good many philosophers today are agreed that it is true of reason, too. Both faith and reason are ways of reading and construing, and both have no other recourse than to invoke historically conditioned models and linguistic artifacts. Faith is

a read we have on the human condition; it is not a supervenient gift coming from on high.[15]

What does that say about philosophical truth in general and the truth of this essay in particular? If it is merely one among a number of valid interpretations, can we term it 'true' at all? If it isn't factually the case, must it be simply this author's relative and nominal construal of life?

Because there is an unavoidable mystery and elusiveness about our lives, an aspect of reality which remains transcendent and hidden and thus can never be grasped, and because there are no solid, certain, univocal foundations for our human perspectives, Jacques Derrida seems to hold that there is no truth at all and that the passionate pursuit of it should simply be given up. This perspective, once again, seems to me to remain mired in the modern bias that if a claim is not verifiably true as a matter of fact then it must be mere illusion. I am arguing for an alternative view that holds that interpretive understanding is neither factually true nor factually false, but a more or less true or false *interpretive understanding* of life as a meaningful whole. At this level, as we have seen, evaluative procedures are quite different from empirical hypotheses and the question of its truth is not something we 'have,' but—if you will—something which 'has' us.

First of all, it seems pretty clear to me that this essay rests on my narrative, hermeneutical sense of being. Just as was the case with modernity, which rested upon a narrative myth concerning human history and destiny, so too this essay is an expression of *my* fundamental identity and way of seeing life. To the degree that I can be clear about this, I would say that what is most fundamental and basic about life for me is the mysterious, extravagant, and remarkably diverse existence of everything and anything at all. That is, wonder at the continuous and profligate creative emergence of my experience as a whole as well as the myriad entities which shine forth through it is that bedrock interpretive understanding which informs and shapes me and my story. The glasses through which I see life have something to do with this existential sense of the beauty and wonder in the concretia of actual experience—what I called "the world of ordinary experience"—and in the possibility of giving voice to (e-voking) various aspects of that experience. To be able to retouch and renew this sense of amazed wonder, to strive philosophically to articulate what's going on, to become as conscious as possible of this mysterious life we are living, to hold it still with words so that it can be langorously and lovingly beheld and appreciated are some of the ways I think I can best and most fully live. I didn't 'argue' myself into this hermeneutical sense, but I could tell you my story with the important events in my life through which it came about. And it underlies or pervades this entire essay as the interpretive standpoint from which the essay has been written.

In this larger sense, the essay is neither a matter of fact nor subjective and nominal, neither objectively 'true' nor merely a human illusion projected upon meaningless matter. Rather, it is as a whole an interpretive religious understanding which should be assessed like any other form of religious understanding—that is, in terms of the evaluative criteria outlined in the last chapter as appropriate to such understanding.

On the other hand, the phenomenological descriptions and claims which arise out of my hermeneutical sense are not in and of themselves hermeneutical. That is, my spiritual understanding of the beauty and wonder of experience drives me to phenomenology, but the actual phenomenological descriptions are true in a phenomenological and not hermeneutical sense. My existential sense is the set of glasses through which I frame this life and through which I see phenomenological reflection as significant and (overall) important and worth doing. (Why else would I do it?) I could never justify the phenomenological project of exploring existence 'phenomenologically,' for it rests on 'me' and grows out of 'my' (and others') interpretive understanding of life. On the other hand, that it rests on such a hermeneutic in no way dilutes the kind of phenomenological truths and understanding (or, for that matter, empirical claims) involved in this essay, including of course the description of religious or mythological understanding itself. Of course, as I indicated earlier, rather than Husserl's foundational sense of apodictic, phenomenological truths, I mean by such phenomenological truth descriptive evocations of experience which more or less display that experience. At any rate, just as empirical truths remain true even though one has questioned the modern mythology which led to them and found them significant, so too our phenomenological descriptions—insofar as they are adequate to their task—remain 'true' even though we know that someone must find them significant and meaningful enough to bother about.

To summarize, then, this essay is neither objectively true nor merely an illusion projected upon reality. It involves two other kinds of truth. First of all, it embodies overall a hermeneutical interpretation or understanding of life which must be assessed in terms of the unique criteria of religious understanding discussed in Chapter Six. But, it also utilizes phenomenological description which claims to be 'true' (like other forms of the human sciences) to the degree that it 'dis-closes' or makes available to reflective consciousness various aspects (phenomena) of our lived experience, including of course the narrative structure of our experience (personal identity) and the dimension of ultimate, narrative religious understanding.

Since this process hides the 'more' which *is* reality beyond that disclosed in the phenomenological description (the 'more' which haunts our lives at the boundaries of reason and which, as Socrates realized, calls us to further disclosures), and since in any case that very project of lovingly articulating aspects of our experience is not itself 'founded' but is generated by an interpretive vision of what is most significant about living, we seem fated to live at the crossroads of wonder. While we are astonished and bedazzled by the mysteriousness of our situation, we seem perpetually cutoff from certainty there, allured and yet confused by the roads which beckon us to try them out, encased and encompassed by ambiguity. And yet, each of us does—because each of us must—set out to journey down one of those roads. When we do, we take up our lives in fear and trembling and hurl them into the future. We set out to make real what until then was merely an interpretive vision of the end of the road by bringing it into being, thereby taking responsibility for it and for ourselves. This is not always an easy matter, and sometimes we try to avoid it by claiming that our perspective is well-grounded, founded, or otherwise a 'revealed truth' guaranteed by God himself. It is, however, at this crossroad of wonder—this bubbling, burgeoning place where we live— that we thread together ourselves in the light of a narrative construal of what is most sacred and real about life. It is an astonishing and creative event, parallel in some ways, perhaps, to God's own creativity. Indeed, perhaps it is a form of that divine creativity.

Reality—being—is our sacred text. We may not always see it, as some have claimed to do, as a perfect, clear, shining order gathered easily into a single story. We may in fact live several stories, or through suffering discover that the story we thought we were was all the while a mere subplot in a larger drama. That is because here there are no obvious foundations, no simple solutions; here there is only ambiguity and risk and bright-eyed wonder at the whole, astonishing affair.

Notes

Preface

1. Brockelman, Paul. *Time and Self: Phenomenological Explorations.* New York: American Academy of Religion Studies in Religion #39, Crossroad Publishing Co. and Scholars Press, 1985.

2. Hauerwas, Stanley. *Truthfulness and Tragedy.* Notre Dame, IN: University of Notre Dame Press, 1977, 73.

Introduction

1. Wolfhart Pannenberg, "Meaning, Religion and the Question of God," in *Knowing Religiously,* ed. Leroy S. Rouner (Notre Dame, IN: University of Notre Dame Press, 1985), 163.

2. Peter Berger, *The Heretical Imperative: Contemporary Possibilities of Religious Affirmation* (Garden City, NY: Anchor, 1980), xi, 21.

3. George W. Cornell, "Scholar Says West Sinks in Paganism," *Portsmouth Herald* (Portsmouth, NH: July 11, 1987), 7.

4. Boris Rumer, "Soviet Writers Decry Loss of Spiritual Values in Society," *The Christian Science Monitor* (Boston: October 7, 1986), 1.

5. Philip Rieff, *The Triumph of the Therapeutic* (New York: Harper & Row, 1966), 65, 70.

6. Robert Bellah, et al., *Habits of the Heart* (New York: Harper & Row, 1985), 295.

7. Peter Berger, *The Heretical Imperative,* 56.

8. Robin Wright, "Jewish Fundamentalism—New Political Force," *The Christian Science Monitor* (Boston: November 5, 1987), 18.

9. New York Times (New York: October 3, 1986).

10. David Tracy, "A Dissenting View," *New York Times Magazine* (New York: November 9, 1986), 24.

11. Francis A. Schaeffer, *He is There and He is not Silent* (Wheaton, IL: Tyndale House, 1982), 13, 16–17. Italics are Schaeffer's.

12. Karl Barth, *Church Dogmatics: The Doctrine of the Word of God,* trans. G.T. Thomson and Harold Knight (New York: Scribners, 1956), 350.

13. Hendrik Kraemer, *The Christian Message in a Non-Christian World,* (Italics are Kraemer's); quoted in Gavin D'Costa, *Theology and Religious Pluralism* (New York: Blackwell, 1986), 53.

14. Hendrik Kraemer, *The Christian Message,* 136.

15. D. Niles, "Karl Barth—A Personal Memory," *The South East Asian Journal of Theology,* Issue Number 11 (1969), 10–11.

16. Mathew Arnold, "Dover Beach," *Arnold: the Complete Poems,* ed. Kenneth Allott and Miriam Allott (London and New York: Longman, 1979), 257.

17. Peter Berger, *The Heretical Imperative,* 155.

18. Peter Slater, *The Dynamics of Religion* (New York: Harper & Row, 1978), xi.

19. Robert Bellah, *Habits of the Heart,* 283.

Chapter One

1. Mircea Eliade, "Myth in the Nineteenth and Twentieth Centuries," in *Dictionary of the History of Ideas,* vol. 3, ed. Philip P. Wiener (New York: Charles Scribner's Sons, 1973), 314.

2. For example, see William Bascom, "The Forms of Folklore: Prose Narratives," in *Journal of American Folklore,* 78 (1965), 4.

3. Mircea Eliade, *Myths, Rites, and Symbols,* ed. W.C. Beane and W.G. Doty (New York: Colophon, 1976), 7.

4. Mircea Eliade, *The Sacred and the Profane,* trans. W. Trask (New York: Harper & Row, 1961), 12.

5. Giles Gunn, "American Literature and the Imagination of Otherness," in *Religion as Story,* ed. James Wiggins (New York: Harper & Row,1975), 74.

6. Avery Dulles, *Models of Revelation* (New York: Doubleday, 1983), 3.

7. Jean Seznec, "Myth in the Middle Ages and Renaissance," in *Dictionary of the History of Ideas,* vol. 3, 287.

8. Robert Oden, *The Bible Without Theology* (San Francisco: Harper & Row, 1987) 40.

9. Arthur C. Danto, *Narration and Knowledge* (New York: Columbia University Press,1985), 142, 183.

10. Donald E. Polkinghorne, *Narrative Knowing and the Human Sciences* (Albany: State University of New York Press, 1988), 62.

11. James P. Mackey, *Modern Theology: A Sense of Direction* (Oxford: Oxford University Press, 1987), 60.

12. Robert Alter, *The Art of Biblical Narrative* (New York: Basic Books, 1983), 23.

13. See Robert M. Grant and David Tracy, *A Short History of the Interpretation of the Bible* (Philadelphia: Fortress Press, 1984), 85.

14. H.A. Wolfson, *Philo: Foundations of Religious Philosophy in Judaism, Christianity, and Islam* (Cambridge, MA: Harvard University Press, vol. 1, 1947), 134.

15. Plato, *The Republic*, 500c.

16. Plato, *Parmenides*, 132c–133a.

17. Mircea Eliade, *Myths, Dreams and Mysteries* (New York: Harper Colophon, 1975), 52–53.

18. Johannes Geffeken, "Allegory," in *The Encyclopedia of Religion and Ethics*, vol. 1, ed. James Hastings (New York: Charles Scribner's Sons, 1924), 330.

19. Note that this "perennial wisdom" is to be distinguished from that of Huston Smith and Fritzhof Shuon in, for example, Frithjof Schuon, *The Transcendent Unity of Religions* (New York: Harper & Row, 1975); and Huston Smith, *Forgotten Truth: the Primordial Tradition* (New York: Harper & Row, 1976).

20. Clifford Geertz, "Religion as a Cultural System," *The Interpretation of Cultures* (New York: Basic Books, 1973), 92–93.

21. E.A. Burtt, *The Metaphysical Foundations of Modern Science* (Garden City, NY: Doubleday, 1932).

22. Martin Heidegger, *Being and Time*, trans. John Macquarrie and Edward Robinson (New York: Harper & Row, 1962), section 32.

23. Langdon Gilkey, *The Sacred and Society* (New York: Crossroad, 1981), 94–95.

24. Stephen Toulmin, *Cosmopolis: The Hidden Agenda of Modernity* (New York: Free Press, 1990), 104.

25. Francis Bacon, *Novum Organum*, Second Book, in *Great Books of the Western World* (Chicago: Encyclopedia Britannica, vol. 30, 1952), 195.

26. Richard Rorty, *Philosophy and the Mirror of Nature* (Princeton: Princeton University Press, 1979), 322. Emphasis mine.

27. Terrence W. Tilley, *Story Theology* (Wilmington, DE: Michael Glazier, 1985), 34.

28. M. Berman, *All That is Solid Melts Into Air* (New York: Simon and Schuster, 1982), 15.

29. Stephen Toulmin, *Cosmopolis: The Hidden Agenda of Modernity*, 75.

30. Walter Kaufmann (ed.), *Religion from Tolstoi to Camus* (New York: Harper Torchbook, 1964), 177.

31. Francis Schaeffer, *He is There and He is not Silent* (Wheaton, IL: Tyndale House, 1982), 17.

32. Cited in Harold Coward, *Pluralism: Challenge to World Religions* (Maryknoll, NY: Orbis Books, 1985), 35–36.

33. G.W.F. Hegel, Foreword to H. Fr. Hinrich's *Die Religion in Inneren Verhaltnisse Zur Wissenschaft* (1822), trans. A.V. Miller, cited in Robert R. Williams, "Hegel and Schleiermacher on Theological Truth," *Meaning, Truth, and God*, ed. Leroy S. Rouner, (Notre Dame, IN: University of Notre Dame Press, 1982), 52.

34. Peter Berger, *The Heretical Imperative* (New York: Anchor, 1980), 10.

35. Peter Berger, *The Heretical Imperative*, 24.

36. See Hans Frei, *The Eclipse of Biblical Narrative* (New Haven: Yale University Press, 1974), 124–142.

37. David Klemm, *Hermeneutical Inquiry*, (Atlanta, GA: Scholars Press, 1986), vol. 1, 12.

39. James P. Mackey, *Modern Theology: A Sense of Direction*, 37.

40. James P. Mackey, *Modern Theology*, 157.

Chapter Two

1. Huston Smith, *Beyond the Postmodern Mind* (Wheaton, IL: Quest Books, 1984), 4.

2. Stephen Toulmin, *Cosmopolis: The Hidden Agenda of Modernity* (New York: Free Press, 1990), 169–270. See also Kierkegaard's notion that "objective truth," posing as Christian faith, is a mere "esthetic" form of self-deception and despair. See also Richard Rorty, *Philosophy and the Mirror of Nature* (Princeton: Princeton University Press, 1979), 361.

3. Hans-Georg Gadamer, *Truth and Method* (New York: Seabury Press, 1975), 244.

4. Timm Triplett, "Recent Work on Foundationalism," *American Philosophical Quarterly*, vol. 27, No. 2, April, 1990, 93–116. Triplett distinguishes some twenty different and distinct forms of foundationalism, some of which he thinks are defensible and some not. In what follows, my claim that the modern reduction of knowledge to matters of fact and matters of reason was "foundational" in spirit (in a variety of ways in different philosophers), and that it failed to meet its own criteria, may not apply to some of the contemporary forms of foundationalism which Triplett isolates.

5. Alvin Plantinga utilizes a version of this argument in his article, "On Taking Belief in God as Basic," in *Religious Experience and Religious Belief*, ed. Joseph Runzo and Craig Ihara (Lanham, MD: University Press of America, 1986), 9–17.

6. Stanley Hauerwas (with David Burrell), "From System to Story," in *Truthfulness and Tragedy: Further Investigations in Christian Ethics* (Notre Dame, IN: Univeristy of Notre Dame Press, 1977), 24. Quoted in Terrence Tilley, *Story Theology* (Wilmington, DE: Michael Glazier, 1985), 35.

7. James Wiggins, "Within and Without Stories," in *Religion as Story* (New York: Harper & Row, 1975), 4.

8. David Klemm, *Hermeneutical Inquiry* (Atlanta, GA: Scholars Press, 1986), vol. 1, 25.

9. Stephen Toulmin, *Cosmopolis: The Hidden Agenda of Modernity*, 84–85.

10. For example, Heisenberg's Principle of Indeterminacy and Bohr's Principle of Complementarity. See Stephen Toulmin, *The Return to Cosmology: Postmodern Science and the Theology of Nature* (Berkeley: University of California Press, 1985), 237-244.

11. Langdon Gilkey, *Society and the Sacred* (New York: Crossroad Books, 1981), 86–87.

12. Barbara Antonia Clarke Mossberg, "A Practical Look at the Humanities," an unpublished talk to the Oregon State Board of Higher Education.

13. E.H. Gombrich, *Art and Illusion* (New York: Bollingen, Pantheon Books, 1960), 84–85.

14. Nikos Kazantzakis, *Report to Greco*, trans. P.A. Bien (New York: Simon & Schuster, 1965), 291–292.

15. Paul Ricoeur, "Existence and Hermeneutics," in *Hermeneutical Inquiry*, vol. 2., 192.

16. Max Black, *Models and Metaphors: Studies in Language and Philosophy* (Ithaca, NY: Cornell University Press, 1962), 41.

17. David Leary, in an unpublished essay entitled, "The Role of Metaphor in Science and Medicine," 3.

18. Sallie McFague, *Speaking in Parables: A Study in Metaphor in Theology* (Philadelphia: Fortress Press, 1975), 49.

19. Gerard Manley Hopkins, "God's Grandeur," *Poems of Gerard Manley Hopkins* (Oxford: Oxford University Press, 1948), 31.

20. John Summerson, *The Classical Language of Architecture* (Cambridge, MA: M.I.T. Press,1986), 12, 13.

21. Sallie McFague, *Metaphorical Theology* (Philadelphia: Fortress Press, 1982), 34.

22. Maurice Merleau-Ponty, "Eye and Mind," in *The Primacy of Perception,* ed. James M. Edie (Evanston, IL: Northwestern University Press, 1964), 164.

23. Hans-Georg Gadamer, "Religious and Poetical Speaking," in *Myth, Symbol, and Reality,* ed. Alan M. Olson (Notre Dame, IN: University of Notre Dame Press, 1980), 87.

24. V.S. Naipaul, "Rednecks," *New York Review of Books,* Dec. 22, 1988, 12.

25. Martin Heidegger, *Being and Time,* trans. John Macquarrie and Edward Robinson (New York: Harper & Row, 1962), Section 44.

26. Harold Fickett, "Flannery O'Connor: Images of Grace," in *Books and Religion,* vol. 14, no. 9, Nov. 1986, 14.

27. Richard Rorty, *Philosophy and the Mirror of Nature* (Princeton: Princeton University Press, 1979), 315.

28. Plato, *Theaetetus:* 155d.

29. Rudolph Otto, *The Idea of the Holy,* trans. John W. Harvey (New York: Oxford University Press, 1958).

30. Karl Jaspers, *Philosophy of Existence,* trans. Richard Grabau (Philadelphia: University of Pennsylvania Press, 1971), 18.

31. Ludwig Wittgenstein, *Tractatus Logico-philosophicus,* trans. D.F. Pears and B.F. McGuinness (Atlantic Highlands, NJ: Humanities Press, 1974), 6.44

32. Norman Malcolm, *Ludwig Wittgenstein: A Memoir* (London: Oxford University Press, 1962), 70.

33. Martin Heidegger, *The Basic Problems of Phenomenology,* trans. Albert Hofstadter (Bloomington, IN: Indiana University Press, 1982), 17–19.

34. Ninian Smart, *Philosophers and Religious Truth* (London: SCM Press, 1964), 14.

35. Parker Palmer, "Good Teaching: A Matter of Living the Mystery," *Change Magazine*, Jan./Feb. 1990, 11.

36. Albert Einstein, *Autobiographical Notes*, trans. and ed. P.A. Schilpp (La Salle, IL: Open Court, 1979).

37. Czeslaw Milosz, from "Consciousness," in *Unattainable Earth* (New York: Ecco Press, 1986.

38. Michael Novak, *Ascent of the Mountain, Flight of the Dove* (New York: Harper & Row, 1978), 55.

39. Soren Kierkegaard, *Concluding Unscientific Postscript*, trans. David Swenson (Princeton: Princeton University Press, 1941), 97.

40. Martha Nussbaum, quoted in Charlotte Bruce Harvey, "The Good Life," in *Brown Alumni Monthly*, Feb. 1989, 24.

41. Langdon Gilkey, *Message and Existence* (New York: Seabury Press, 1979), 81.

42. Richard Rorty, *Philosophy and the Mirror of Nature*, 360.

43. Richard Rorty, *Philosophy and the Mirror of Nature*, 370.

44. Albert Camus, *The Myth of Sisyphus*, trans. Justin O'Brien (New York: Vintage Books, 1955), 10.

Chapter Three

1. Paul Ricoeur, "Phenomenologie et Hermeneutique," in *Man and World*, vol. 7, no. 3, 1974, 236; See also "Existence and Hermeneutics," in *Hermeneutical Inquiry*, vol. 2, ed. David Klemm (Atlanta, GA: Scholars Press, 1986), 185–202.

2. Maurice Merleau-Ponty, *Phenomenology of Perception* (New York: Humanities Press, 1962), x.

3. Edmund Husserl, *The Crisis of European Sciences and Transcendental Phenomenology*, trans. David Carr (Evanston, IL: Northwestern University Press, 1970), 122.

4. David Klemm, *Hermeneutical Inquiry*, vol. 1, 23.

5. Cowley, *Critique of British Empiricism* (New York: St. Martin's Press, 1968), 19.

6. Paul Ricoeur, "Philosophy of Will and Action," in *Phenomenology of Will and Action*, ed. Straus and Griffith (Pittsburgh: Duquesne University Press, 1967), 17.

7. Maurice Merleau-Ponty, *Phenomenology of Perception,* vii.

8. Richard Rorty, *Philosophy and the Mirror of Nature* (Princeton: Princeton University Press, 1979), 319.

9. Mircea Eliade, *The Quest* (Chicago: University of Chicago Press, 1969), 10.

10. Mircea Eliade, *The Quest,* 6.

11. Wayne Proudfoot, *Religious Experience* (Berkeley, CA: University of California Press, 1985), 192.

12. Wayne Proudfoot, *Religious Experience,* 196.

13. Wayne Proudfoot, *Religious Experience,* 196.

14. Wayne Proudfoot, *Religious Experience,* 197.

15. Donald Polkinghorne, *Narrative Knowing and the Human Sciences* (Albany, NY: State University of New York Press, 1988), 111.

16. Stephen Crites, "Angels We Have Heard," in *Religion as Story,* ed. J. Wiggins (New York: Harper & Row, 1975), 30–31, 53–54.

17. Much of what follows can be found in a more leisurely and expanded form in an earlier book of mine, *Time and Self: Phenomenological Explorations* (New York: Crossroad and Scholars Press, 1985).

18. Karl Jaspers, *Philosophical Faith and Revelation* (New York: Harper & Row, 1967), 5.

19. Martin Heidegger, *Being and Time,* trans. John Macquarrie and Edward Robinson (New York: Harper & Row, 1962), 187.

20. Paul Ricoeur, "The Human Experience of Time and Narrative," in *Research in Phenomenology,* 1979, 28.

21. Donald E. Polkinghorne, *Narrative Knowing and the Human Sciences,* 11.

22. Steven Crites, "Myth, Story, History," in *Parable, Myth, and Language,* ed. Tony Stoneburner (London: Church Society for College Work, 1968), 68.

23. Linnia Marsh Wolfe, *Son of the Wilderness: The Life of John Muir* (New York: Alfred Knopf, 1946), 88, 96, 104, 105.

24. Hannah Arendt, *The Human Condition* (New York: Anchor, 1958), 286.

25. Paul Ricoeur, *Time and Narrativity,* vol. 1, trans. Kathleen McLaughlin and David Pellauer (Chicago: University of Chicago Press, 1984), 54, 55, 56, 64. See also Paul Ricoeur, "The Human Experience of Time and Narrative," 34.

26. Alasdair MacIntyre, *After Virtue* (Notre Dame, IN: University of Notre Dame Press, 1981), 117.

27. Paul Ricoeur makes a similar point in *Time and Narrative*, vol. 1, 54–60.

28. Donald E. Polkinghorne, *Narrative Knowing and the Human Sciences*, 111.

Chapter Four

1. A.L. Basham, *The Wonder That Was India* (New York: Grove Press, 1954), 257.

2. Donald E. Polkinghorne, *Narrative Knowing and the Human Sciences* (Albany, NY: State University of New York Press, 1988), 18–19.

3. Roland Barthes, "Introduction to the Structural Analysis of the Narrative," occasional paper, Centre for Contemporary Cultural Studies, University of Birmingham, 1966, quoted in Polkinghorne, *Narrative Knowledge*, 14.

4. *Christian Science Monitor*, Feb. 12, 1991, 13.

5. George S. Howard, "Culture Tales: A Narrative Approach to Thinking, Cross-Cultural Psychology, and Psychotherapy," *American Psychologist*, March 1991, 196.

6. Ninian Smart, *The Long Search* (Boston: Little, Brown & Co., 1977), 107.

7. Clifford Geertz, "Religion as a Cultural System," in *The Interpretation of Cultures* (New York: Basic Books, 1973), 123–4.

8. Michael Barnes, *In the Presence of Mystery* (Mystic, CT: Twenty Third Publications, 1984), 138.

9. Mircea Eliade, *Ordeal by Labyrinth* (Chicago: University of Chicago Press, 1982), 156.

10. David Tracy, *Plurality and Ambiguity* (New York: Harper & Row, 1987), 84.

11. Sallie TeSelle, "The Experience of Coming to Believe," *Theology Today*, vol. 32, no. 2, July 1975, 160.

12. David Klemm, *Hermeneutical Inquiry*, vol. 1, (Atlanta, GA: Scholars Press, 1986), 42.

13. David Klemm, *Hermeneutical Inquiry*, 6.

14. Martin Heidegger, *Being and Time*, trans. John Macquarrie and Edward Robinson (New York: Harper & Row, 1962), 189. On "seeing...as," see Ludwig Wittgenstein, *On Certainty*, trans. Denis Paul and G.E.M. Anscome (Oxford: Basil Blackwell), 1969.

15. Gordon Kaufman, "Religious Diversity, Historical Consciousness, and Christian Theology," in *The Myth of Christian Uniqueness*, ed. John Hick and Paul Knitter (Maryknoll, NY: Orbis Books, 1988), 7.

16. John Hick, *Faith and Knowledge* (Glasgow, Scotland: Collins-Fontana Books, 1974), 133.

17. Martin Heidegger, *Being and Time*, section 44. See also Robert Scharlemann, *The Being of God* (New York: Seabury Press, 1981), 13.

18. Cited in Terrence Tilley, *Story Theology* (Wilmington, DE: Michael Glazier, 1985), 211–212.

19. Paul Ricoeur, *Interpretation Theory: Discourse and the Surplus of Meaning* (Fort Worth, TX: Texas Christian University Press, 1976), 31–32.

20. Martin Heidegger, *Being and Time*, 185.

21. David Klemm, *Hermeneutical Inquiry*, 23.

22. Stanley Fish, *Is There a Text in this Class?* (Cambridge, MA: Harvard University Press, 1980), 327.

23. Paul Ricoeur, *Interpretation Theory*, 31.

24. Hans-Georg Gadamer, "The Universality of the Hermeneutical Problem," in *Hermeneutical Inquiry*, ed. David Klemm, 183.

25. Wolfhart Pannenberg, "Meaning, Religion, and the Question of God," in *Knowing Religiously*, ed. Leroy S. Rouner (Notre Dame, IN: University of Notre Dame Press, 1985), 161.

26. Gordon Kaufman, "Reconceiving God for a Nuclear Age," in *Knowing Religiously*, 135–6, 144.

27. John Hick, "A Philosophy of Religious Pluralism," in *Religious Experience and Religious Belief*, ed. Joseph Runzo and Craig Ihara (Lanham, MD: University Press of America, 1986), 111, 113.

28. M. Mair, "Psychology as Storytelling," in *International Journal of Personal Construct Psychology* vol. 1, 1988, 127.

29. Quoted in Charles A Radin, "Scholars Seek Link of Ecology and Theology," *Boston Globe*, Sept. 17, 1990, 27.

30. Wendell Berry, *What Are People For?* (Berkeley: North Point Press, 1990), 96.

31. Stephen Toulmin, "Cosmology as Science and Religion," in *On Nature*, ed. Leroy Rouner (Notre Dame, IN: University of Notre Dame Press, 1984), 35.

32. Stephen Toulmin, *The Return to Cosmology: Postmodern Science and the Theology of Nature* (Berkeley: University of California Press, 1985), 237.

33. Stephen Toulmin, *The Return to Cosmology*, 268.

34. Stephen Toulmin, *The Return to Cosmology*, 272, 274.

35. Much of the material for this story comes from Sean McDonagh, *To Care for the Earth* (Santa Fe, NM: Bear and Company, 1986); Thomas Berry, *The Dream of the Earth* (San Francisco: Sierra Club Books, 1990); Brian Swimme, *The Universe is a Green Dragon* (Santa Fe, NM: Bear and Company, 1984); and from an unpublished manuscript by Albert LaChance, *Greenspirit*. I owe the term "originating mystery" to Albert LaChance.

36. Sara Maitland, "Daughter of Jerusalem," in *Writers Revealed: Eight Contemporary Novelists Talk About Faith, Religion and God*, ed. Rosemary Harthill (New York: Peter Bedrick Books, 1989), 127.

37. Black Elk, *The Sacred Pipe* (New York: Penguin Books, 1979), xx.

38. Quoted in Charles A Radin, "Scholars Seek Link of Ecology and Theology," 27.

39. Meister Eckhart, *Breakthrough: Meister Eckhart's Creation Spirituality* (New York: Doubleday, 1980), 84.

40. Erazim Kohak, *The Embers and the Stars: A Philosophical Enquiry into the Moral Sense of Nature* (Chicago: University of Chicago Press, 1984), 60–61.

41. Edgar Mitchell, in *The Home Planet*, ed. Kevin W. Kelley (Reading, MA and Moscow: Addison-Wesley and Mir Publishers, 1988), 138.

Chapter Five

1. Blaise Pascal, *Pensees* (New York: E.P. Dutton, 1958), 78.

2. Sören Kierkegaard, *Concluding Unscientific Postscript*, trans. David Swenson (Princeton: Princeton University Press, 1944), 165–6. Emphasis mine.

3. Sören Kierkegaard, *Concluding Unscientific Postscript*, 194.

4. Sören Kierkegaard, *Concluding Unscientific Postscript*, 192–3, 291.

5. Sören Kierkegaard, *Journals*, trans. Alexander Dru (London: Oxford University Press, 1938), 15.

6. Sören Kierkegaard, *Concluding Unscientific Postscript*, 182.

7. Sören Kierkegaard, *Concluding Unscientific Postscript*, 30, 33, 118.

8. H. Richard Niebuhr, "The Story of Our Life," in *The Meaning of Revelation* (New York: MacMillan, 1941), 58–59.

9. Paul Ricoeur, "Existence and Hermeneutics," in *Hermeneutical Inquiry,* ed. David Klemm (Atlanta, GA: Scholars Press, 1986), vol. 2, 201.

10. Wayne C. Booth, "Systematic Wonder: The Rhetoric of Religion," in *Journal of the American Academy of Religion,* vol. 53, No. 4, December 1985, 683.

11. Leo Tolstoy, "A Confession," in *The Portable Tolstoy,* ed. John Bayley (New York: Penguin Books, 1978). I have considerably abridged this material from pages 676, 678, 679, 704, and 715–716.

12. Mircea Eliade, *Fragments d'un Journal* (Paris: Gallimard, 1978), 547.

13. Thomas á Kempis, *The Imitation of Christ,* I, 3.5; cited in John Hick, *Truth and Dialogue in World Religions: Conflicting Truth Claims* (Philadelphia: Fortress Press, 1974), 144.

14. Nelson Pike, "St. John of the Cross on Mystic Apprehensions as Sources of Knowledge," in *Religious Experience and Religious Belief,* ed. Runzo and Ihara (Lanham, MD: University Press of America, 1986), 89, 93.

15. Black Elk, *The Sacred Pipe* (New York: Penguin Books, 1971), 13, 14.

16. Peter Slater, *The Dynamics of Religion* (New York: Harper and Row, 1978), 176.

17. Hendrik M. Vroom, *Religions and the Truth,* trans. J.W. Rebel (Grand Rapids, MI: Wm. B. Eerdmans Publishing Co., 1989), 311.

Chapter Six

1. Wilfred Cantwell Smith, *Questions of Religious Truth* (London: Victor Gollancz, Ltd., 1967), 73.

2. R.B. Braithwaite, "An Empiricist's View of the Nature of Religious Belief," in *The Philosophy of Religion,* ed. Basil Mitchell (Oxford: Oxford University Press, 1971), 89.

3. R.B. Braithwaite, "An Empiricist's View," 86, 78, 80–81, 90.

4. Merold Westphal, "Phenomenologies and Religious Truth," in *Phenomenology of the Truth Proper to Religion,* ed. Daniel Guerriere (Albany: State University of New York Press, 1990), 107, 109.

5. Terrence W. Tilley, *Story Theology* (Wilmington, DE: Michael Glazier, 1985), 184.

6. David L. Wolfe, *Epistemology: The Justification of Belief* (Downers Grove, IL: InterVarsity Press, 1982), 46, 55. On this same topic, see also Frederick Ferré, *Basic Modern Philosophy of Religion* (New York: Scribners, 1967), especially chapters 13 and 14.

7. Paul Tillich, *Dynamics of Faith* (New York: Harper & Row, 1957), 97.

8. Robert Coles, *The Spiritual Life of Children* (Boston: Houghton Mifflin Co., 1990), 25–26.

9. Stanley Hauerwas, *Truthfulness and Tragedy* (Notre Dame, IN: University of Notre Dame Press, 1985), 71.

10. John Hick, "On Grading Religon," in *Religious Studies* 17 (1981), 461.

11. Stanley Hauerwas, *Truthfulness and Tragedy*, 80.

12. Terrence Tilley, *Story Theology*, 191–192.

13. Norman Perrin and Dennis Duling, *The New Testament: An Introduction* (New York: Harcourt Brace Jovanovich, 1982), 53–54.

14. R.M. Hare, "Theology and Falsification," in *Philosophy of Religion*, ed. Louis P. Pojman (Belmont, CA: Wadsworth, 1987), 360.

Chapter Seven

1. Stephen Toulmin, *Cosmopolis: the Hidden Agenda of Modernity* (New York: Free Press, 1990), 168.

2. Brian Swimme, "The Cosmic Creation Story," in *The Reenchantment of Science*, ed. David Ray Griffin (Albany, NY: State University of New York Press, 1988), 53.

3. John E. Smith, "Faith, Belief, and the Problem of Rationality in Religion," in *Rationality and Religious Belief*, ed. C.F. Delaney (Notre Dame, IN: University of Notre Dame Press, 1979), 57.

4. John E. Smith, "Faith, Belief, and the Problem of Rationality," 56.

5. Paul Tillich, *Dynamics of Faith* (New York: Harper Colophon, 1957), 123.

6. Thomas Sheehan, *The First Coming: How the Kingdom of God Became Christianity* (New York: Random House, 1986), 166. See also 169 and 170–173.

7. Thomas Sheehan, *The First Coming*, 170.

8. Thomas Sheehan, *The First Coming*, 172.

9. Thomas Sheehan, *The First Coming*, 172.

10. Thomas Sheehan, *The First Coming*, 172, 173. Underlining is Sheehan's.

11. Thomas Sheehan, *The First Coming*, 173.

12. Annie Dillard, *Pilgrim at Tinker Creek* (New York: Harper's Magazine Press, 1974), 9.

13. Paul Ricoeur, *The Symbolism of Evil*, trans. Emerson Buchanan (New York: Harper & Row, 1967), 352.

14. Robert Bellah, *Habits of the Heart* (New York: Harper & Row, 1986), 296.

15. John Caputo, "Radical Hermeneutics and Religious Truth: The Case of Sheehan and Schillebeeckx," in *Phenomenology of the Truth Proper to Religion,* ed. Daniel Guerriere (Albany, NY: State University of New York Press, 1990), 164.

Index